PROPHETIC
SISTERHOOD

Revs. Caroline Bartlett Crane (standing, right), Florence Buck (with guitar), and
Marion Murdock (with hymnal) in Kalamazoo, early 1890s. Caroline Bartlett Crane
Papers, Western Michigan University, University Archives and Regional History
Collections, Kalamazoo, Michigan.

PROPHETIC
SISTERHOOD

Liberal Women Ministers of the Frontier, 1880–1930

CYNTHIA GRANT TUCKER

INDIANA UNIVERSITY PRESS
Bloomington and Indianapolis

The paper used in this publication meets the minimum requirements of American National Standard for Information Sciences—Permanence of Paper for Printed Library Materials, ANSI Z39.48-1984.

∞™

Manufactured in the United States of America

Library of Congress Cataloging-in-Publication Data

Tucker, Cynthia Grant.
    Prophetic sisterhood : liberal women ministers of the frontier,
1880–1930 / Cynthia Grant Tucker.— 1st Indiana University Press
ed.
        p.   cm.
    Originally published: Boston : Beacon Press, c1990.
    Includes bibliographical references and index.
    ISBN 0-253-20822-X (alk. paper)
    1. Unitarian Universalist churches—Great Plains—Clergy—
Biography.   2. Women clergy—Great Plains—Biography.   3. Great
Plains—Biography.   I. Title.
[BX9867.T83   1994]
289.1'78'8'082—dc20   93-22699

1 2 3 4 5 98 97 96 95 94

For my mother
Ruth Marks Grant
1908–1988

CONTENTS

viii   *Contents*

LIST OF ILLUSTRATIONS

ACKNOWLEDGMENTS

I should like to thank Memphis State University, the Murray Research Center at Radcliffe College, and the National Endowment for the Humanities for awarding me research and travel grants in support of this work. I am also indebted to numerous public libraries, churches, schools, and historical groups for the use of their archives and many courtesies: the Andover-Harvard Theological School Library; the Bentley Historical Library at the University of Michigan; the Brister Library at Memphis State University; the Chicago Historical Society; the Denver Public Library; the Des Moines Unitarian Church; the Garnavillo, Iowa, Historical Society; the Iowa State Historical Society; the Iowa State Historical Department and Library; the Library of Congress Manuscript Division; the Meadville-Lombard Theological School Library; the Orlando, Florida, Public Library; the Orlando Unitarian Church; the Regenstein Library at the University of Chicago; the Schlesinger Library at Radcliffe College; the Swarthmore College Peace Collection; the Unitarian Universalist Association; the University of Illinois at Chicago; and the Western Michigan University Archives.

More than to institutions, however, my debt is to people—colleagues, students, friends, and family—who have nurtured this book and its author since its inception. For their scholarly guidance, professional help, and manifold personal kindnesses, thanks go to Meredith Anderson, Helen Bullard, Mary Jo Buhle, Allen Davis, Robert Forrey, Marta Flanagan, Neil Gerdes, Evelyn Glazebrook, Mary Bell Glick, Donald Gordon, Betty K. Gorshe, Thomas Graham, Lida L. Greene, Mary-Ella Holst, Helen Hoagland Johnson, Kenneth P. Johnson, Wayne Mann, Audrey May, Colleen McDannell, Larry Peterson, Nancy and Claude Phillips, O'Ryan Rickard, Alan Seaburg, Nora Staton, and Angie Utt. The early encouragement of two professors, Kenneth B. Marshall and Rosalie Colie, must also be acknowledged, as must the heroic support of my graduate assistants, Jane Shirley and Douglas Wilson.

Above all, thanks go to my father, Phillip Grant, for expecting the best from his daughters; to my husband and live-in historian, David, for his unfailing humor, love, and support; and to our children, Hope and Grant, for reminding me that there really is life after authorship.

INTRODUCTION

It was not so long ago that our only accounts of recent church history were so preoccupied with the male personnel and their perspective that one would have thought that women, whose numbers accounted for most of the active membership, never existed or made a difference worth mentioning. Emerging revisionist scholarship has already done much to correct this impression, showing that, during the nineteenth century, the church's female majority feminized not only corporate worship and congregational life but the character of the pastoral office from which their sex was barred. Indeed, the expanded record establishes that, in the guises of ministers' wives, missionaries, deaconesses, and all-round lay workers, many ambitious and capable women were actually running their churches and engineering their social outreach, virtually doing what ministers did without the recognition or the salary.[1]

The present study, a group biography, broadens the picture still further by turning to the experiences of women who did gain the title and office of minister in the decades that followed the Civil War. The unqualified if reluctant authorization for females to take on this role was available in both the Universalist and the Unitarian folds, whose liberal traditions put up no impassable creedal barriers and contained theological elements that encouraged such female ambition. The Universalists, who maintained that salvation was open to all, had harnessed to their iconoclasm a loose institutional structure and a tradition of experiment that relaxed the historical strictures on women and gave them more latitude in public service. The Unitarians, more individualistic, cerebral, and citified, also brought with them a strong commitment to freedom of thought, stressed education, and insisted on a rational reading of Scripture. Rejecting original sin, they absolved Eve of having corrupted the race. Discarding the Trinity and placing Jesus on an entirely human plane, they allowed for a more androgynous concept of deity. At least in this creedal revamping of orthodox Christian construc-

I

tions, liberal religion released women from their inferior station and cleared
the way for their ascent in the church.

Not that these two communities, who finally merged to become the
Unitarian Universalists in the later twentieth century, were altogether at
ease in their liberal proximity. Universalists, largely rural and less prosperous, tended to see Unitarians as privileged academic elitists whose
rational bent drained their faith of Christianity's warmth and vitality.
Temperamental, as well as insistent, if minor, theological differences also
made it hard for Unitarians to draw close to their Universalist cousins,
though this was less true of the women who sought leadership roles in their
churches. For these it was more important to stress what united them than
what still set them apart. They all believed that their liberal faith, a legacy
from the Enlightenment, gave them, no less than their brothers, a mandate
to seek principles of individual freedom and growth and democracy in their
relationships. They also found sanction for their striving in the mystical
thought of the New England Transcendentalists, who not only saw the
divine as androgynous and present in all humanity but expected that
women would be the prophets of the future, a powerful recommendation for
women who wanted to preach and lead churches. Thus, the pioneers of the
female ministry—Olympia Brown, Phebe Ann Hanaford, and Augusta
Chapin—were Universalists who also cheerfully served Unitarian parishes,
and the women on whom this study is focused carried the Unitarian banner
to new congregations while trying to strengthen their ties to their Universalist kin.

The language of liberal religion, used in this book in the ways that its
Unitarian principals used it, has as its referents an overarching commitment to human freedom and a specific rejection of orthodox Christianity. A
century ago, this complex of meanings, while not as large as today's, already
contained ambiguities that had been gathering since the start of the century, when the churches of the "Standing Order" in Massachusetts split over
the Calvinist doctrines of election. The dissenters, who believed in free will
and human dignity, chose to call themselves *rational Christians* or *liberal
Christians* rather than *Unitarians,* a term that their adversaries applied, and
made stick, as an epithet. But even then, the liberals themselves disagreed
about the inflection. Insurrectionists like William Ellery Channing put the
accent on *liberal* to emphasize the distinction from orthodoxy, while others
like Henry W. Bellows stressed the *Christian* component to distance themselves from the radicals' ethically based humanism. As for the female clergy,
who allied themselves with the radical wing for reasons that were as politi-

cal as theological, they charged that the self-described "liberals" who clung to the old patriarchal concepts of deity and excluded women from leadership roles were misrepresenting themselves.

Part 1 of this book introduces its principal figures into the network that helped them survive in an isolating and most lonely calling. While it might be tempting to think of this early emergence of female clergy as part of the same rising movement that has carried significant numbers of women into the pulpits in recent years, to do so would be to suggest that the influx was much larger and more sustained than it was and thus to obscure two of its most telling features: its sparseness and its vulnerability. As these first chapters show, even within a tradition that freed women from the inhibiting creeds of the past and enhanced their image profoundly, there was no great rush of females into the ministry in the late nineteenth century. However unorthodox in their theology and committed to other reforms, the liberal religionists were as a rule quite reluctant to alter the sexes' assigned roles, and this was especially true when it came to the ministry. The number of women who had the interest and nerve to take on the opposition and prove themselves in pastorates was a minuscule cluster that seemed like a great gathering only to the women themselves when their hopes got the better of them.

In 1870, only five women had sought a place alongside the 600 male liberal clergy. Twenty years later, the Universalists and Unitarians together had ordained only about seventy, and far fewer actually had a chance to use their credentials in full-time, paid pastorates. Called to only the small or shakier congregations that the men would not take, often married to ministers whose position obscured or reduced their own, and regarded by the denominational leadership as a blotch on their image and best kept on the organizational sidelines, the women in ministry were a largely unnoticed presence whose existence came to be known primarily through the efforts of a still smaller group who banded together on the frontier in the 1880s and 1890s. These twenty or so Unitarian women, some of whom first met when they were young girls, were held together for half a century by a webbing of common ideals and shared history. As the focal point of this book, the story of this Western sisterhood dramatizes the female ministers' isolation and lonely struggle for recognition, their unique contributions to church and community leadership, and the power and complexities of female affiliation.

It was no accident that this sisterhood should emerge in Iowa and the states surrounding it rather than in the East, the Mecca of Unitarianism, for the colonists who had come to the Great Plains to start new lives from scratch were less bound to old ways of doing things. They brought their states into the Union with new sets of ground rules, laws that gave females unprecedented domestic rights and political voice, and, as men were in chronically short supply, the women were also given a chance to break out of old roles and enter professions. Female doctors, dentists, and lawyers who could not get licensed back East were given a hearty welcome in the frontier communities. This shortage of men also opened the way for liberal women to enter the ministry after the war when the Unitarian leadership targeted Western fields as the most promising for planting enlightened religion. When few men stepped forward to take on the grueling and low-paying job of organizing and tending new congregations, the women moved in and took command of denominational growth for two decades.

In part 2, which examines this pioneer clergy's methods of pastoring, there emerges the irony that this group's break with conventional roles was hardly as radical at the grass roots as the opposition suggested. Actually, while their vocation removed them from much of their lay sisters' work, their practice of ministry did not repudiate woman's sphere but allied itself with it in order to make it broader and more androgynous. Committed to a ministry that went beyond once-a-week pulpit appearances, they devoted themselves to raising church families all during the week, to moving the concept of "church home" beyond the popular metaphor as few of their brother clergy had thought to do. Their sermons and worship services, Sunday School programs, and church sociables enunciated the ideals and practical needs of family and home, as did the down-to-earth architecture, utilitarian furnishings, and domestic use of interior space in the church buildings that they designed. This emphasis gave the historically male role of pastor a new shape the women wore well. It eased the people's anxieties about putting females in charge of the church and proved itself decisively in terms of strong congregational life, impressive membership growth, and financial prosperity.

The women's androgynous blend of business management, sound preaching, and maternal caretaking met the distinctive demands of those who broke with the orthodox church in the West. Not only did frontier parishioners face the problems of poverty, sickness, and climate, but they were regarded as heretics of the worst kind by their orthodox neighbors, the Presbyterians, Methodists, Baptists, and Calvinist Congregationalists, all of whom had preceded them in the region. Nontrinitarians were ostracized and persecuted; they were made the object of scorn at public revivals and had their businesses boycotted. What they longed for was not academic orators but sympathetic ministers with an optimistic faith to enfold them in tight, supportive communities and lighten their everyday load. Though the women clergy were barred from attending the Unitarians' Harvard, this very exclusion help educate them as no Eastern school could have about what it meant to be a minority of outsiders on the frontier and not the established religious group in New England. They knew and addressed the need for their churches to serve as rural outposts of rationality and human warmth that could offer protection, comfort, and nourishment. All this is to say that much more than the law of supply and demand explained their success in the local parishes.

Part 3, which takes up the sisterhood's struggle within the institutional frame, explains that the women's grass-roots success did not bring the same recognition and backing at the church's national levels. Indeed, the Unitarians' East Coast bureaucracy, while forced to admit that the women had built an impressive record in church expansion, was nonetheless adamant that their presence was doing the cause more harm than good. These chapters describe the denominational contexts in which this tension developed, examining how it sharpened the women's sense of themselves and their place in their larger fold. Tracking the conflict along the contours of Unitarian landscape, this section first illuminates how the collision between the sisterhood and the male power base came to reflect a larger complex of warring values and temperaments that distinguished Eastern liberals from those pioneering outside New England. As pastors who had been reared and summoned to ministry on the frontier in an atmosphere of freedom and egalitarianism, these women became acutely aware of how deeply attached they were to their region and all that it stood for when church business put them in contact with the conservative Eastern mentality. They felt their roots keenly each time they were slighted or patronized by the central administration and treated with open hostility by the men at the ministers' meetings in Boston. They felt what geography meant in the movement whenever a young seminarian came to their district from Harvard and ran off the people with pulpit abstractions and condescending ways.

The Unitarians' long and fiery argument over their shared beliefs also helped to refine the sisterhood's sense of place in the institutional scheme. This denominational struggle for theological definition firmly positioned the sisterhood close to the Western "radicals" who had been shucking off the old christological elements and patriarchal features of deity that most Eastern liberals still clung to. The clergywomen who labored constantly

under the burdens of sexist oppression were passionate and articulate cele-
brants of this freer, egalitarian faith that spoke most directly to Westerners
who had broken away from the orthodox church.

Then, too, while the women had entered the pulpits in hopes of remov-
ing the question of gender, in time they were forced to concede that it was
the major issue, that their struggle for real religious integrity was a fight
against patriarchy. As the nineteenth century drew to a close, they watched
the reassertion of male authority in the culture at large change the West
from a haven for women in ministry to an annex of Eastern resistance to
them.[2] The Unitarian leadership, thinking that it could recover its lost
institutional vigor by building a "manlier" ministry, strengthened its central office in Boston and did its best to dislodge female clergy while block-
ing others from joining them. The central administration, backing Harvard Divinity School in its policy of turning down female applicants, tried
to steer them into new schools created to certify parish assistants. Abetted
by population shifts to the cities that wiped out the sisterhood's base, the
effort to put women back in their time-honored place soon produced its
desired effect. The female ministry that had appeared to have come out of
nowhere to take command of Western expansion twenty-five years before
seemed to disappear just as abruptly shortly after the century turned when
its members scattered across the country to other fields of public service.

While these pastors blamed sexist bias the most for their exodus from
parish ministry, they knew that their congregations' indifference to what
they were preaching was also a factor. Sensitized to the need for reform by
their own oppression as women, these preachers had become increasingly
outspoken social gospelers who called for radical changes in the structures of
business and government and tried to rouse their people to get involved.
Unlike the Universalists, however, the Unitarians had never been given to
active involvement despite their disproportionate numbers in many social
reforms, and the women preachers who tried to prod their parishioners in
this direction watched the younger generations—whose greater distance
from Calvinism made them more casual about their liberal faith—defect to
fashionable mainline churches where the orthodox teachings had softened.
Frustrated by the laity's failure to take their sermons to heart, and weary of
being anathematized by an institution that wanted them out, the clergywomen reluctantly shifted their ministry to the secular fields of settlement
work, municipal housekeeping, suffrage, and world peace.

Part 4 begins by considering how these preachers' prophetic message
evolved and then looks at how the group endeavored to put what they

preached into practice outside the church not by abandoning but by reshaping the work to which they had been ordained. As residents of social settlements, and as public health reformers, they carried the principle of the domestic ministry one step farther by trying to make society a better home for the larger family out in the community. As the leaders of suffrage campaigns and as workers for peace during World War I, they evangelized for the same ideals of democracy, freedom, and balance in human relations that they had consistently preached from their pulpits. Yet, being as fraught with disappointments as pastoring congregations had been, these alternate ministries brought out the limits of any reform methodology. When the programs for institutional change that were offered by suffrage and social work failed to deliver the promised results and "the war to end all wars" turned out to have been a corrupt crusade, the sisters returned to the old solutions, putting their hopes if not absolute confidence in the individual uplift that they had practiced as pastors.

Misleading as it would be to suggest that this group of feminist clergy was a large wave that broke down the barriers of male privilege in the Protestant church, it would be too narrow and just as much a distortion to describe their story as essentially a denominational history. For, while this ecclesia was but a tiny and brief presence within a small sect that stood on the Protestant outskirts, its sparseness, marginality, and defeat as well as its resilience belong to the broader fabric of women's experience and reform in America. Its small proportions remind us, for one thing, that women's sphere has been narrow, and narrowest in our traditional institutions. While their unique access to full ordination set the Unitarian and Universalist women apart from the others on paper, they nevertheless shared much of the same frustration and anger at being cut off from centers of influence as their evangelical sisters who were refused a place in the ministry outright. Again, with their entry into the secular spheres of progressive reform, the pastors became part of an ecumenical liberal community that shared a common ground of ideals and disillusionment. In short, as a record of people who were at once influential and impotent, conspicuous and invisible, highly vocal and effectively silenced, this study illuminates the interplay between personal and systemic power and the mixed blessings of standing outside the establishment. These are not denominational characteristics but human complexities that continue to shape our social institutions.

This book's final chapter, which focuses on the women's own efforts to tell their story, addresses the issue of history's value as a usable ground and the

problem of its elusiveness. It documents the ease with which our past is lost
or revised and the difficulties of preserving it for a dialogue with the present
and future. Finally, it speaks of the deep and sustaining power that comes
from affirming our place in an unbroken line of kindred seekers and prophets. Though they fought hard against being silenced and shoved aside, the
women in this biography ended up in almost total obscurity, their presence
expunged from the record by a conspiracy of forgetfulness. It was only by
chance that their story was not lost forever but slowly began to resurface in
1973, when one of the ministers' memoirs turned up in an archive in
Memphis, Tennessee, six hundred miles and a century downriver from
where it all began.[3] Though its references to a mentoring sisterhood were all
too brief and often opaque, this document served as a guide for excavating
the rest. As widely scattered remnants were found and rejoined, the more
complete version emerged that now takes its place in our annals and broadens the frame for today's renewed debate about the changing face of the
church and its ministry.

Those who speak of the changing church have impressive statistics to
back them up. In these waning years of the twentieth century, women make
up about 10 percent of the clergy and occupy pulpits in virtually all the
mainstream Protestant groups. They appear in yet greater numbers preparing to enter the pastoral field: on average, a third of the students in major
seminaries are female, and at the Harvard Divinity School women not only
have gained full admission but actually outnumber men.[4] These recent
and rapid developments are all the more striking when viewed in the
longer context that these pages have reconstructed. Yet this history's
most compelling effect is not that it distances us from the past by sharp-
ening contrasts between then and now but that it envelops us in a sensa-
tion of déjà vu, seizing us with a sense of how very little of substance
has changed. Even as this text was being composed, its author was able to
look out her office window and watch as a small Southern Baptist church
that stands just across the street made national headlines by drawing denominational wrath for calling a woman as pastor. This same biographer
listened ruefully as some Unitarian congregants balked at amending a
patriarchal text that has long been a fixture in their weekly services. Attitudes have not changed nearly as much as the numbers of women ordained
might suggest.

Today, as in the past, clergywomen complain that, if they are not looked
on as imposters or heretics, they are at best treated like the second-class

citizens of their profession. They note that their brothers earn upward of 30 percent more on the average and have an easier time getting full-time positions as pastors, while with the same or stronger credentials they themselves are likely to end up working as interim or assistant ministers, chaplains, or social workers.[5] While there may now be greater intellectual acceptance of the authority carried by an individual's sense of calling to ministry, there is nonetheless much of the same resistance to female leadership that there was when Olympia Brown, Anna Shaw, or Mary Safford started to preach. Without clear support from the rest of the culture, feminist theologians have yet to free the church-going public from their dependence on strictly male forms of worship and leadership. There remains, too, the old way of seeing a church as a chain of command, with discreet power centers for each of the sexes encased in their separate spheres, and this territorial view sets both men and women against putting females in charge.

Like their nineteenth-century sisters who blazed the trails and tried to clear the brush for them, women pastors today reaffirm the importance of women's traditional work and seek to return ministry to its domestic imperatives of building church families, making good homes for them, and preaching a practical gospel of neighborliness. While they object to the bias that gives them scant choice in the matter of size, feminist clergy do not think they have to be "tall-steeple" preachers to be a success; rather, they want to abolish hierarchical systems that tend to impede good domestic relations and frequently say they prefer smaller churches that foster a family spirit. Their inclination is toward a "more circular rather than top-down management" style.[6] Recognizing as equally vital the pastorates of all their members—whether they chair the church board or bake the cakes that pay for the pews—they encourage more congregational ministry, more lay presence in the pulpit, peer support groups, and intergenerational services. This return to the old meaning of *the church home* comes as a timely corrective to the growing consumer mentality that wants its religion catered.

Again like their sisters before them who spoke of the problems of worship by proxy, women in pulpits today have us question the worth of the kind of theology that has been most respected by the establishment. Many if not all insist that useful religious belief must be a theology of "dailyness" that is written in the vernacular of familiar experience.[7] They will argue that erudite sermons will not satisfy the hunger for greater spirituality and community in the church and that, to meet the need, preachers will have to start seeking their texts in the life of the parish, past and present, and build on the theology that they discover among the people. This religion "of doing and being" that the feminist clergy articulates requires that we befriend our history as the ground of a meaningful faith. In reading the narratives of past lives like the one offered here in this larger way, we find ourselves part of a timeless community of courageous dreamers, with whom we can anchor our common visions and hopes of a better world.

Part One

LIBERTY'S DAUGHTERS

Rise up! rise up! oh, woman,
No longer sit at ease,
The banner of thy freedom,
Is lifting to the breeze.
Be ready for the morning,
That breaks thy long, dark night.
Up, ignorance and bondage
And hail the coming right.
—Rev. Ada C. Bowles

Chapter One

THE ENTERING WEDGE

All endings imply a beginning. All accomplishment suggests preparation.
—Rev. Eleanor E. Gordon

I

When she was a child, Mary Augusta Safford often amused her family by preaching to them from a tree-stump pulpit that stood on their Hamilton, Illinois, farm, not far from the bank of the Mississippi River. These performances seemed to be harmless enough in the 1850s, when it was still hard to imagine their leading to anything serious. Mary's mother, Louisa Hunt Safford, having learned from her own Presbyterian parents that woman's nature and sphere had been clearly and permanently defined, expected her daughter to work for the church in the kitchen and pray from the pews. That she step to the front and deliver the sermons was simply unthinkable. In time, however, Louisa came to regret her trust in convention and consequent failure to outlaw her little girl's game, for the tree-stump preaching turned out to be the genesis of a life's work to which the Hunt side of the family could never be reconciled.[1] By the time Mary Safford was twenty-eight, she stood with full authorization in a Unitarian pulpit, the pivotal figure in an emerging constellation of clergywomen who dominated their church's development on the frontier for the rest of the century.

Actually, Mary's parents themselves helped seed the religious aggressiveness that took hold of their daughter and some of her friends just after the Civil War. For, while Louisa was teaching her daughter conventional wisdom about her proper place, her husband was introducing the children to new and disruptive ideas. In fact, at the time of his death in 1860, when Mary was nine years old, Stephen Safford, a farmer and teacher,

13

MARY A. SAFFORD
Pastor of the First Unitarian Church in Sioux City, Iowa, ca. 1890.
Courtesy of the Unitarian Universalist Association, Boston, Massa-
chusetts.

had become so outspoken in his defense of radical notions like biblical fallibility, abolition, and the new Darwinian theory that he was repeatedly called before his church board to justify them. After his death, his daughter discovered his library and the thinkers who had stirred him most and shaped his "heresies."[2]

From her father's books and radical journals, Mary began to grasp the breadth of possible religious belief. She was startled at first to find that some of her greatest revolutionary heroes like Franklin and Jefferson had withdrawn from established religion in favor of a more rational faith. She saw sense in their views that God had created the universe to run by natural laws and did not perform miracles or intervene in people's daily lives and that nothing was served by believing in Christ's divinity, people's corruption, or the Bible's status as divine revelation. It was best, they said, just to make ethical living the basis of Christianity. With Thomas Paine, her heroes renounced the orthodox churches as "human inventions set up to enslave and terrify" the race.

The indictment struck a responsive chord in the Safford girl at a time when she, too, rebelled against stern and depressing theology. Then, too, there were the unorthodox clergymen William Ellery Channing, Ralph Waldo Emerson, and Theodore Parker, who, by challenging the absolute authority of Scripture and making reason the final test of its validity, lifted the Pauline injunctions against women speaking or teaching. Their affirmation of all people's dignity and capacity for great service offered absolution to the Safford girl, who had always been taught to suppress as sinful— especially as she was a female—her nagging sense of self-worth and her ambition to make herself heard in public.

As Mary grew older, her mother's example as head of the household itself argued eloquently for woman's stature and potential for doing "a man's work" and more. In fact, throughout her adulthood, Mary most often described her mother as a "*most able farm manager*" who had single-handedly cleared the estate's indebtedness after her husband's death while rearing and educating her six children.[3] But during her childhood and adolescent years, when her mother's verbal promotion of True Christian Womanhood neutralized the message sent by her actions, Mary would have found it hard to reject the mystique had it not been for her friendship with Eleanor Gordon.

Just nine months younger than Mary, Eleanor lived on a neighboring farm in Hamilton, where her family's colorful religious diversity made them the perfect cast for a grass roots parliament of religions. Her father

ELEANOR E. GORDON
*Associate pastor of the First Unitarian Church in Sioux City, Iowa,
ca. 1890. Courtesy of the Unitarian Universalist Association, Boston,
Massachusetts*

moved out west from New Hampshire in the 1830s, but her Uncle William had since become a "radical Unitarian," her Aunt Caroline a self-described "Channing Unitarian," and her Uncle James a Spiritualist. Her mother's family were all Baptists, but divided between the free will and the regular or close communion wings, and the house was always strewn with the different religious journals they brought as their briefs. Eleanor, who by the age of eight was reading everything she could find, greatly looked forward to the occasions when all the relatives got together and the debates were resumed.[4]

Of the younger set, it was Eleanor who most displayed the intellectual independence that had run through the clan for generations. This dominant family trait was not only fostered by the climate of good-natured pluralism in which she was growing up but also encouraged by her position as the eldest of six children in a home where the mother was almost an invalid. Even before her father went off to war in the early 1860s, the girl, not yet in her teens, had assumed a large part of the household management. With a chronic shortage of money and time, she had to develop a keen business sense and learn to juggle a hundred things that needed tending at once: "fires had to be made, meals prepared, socks darned, dishes washed, and children put to bed and sat by until they had fallen asleep."[5] The responsibilities tested Eleanor's capacity to think and do for herself, gave her a healthy and enduring respect for hard work, and, most important, fed her already abundant belief in her own abilities.

Though her immediate family attended the local Baptist and Presbyterian churches—more by default than by conviction—and heard the standard religious point of view expressed everywhere except at the family conclaves, Eleanor had been impervious to the influence of the traditional church as far back as she could remember. She simply did not believe what she heard and was even less ready to do so after being served notice that there was no room for discussion. When she once raised a question in Sunday School that opened a door for debate, the abruptness with which the door was closed "ended all search for light in that direction": she "never tried it again." Eleanor's confident analytic mind and "utter indifference" to the specters of hellfire and damnation—which she doused in waves of laughter—provided Mary Safford with the very brace and antidote she needed to move ahead in her own, less steady "search for light."[6]

From all evidence, no two friends could have been more devoted or a better study in contrasts. Mary was a sprightly youngster, tall, thin, and fair, with pale blue eyes, straight blond-brown hair, and a radiance that made her appear all through life "more attractive than she really was."[7] Her enthusiasm and drive for success generated surprising reserves of energy, but her physical delicacy was what struck people most and caused them to speak of her as "spiritual looking" and "saintly," terms they never applied to her closest friend.[8] Eleanor had nothing of the otherworldly about her but was average in height and sturdily built, as steady in body as in temperament. More darkly complected than Mary, she had thick brown hair and a broad mouth with full lips that seemed tailored specially for her expansive laugh. Where Mary dressed fashionably and wrote in a graceful cursive, Eleanor, making no concessions to what she considered to be nonessentials, wore whatever was most comfortable and scrawled in an almost illegible hand.

Then, too, while Mary continued to show her early flair for public speaking and won commendations for "faultless declamations" and "charming recitals," Eleanor, while lacking Mary's presence on the platform, was a natural conversationalist and much admired student. Since Eleanor, an insatiable reader, had little in her own home to feed on aside from the religious periodicals and *Our Young Folks* magazine, she was as happy in the Safford home, with its remarkable library, as Mary was at the Gordons' place, with its good humor and open atmosphere. In these early years, when the girls' complementary talents and needs kept their friendship free from the rivalries that developed inevitably as time went on, the conditions were ideal for laying a base strong enough to support a lifelong devotion.

One summer day in the mid-1870s, when they were in their early twenties, Mary and Eleanor sat in their usual meeting place under an old apple tree in the Gordons' orchard and made a pledge that they would spend their lives together serving the world as a team.[9] After toying with the idea for some time, Mary had announced her intention of becoming a Unitarian minister. Eleanor, who had recently been elected an assistant high school principal after teaching for several years, seemed well on her way to a career in education and imagined herself helping Mary spread their enlightened religion along the frontier.

Like most of the professional women with whom they identified, Mary and Eleanor also concluded that marriage was not for them, having settled the matter while reading George Eliot's *Middlemarch*. Comparing themselves to Eliot's Dorothea, who was the same age as they when the story began, they were struck by the contrast between the limited opportunities for women in England in the early years of the century, and "the outlook for the ambitious American young woman" in 1874. To be sure, they conceded, even in their day the female's prospects were "dreary enough," but "inch by inch she was finding her way to a greater opportunity," and "at least she did not have to marry a Mr. Casaubon in order to find a mission." In fact, they told themselves proudly, the modern-day woman did not have to marry anyone. As Eleanor factored it, she had two hands and a brain of her own, and no one was going to tell her how to use them. [10]

The two had already learned something about how easy it was for a woman's pursuits to be derailed even without the inhibiting cargo of marriage, for both had been thwarted in their attempts to get a college degree. Though Mary's mother had had the money to send her to Iowa's state university when she was seventeen, first her own poor health and then an older sister's illness and need of care conspired against her remaining. Permelia Gordon had also done what she could for her daughter to follow her friend but could borrow from a neighbor only enough to pay the first year's tuition. The following year therefore found both Mary and Eleanor back in Illinois teaching and trying to get the equivalent of a college education on their own. [11]

Not knowing how else to go about it, the young women studied without any organized program, reading whatever seemed to be worthwhile. Both were already students of Emerson, Eleanor having first read "Society and Solitude" in her late teens on the urging of a "radical" cousin and later having added *Representative Men* to her personal library. These books seemed the staples for any "ordinary education," and she valued them principally as a part of the cultural cannon. "The American Scholar" and "The Divinity School Address," however, meant something quite vital to her. When she read them, she felt "a thrill of moral and religious enthusiasm" that compelled her to speak the words aloud and make their truth fully hers by substituting *woman* and *women* for the words *man* and *men*. [12] In appealing to scholars not to hoard their book learning but to use it to make the world better, Emerson set up her life's agenda, and, in challenging theological students to look for divine revelation in themselves no less than in the historical person of Jesus, he codified the evangel of self-reliance and human progress that she would carry as her equipment.

Eleanor and Mary also savored the optimism of John Greenleaf Whittier and Robert Browning, but their greatest hero, the one who inspired Eleanor's first real sermon and never fell down from his pedestal, was the Unitarian clergyman Theodore Parker. Eleanor had first learned of Parker and his controversial views from the *Dial* and the *Christian Examiner* about the time of his death in 1860, when she was still a young girl. The passion and courage he showed in taking unpopular positions on social responsibility had captured her affection even then, and her feeling for the man had grown and deepened into respect as she matured and gained a real understanding of his message. Parker's theological and political radicalism, leaving room for an intuitive knowledge of the divine yet heavily influenced by Comte's empiricism, connected her and Mary, as it did other religious liberals, with the new science of society that could furnish the data for social reform. In teaching them Comte's definition of God as "Collective Humanity," Parker strengthened their view that religious communities ought to spend less of their time in prayer and more in ethical action.[13]

In 1871, Mary, already displaying her mother's executive bent, started the Hawthorne Literary Society, which served her as a training ground for testing and expressing ideas. Mary had Eleanor, most of their siblings, and several sisters-in-law sign on as charter members; and, though everyone held an office at one time or another, Mary was the most active in writing the sets of constitutions and bylaws that were adopted, tried out, and soon replaced. Meeting weekly, they debated "Whether Deception is Ever Justified," if "Congress Ought to Assume the Alabama Claims," and of course "The Duties and Benefits of the Hawthorne Literary Society." The group presented book reviews, essays, poetry readings, and plays and occasionally brought in guest lecturers.[14]

A favorite speaker was Oscar Clute, a Unitarian minister who had recently taken the church in Keokuk, Iowa, just across the river, and had caused quite a stir by giving a Town Hall lecture in Hamilton on "The Evolution of Religion." In 1874, when he spoke, the topic was being hotly debated among liberal as well as orthodox clergy, all of whom were trying to reconcile their religious beliefs with Darwin's theory of biological evolution and Herbert Spencer's application of it to social principles.[15] Responding in a way that his Western colleagues considered conservative, Clute's sermon welcomed the idea of natural progress but not the Spencerian speculations about the limits of what could be known. These he rejected as unjustified and damaging to religion and instead reaffirmed his avowedly theistic Unitarian faith.[16]

The Keokuk minister's first presentation went over so well that he was asked back to explain his religion in the light of "The Age of the Earth." Before long, he was speaking regularly, both in the Town Hall and before an admiring Hawthorne Literary Society.[17] Clute gave Mary Safford and Eleanor Gordon the needed encouragement to start their first church in Hamilton, and, by the spring of 1879, the women were planning the services. The Gordon nephews and nieces remembered years afterward how they had sat by excitedly while their Aunt Eleanor and her friend Miss Mary worked out all the details.

As word got around, a number of veteran organizers came forward to help, the most attentive of these being Jenkin Lloyd Jones, the Unitarians' Western secretary. As the general missionary officer, Jones had cause enough to encourage these eager women in the 1870s, when it was almost impossible to get any male clergy to come to work in his district. As his predecessor, H. H. Hunting, had laid out the problem, the spirit of sacrifice had evidently gone out of vogue, and the young seminarians and married ministers who "would gladly have taken places in flourishing railroad towns, with established churches, inviting sanctuaries, and a salary from $800 to $2000 a year," could simply not be induced to go to "the border of civilization," where they were most desperately needed.[18] Yet, at thirty-five, the Western secretary was also destined by background and temperament to become the sisters' most ardent and steadfast male ally.

The son of Welsh immigrants who had spent many years carving out a small farm in Wisconsin when he was a boy, Jones had grown up within a tradition of hard work, resolve, and a high-mindedness that inspired the neighbors to tag the family "The God-Almighty Joneses." As both of his parents had come from long lines of educators and liberal clergy, Jones had also grown up with a burning desire for learning and an absorbed expectation that he would train for the Unitarian ministry. His dream of a university education was dashed, however, by the Civil War, in which he enlisted to spare his brothers from having to leave the farm; and, when he was finally able to enter the Meadville Theological School, he had to start off in a preliminary division because of extensive academic deficiencies. Later, as field secretary, Jones took up the Hamilton women's cause as he did because he not only shared their ideals but also understood the struggle of trying to get the education a liberal minister needed.[19]

Jones's sympathies with the Hamilton movement emerged as well from a deep respect for women and their abilities. This respect was anchored in his relationship with his wife, Susan Barber Jones, whom he had married right after his graduation from seminary in 1870. From the start, the marriage had been a working partnership in which there was never a question of whether the wife was her husband's equal. Nine years older than Jenkin and better educated as well as more cultured, Susan had been the secretary at Meadville when the couple met and worked for her husband in the same capacity during his ministry. But she also served as his tutor, exposing him to art and poetry, and achieved status as a leader in her own right, sometimes filling her husband's pulpit when he could not preach. As colleagues, the couple coauthored tracts and collaborated in numerous efforts from starting the Western Unitarian Sunday School Society and the Western Women's Unitarian Conference to crusading for temperance and suffrage. Jones's manifest sympathy and respect for females throughout his life was to win the devotion of sister reformers like Jane Addams, who spoke of him when he died as "a brother, helper, and defender" to women like herself and those who had served in the frontier pastorates "and did not always have an easy time."[20]

Jones clearly had every reason to expect that the women in Hamilton would be the hope of liberal expansion in the Western Conference and, as soon as he heard of their venture, began to promote it vigorously as a worthy work in its own right and as an incentive to others. In the fall, his new weekly publication *Unity* started to spotlight the gifted woman who in just a few months had shown such a knack for disarming the opposition that she was now preaching to a small but stable congregation every week. After spending a day on location himself and watching the preacher in action, Jones was convinced that her group would grow steadily. As it turned out, his expectation was not only met but exceeded. By year's end, the Sunday attendance in Hamilton was running well over 150 and sometimes as high as two hundred, and, during the week, the circle was sponsoring lectures and plays in the evenings. If this were not gratification enough, Jones reported, the minister and her assistant Miss Gordon were also holding services for a satellite group eight miles out in a little country church that was "crowded to overflowing."[21]

This was precisely the kind of talent that Jones had been looking for, not only to build new societies, but also to serve such leaderless parishes as the one in Humboldt, Iowa, where an exceptionally promising group was in the process of building a church but had not yet been able to keep a permanent minister. Jones, who had been to the town several times and was determined to help, asked Safford if she would be willing to go; and when it turned out that the town also needed a principal for its school, the matter was settled to everyone's satisfaction. The women saw this as their chance really to start fulfilling their pledge. "We had decided four years before to work together," Gordon wrote later, "and now the opportunity had come for establishing our home."[22]

II

Humboldt was a natural training ground, or, as some said, "a nursery," for women who had unorthodox aspirations. The town was itself an anomaly, a pocket of some of the most extreme liberal dissenters surrounded by staunch evangelicals out on the prairies of northwestern Iowa. In 1880, seventeen years after being carved out in a little valley right where the rushing Des Moines River came to a fork, the colony of six hundred still lay at the edge of an untamed frontier. Its founding father, Stephen H. Taft, a defector from the Methodist ministry in upper New York State, had harnessed the white water for a saw and grist mill and forged from the wilderness a modest commercial center. Besides stores and shops and a public school, Taft's followers had established a college and etched in a network of roads that joined the hub to its nearest neighbors. When the railroad connected the town to the outside world within a few years, a steady stream of Taft's former parishioners came through the conduits to find new prosperity in his "western paradise."[23]

Taft had dedicated his colony to "freedom and unity in religion," temperance and social responsibility, and "equal rights for all, both black and white, male and female." As soon as the group had settled in, he began holding noncreedal services to promote these values and, using whatever space he could find, simply carried his pulpit and family melodeon from storeroom to schoolhouse to vacant shops.[24] It was only after the Catholics and orthodox Protestants moved into town and began to present a significant opposition that Taft's constituency took steps toward improving their image and broadening their base. In 1875, they reorganized as the Christian Unity Church and extended a welcome to anyone wanting to study and practice religion "as taught by Christ."[25] To ease their isolation and improve their congregational life, they also decided to enter the national fellowship of Unitarians and build a permanent place to meet. Taft himself raised the money, superintended the framing, and, as he was ready to be relieved of his pastoral duties, sent out the call that brought in the two spunky women from Hamilton.[26]

On 29 June 1880, even before the building was finished, Mary Safford received ordination in Humboldt's Unity Church. After voting unanimously to accept in the absence of any advanced education the candidate's proven ability as sufficient ground for credentialing, the Iowa Unitarian Association had decided to make the ceremony the highlight of its third annual conference. The church, according to one witness, "fairly oozed audience at every pore." Since the pews had not yet been installed, the townsfolk and visitors had to squeeze onto the long recitation benches that had been borrowed from the school, and the children, eager to see the lady preacher, competed for room on the floor or outside the open windows. Flaring kerosene lamps fanned by June breezes lit the dim hall, revealing a makeshift platform that had been lavishly covered with flowers.[27]

Safford had arranged the simple order of service herself as a kind of wedding in which she was giving herself to her faith, and, in keeping with this not uncommon conception, the mood was familial instead of ecclesiastic. As one of the organizers wrote slyly, this bride of enlightened religion was never in danger of being "led trembling" to the altar past "solemn-faced divines" who brandished "the five points of Calvin" but knew she would be greeted warmly by her "large-hearted" family of liberal workers. Jenkin Lloyd Jones gave the ordination sermon and Oscar Clute the "Right Hand of Fellowship."[28] Iowa Unitarian Association secretary Cordelia Throop Cole had been the obvious choice for presenting the "Charge." For Cole's marriage to a minister had convinced her years before that women were the unsung talent that kept churches running and should be given not simply more credit but full access to the clerical office. She saw Mary Safford's request for this authorization as a breakthrough and was deeply gratified to have the chance to offer herself as a "friend, sister woman, and possible mother."[29]

As a feminist, Cole's evolution had been a practical, not polemical one. Her ambitions for women, however iconoclastic they seemed to some, emerged from the standard assumption that females had special attributes rather than from the denial of any essential distinctions. Proud of the differences and convinced that they would account for her sister's effectiveness, she warned Safford not to diminish herself by accepting the male way of doing things as the model for success, not to suppress or conceal her unique capabilities out of some sense of female weakness or "insufficiency." Rather than trying to wear a "man's armor," Cole cautioned, the novice must trust in her "own simple sling," and "the slender woman's arm" would reach its target. By answering this sacred call in her own terms, Safford would prove that the power of ministry was no more limited to a particular sex than to one race or region. This said, in a charge that repeated the essence of Rev. Olympia Brown's to Rev. Phebe Hanaford ten years before, Cole reminded the minister that in her mothering role she must not neglect rearing new offspring, especially daughters, to carry the ministry forward.[30]

While neither Safford nor Gordon put much stock in Cole's linking of gender to traits like spirituality or business sense, they both took to heart her advice about trusting themselves enough to fashion new and better methods of ministry shaped by their unique insights as women. The new pastor and principal took up their duties in Humboldt in August 1880, beginning what turned out to be a five-year residency and a lifelong attachment. Though both had grown up on farms and lived in the backwoods while teaching in country schools, the newcomers found life in Humboldt harder than anything they had ever known. The best living quarters that they could rent were a second-floor flat of five rooms, and keeping house in an upstairs apartment in the days before modern conveniences meant lugging up all the water and fuel and carrying garbage and ashes back down. When the cold weather came and the blizzards swept over the prairies one after another, "just staying alive" was a struggle, and there was much more than survival to think of. With all their responsibilities in the church, the school, and the community, it was not unusual for the women to work eighteen hours a day, from six in the morning until midnight. Gordon earned $40 a month for her work, well above the national average for teachers at the time; but Safford earned only a little more, which put her under the $80 monthly minimum that most men demanded before they would take a Unitarian church.[31] The enthusiasm that often comes with new ventures no doubt blocked out much of the hardship, for, by all accounts given then and later, the women's high spirits and energy brought the town a tremendous vitality.[32]

On Sundays, when the farmers' horses and buggies jammed the sheds outside and the people milled about before and after the services, it was plain that Unity Church was the town's fastest growing attraction. The combination of the preacher's novelty, pulpit power, and charm drew in new members steadily until the weekly attendance started to strain the little church, which could seat no more than three hundred at most. While those who came knew that they worshipped freely and not bound by any creed, they were always reminded of the ideals that united them by the words on the walls: "Freedom, Fellowship, Character in Religion"; "Truth for Authority, Not Authority for Truth."[33]

The minister's sermons, beginning with Scripture but going beyond standard exegeses, elaborated on what these inscriptions meant. In the modern world of reason and experiment, Safford explained in a paper that served her as a staple for many years, "experiencing religion" entailed something quite different from the sudden, supernatural change that was commonly thought to save corrupt souls instantaneously. Indeed, such a notion was probably more inhibiting than conducive to reform. True religion, she submitted, must first of all be "free" religion, free from irrational dogma that discouraged personal growth. Then, too, it must be understood as a part of human experience, as something "as real as the law of gravity or as the solar system." It must be put to the test of reason in people's everyday living and, like the modern world, was best understood as a process that worked through community. The human soul would evolve, Safford said, not in solitude but in society as people made their common tasks divine "by doing them in the spirit of love and helpfulness."[34] In these early 1880s, Safford's ethically based, humanistic approach to religion would have displeased the many Unitarians, primarily back in the East, who still felt a strong attachment to the old christological underpinnings. It was, however, precisely what Taft's mavericks and the frontier's "come-outers" from orthodoxy were looking for: a guide for upright living that held out a hope of immortality as a reasonable inference from modern scientific thought.

By necessity, Safford's society took an active part in the services, for the pastor had come with the understanding that she would preach alternate Sundays in Algona, a smaller town twenty-eight miles away. The vacancy that this arrangement created in Humboldt every other week inspired a novel system of lay preaching that proved so beneficial that other societies in the area started to use it. The idea was to have five or six members take turns conducting the programs, using initially borrowed sermons by favorite preachers like Channing and Emerson. Though the papers presented were seldom original, just the opportunity to lead the services and preach gave the stand-ins a pulpit apprenticeship that stood the church in good stead for many years.

As one of the cadre of substitutes, Gordon was fully aware that she lacked her friend's striking delivery, but she came to discover that she had her own strengths and poise in the pulpit and derived an immense satisfaction from her efforts there. It was a kind of fulfillment that crystallized in her memory of the morning she gave a sermon called "Snow" by William Channing Gannett, a close colleague of Jones's. "I had read and reread the sermon until practically it was my own," she remembered, and then had spent days choosing readings and hymns to harmonize with the theme. When Sunday arrived, she awoke to find that Mother Nature had extended a helping hand during the night by spreading a blanket of white down on top of the old frozen drifts to spruce up the setting. When, in time, Gordon felt ready to give an original sermon, she made it a tribute to Theodore Parker, her spiritual mentor, and wrote it with such intensity that she could still feel the rush of emotion when she read it again more than fifty years later.[35]

For the liberal preachers in Humboldt, who recognized that every part of the service was vital, trying to find appropriate texts for the hymns was a major frustration. It was easy enough to accept the spirit of the traditional music, but they felt that they must draw the line when it came to the words. It was ludicrous, they pointed out, to step to the pulpit and offer a Unitarian invocation and then ask the choir and congregation to sing "The Old Rugged Cross" or "Oh, Sacred Head Now Wounded." Safford developed a knack for rewriting the old hymns and liturgy, and most of the congregation were agreeable to the changes, with only occasional protests when some special favorite was tampered with. Gordon always remembered a worshiper grumbling after a service, "The next thing we know, you'll be trying to improve the Lord's Prayer!"[36]

The minister carried her love of experiments into the programming during the week as well and started, among other church groups, an organization called the "Unity Club." She suggested this name as a shortening of "Unitarian" to announce that the group, like the church, welcomed all people of goodwill, regardless of religious connection. The name was also meant to affirm that the study of culture, in its broadest sense, was the "handmaiden of religion," as the minister liked to say. As she conceived it, the Unity Club would draw no sharp lines between sacred and secular but would try to discover God, "the power that makes for righteousness," in whatever learning and truth its members could find.[37] It was in this spirit that thirty-odd Unity scholars, both men and women, primarily adult but also a few youngsters, started applying themselves to getting all the "mental culture" they could. According to Gordon, who rarely missed, there were always a few faithful souls who turned out, no matter how deep the drifts or how low the mercury. They were "afraid of no subject," she remembered proudly, and tackled the ancient and modern philosophers, higher biblical criticism, and at least enough Darwin to know that "the universe had changed front, so to speak."[38]

Early the first year, Gordon reviewed Herbert Spencer's "Data of Ethics." Others followed with programs on "Religion in Art," world religions, "The Relation of Disease to Morality," revolutionary heroes, Victor Hugo, and

Browning.[39] Given the leadership's gender, it was assumed that the group would also study the works of George Eliot, which were recommended to them as some of "the noblest" in all English literature.[40] Like other nineteenth-century feminists, Safford and Gordon revered Eliot as a writer who had been "dignified and transfigured" by the positivists' concern for humanity. They praised her "genial altruism," which took the place of creeds, and her "scientific knowledge of the natural sequence of law," which replaced "a blind faith in an irresponsible arbitrary something."[41]

What set this inquiring spirit in Humboldt apart from the intellectualism that tended to characterize old Unitarian pulpits back East was its vigorous integration with current affairs and community service. Unwilling to let the congregation settle into a church life of "all reading poetry or studying modern science," the pastor encouraged the people to form a philanthropic society and adopt a number of charities.[42] A woman's Unity Circle was formed and in a typical year sent donations to the Post Office Mission which kept in touch with unpastored families, the Benedict Home in Des Moines for abandoned and destitute women, a local humane society, and the Unitarian Women's Conference.[43]

From the start, Safford also promised herself that she was going to make the church self-sufficient and not ask to be helped along by the Unitarians' main offices in Boston. This aversion to being dependent on others— especially on the Eastern establishment, which she had already found too patronizing and "high church" to suit her—was to be a salient feature of her long career. She and Gordon had both grown up watching their mothers struggle to keep their families free of debt and thus self-respecting. Now placed in a mothering role herself, Safford kept close track of every cent that went in and out of the church's coffers and made sure her people remembered that, as a family, they had obligations to help pay its household expenses. With her associate's help, she succeeded where others had failed, year after year. During their five years in Humboldt, the congregation repaid all but $300 of the $1,500 it had borrowed to build the church, no small feat in a community where the people with any assets worth talking about were all "land poor."[44] As a later parishioner analyzed it, "when Miss Safford's charm and emotional appeal did not reach . . . the heart or the pocketbook of 'the practical business man,' the scientific knowledge, touch of humor and 'hard common sense' of Miss Gordon appealed to his reason" and opened his purse.[45]

Chapter Two

LENGTHENING CORDS AND STRENGTHENING STAKES

Enlarge the place of your tent . . .
hold not back, lengthen your cords
and strengthen your stakes.
For the Lord has called you like a wife forsaken.
—Isaiah 54:2, 6

I

Looking back from a distance of well over half a century, it seemed to Gordon that she and Safford had been much too busy in Humboldt to think about being exiled halfway across the continent, hundreds of miles from the rest of the liberal fold.[1] Yet, to judge from the effort they made to get to distant conferences and their pleadings with friends from the outside world to come visit with them in Iowa, the women were always aware of their isolation and even were vitalized by it. As the powerful impetus for even greater unification at home and a simultaneous reaching out, the feeling of being cut off from the larger denominational family inspired a motto that often appeared on their orders of service: "Lengthen the cords," it commanded, "and strengthen the stakes!"

The Iowa Unitarian Association served as a bridge between Humboldt's Unity Church and a half dozen other societies. Liberals from Keokuk, Burlington, Dubuque, Mount Pleasant, Davenport, and Des Moines met several times a year to organize missionary efforts and cooperative fieldwork in the territory.[2] Unable to resist the administrative challenge, Safford had quickly become involved in building the organization and before long was asked to serve as executive secretary. The position, which grew with Saf-

29

ford's ideas about what could be done with it, put Humboldt at the center of the state movement and primed Safford for the presidency, to which she moved rapidly.

Humboldt's minister and her associate also lengthened the cords by arranging for pulpit exchanges and visits from colleagues like Jenkin Lloyd Jones and Oscar Clute. A three-day visit one year by the temperance reformer Mary Livermore was particularly memorable, for, when the guest was not at the church speaking, she and her hosts retreated to the upstairs parsonage and talked for hours about their lives and goals as sister crusaders. "We would sit down close to the hard coal base burner, for it was intensely cold, and listen to her wonderful experiences," Gordon always remembered. For the young idealistic hosts, who usually could admire such people only from a great distance, these visits served as a lifeline to a vital, inspiring community.[3]

Meanwhile, Safford and Gordon were also strengthening the stakes. They expanded their two-person home to a household of half-a-dozen females by taking in four teenage girls from Illinois, presumably former students of Gordon's, who helped as parish assistants and teaching aides while attending the town's Normal College. While this "family" of six stands out as unique in the Humboldt County census, the arrangement was actually but an extension of well-established nurturing structures that had long connected women across generations. In the female world, girls had always been systematically, almost ritualistically, trained by mothers and other older women in the domestic arts that they would need in their adult roles;[4] and, now that Safford and Gordon saw that women had real alternatives to housewifery and motherhood, they felt compelled to tutor younger sisters who wanted to enter the work that they had chosen for themselves. At the same time, of course, the younger generation increased their mentors' effectiveness by relieving them of the routine tasks that claimed energy better spent elsewhere.

To be sure, the parsonage welcomed all the young people to its extended family. There were boys like Frank Bicknell, who lived with his parents across the street and by age fourteen had become a permanent fixture at the pastor and principal's "headquarters." The young Bicknell carried the women's wood, coal, and water up the long flight of stairs and spent long afternoons helping Gordon mark younger students' papers and talking about the world and the future, cementing a friendship that lasted for sixty years, until Gordon's death.[5] For the most part, however, it was the girls

whom Safford and Gordon attracted and took under wing with the uncon-
cealed hope of recruiting a new line of liberal ministers.

One of these girls was Mary Collson, who was just nine years old when
Safford and Gordon began their work in Humboldt. A bright and sensitive
child from a poor family, Mary was quickly won over by the nurturant
atmosphere at the parsonage and transformed into one of the parish's most
conscientious lay workers. She attended the meetings of Unity Club, joined
the Sunday school, and down at the schoolhouse became one of Eleanor
Gordon's most promising students. By the time she had finished the tenth
grade, her future was clearly mapped out. First the principal helped her
finance a move to Fort Dodge, where the school was bigger; then, when it
was time for college and seminary, Gordon again squeezed enough from her
small salary for additional loans. There was never the slightest doubt in
Mary's mind that she would follow her mentors; for, seeing them daily as
able and confident leaders in the community, she developed a certain forgetfulness of gender that seemed to make all things possible. Through their
example and support—the "laying on of hands" by which feminists have
long been consecrated—Mary and other girls like her were "destined" from
"early childhood," as Collson expressed it, to join the procession of women
who were entering liberal pulpits.[6]

As the Humboldt parish developed into a magnet for women called to
the ministry, it began also to serve as a hub for a pastoral network that
spread throughout Iowa and into neighboring states. The branching out
started in 1882, when Ida Hultin, a twenty-six-year-old Michigan lay
preacher, came to Algona to step in for Safford, who was already overex-
tended and no longer able to juggle two pastorates. Safford's strength had
given way once already before a week of state meetings. Forced to swallow
her pride, she told Jones she had had "to give up, be sick and ask for a leave
of absence," though a little rest surely would put her back on her feet in
time for the conference.[7] The field secretary could see that his sister was
going to need more than that; and having heard good things about Ida
Hultin, he offered to ask her to take on Algona and soon had arranged for a
changing of the guards.

Safford's new neighbor and colleague had been raised as a Congrega-
tionalist and moved to liberal religion in her teens. Soon after, she had set
out on her own, done some teaching, and then turned to public speaking,
for which she showed a natural aptitude. Only recently, however, had she
come to accept her calling as "ministry." Being conditioned to think of

IDA C. HULTIN
Courtesy of the Unitarian Universalist Association,
Boston, Massachusetts

"preaching" as "something men did," she initially spoke of what she did as "talking" and never thought more ambitiously.[8] As she became more involved in shepherding small congregations, however, she came to acknowledge the full character of her work and even began to consider the possibility of ordination.

Like Safford and Gordon, Hultin had been defeated repeatedly when she had sought the advanced education that she felt she needed to be a good all-round minister. Once in the early 1880s, the woman had signed up to take several courses at the university in Ann Arbor, intending to finance her study through free-lance preaching. But having to drive her carriage as far as forty miles a day for services three or four times a week made it impossible for her to get to classes regularly, and at the term's end she had little more than frustration to show for her trouble.[9] Though she knew that she had the intelligence to understand the work, her inadequate background and poverty continued to get in her way, thwarting her again when she tested the idea of entering Meadville Theological School a few years later.[10] Unable to get her credentials through the preferred educational channels, Hultin grabbed at the chance to go to Algona and prove herself there.

There was plenty to test Hultin's pastoral skills in the situation awaiting her. Not only was there not yet any fixed meeting place for the services and Sunday school, but there were a number of factions within the Algona congregation and one or two people who seemed bent on turning out any minister who was brought in. Her neighbors in Humboldt were well aware of how much she had to contend with and wanted to help, but, as Hultin was clearly accustomed to working independently, it was difficult to know how to go about it.[11] With few traditions to guide them, Safford and Gordon could only discover through trial and error the best way to build a new kind of professional sisterhood. In her letters to Jones, to whom she unburdened her parish concerns, Safford spoke of her quandary. Sometimes, she told him, she feared that, in trying to pave her successor's way and smooth the transition, she had actually made things more difficult for her. "Being Miss Hultin's friend," she told Jones, she "wished only to aid her in every way," as she wished "to stand side by side and join hands with every worker for the cause." Even in sharing these confidences, Safford worried that she might be harming her colleague by giving some "wrong impression" about her ability and earnestness. "I think the same one who made it hard for me makes it hard for Miss Hultin," she said, adding that she believed that her new neighbor was "liked better in the pulpit" and would be able to reach many whom she herself had failed to reach.[12]

Despite Safford's fears, and whatever the actual difficulties, Hultin's job and her own became easier with the two of them working as neighbors. While Safford was able to concentrate on the state conference and pulpit duties at home, Hultin was making enough progress in Algona to feel optimistic. She was getting good turnouts for the Sunday school and services, had more requests to preach in outlying areas than she could answer, and found a sustained interest in the Young People's Club and a Tuesday night reading group that she had been asked to lead.[13] The neighboring pastors filled in for each other when illness or business kept them from preaching, and, by taking turns as speakers and delegates to the state and regional meetings, they lightened the load of professional duties that each would otherwise have carried alone.

With Hultin carefully tending the field that her predecessor had planted, Algona was soon sprouting growth of its own for the sisterhood's future expansion. As a way of preparing the ground, Hultin put special energy into youth programs, and, at the first signs that some future ministers might be emerging, she wrote Jones excitedly. "They are girls yet," she explained cautiously, weighing the prospects for bringing them in, but, if they decided to enter the pulpit, she could promise them solid support from the women ministers like herself who had never had the mentoring of a professional network themselves.[14]

Hultin's most promising candidate was "Minnie Belle" Rowena Morse, who was just about the same age as Gordon's protégée Mary Collson and whose family background and situation were also much the same. Born in Ithaca, New York, in 1870, Minnie was the youngest of five children in a family that had lost heavily in the stock market crash of 1880. As her father had broken off from the orthodox church some years before and cast his lot with the Unitarians' radical Parkerites, he had chosen to make a new start for his family on the government land near Humboldt, where other like-minded liberals had immigrated.[15] Though it lacked the urban East's polish, the Morses' new parish did offer a cultural life that was bound to have stimulated the young girl's ambition. Under Hultin's supervision, the Unitarian Sunday school and Young People's Club promoted egalitarian principles and reformist ideals.[16] The pastor joined Humboldt's in waving down speakers who came riding through on the lecture circuit, giving Minnie the chance to hear people like Ralph Waldo Emerson, Frederick Douglass, Anna Dickinson, Clara Barton, Amelia Bloomer, and Carrie Chapman Catt.[17] Minnie's teachers at school appear to have reinforced the liberal perspective, urging the girls as much as the boys to leave their mark on the world. They warned Minnie not to succumb to the passive behavior promoted as "ladylike" and encouraged her to make her life "as a *woman*" an "active song," to "*do* noble things and not *dream* them." [18]

Given the parish's feminist leanings and Hultin's special interest in the girl, it is strange to discover that, when M. Rowena Morse later described the formation of her call to the liberal ministry, she never once mentioned either Algona or the Iowa sisterhood but deliberately left the impression with her biographers and publicists that she and her family had spent all these early years in the properly "civilized" university setting of Ithaca, New York. This was not inconsistent with her lifelong habit of trying to make a success of herself by courting the male establishment and bending the facts to gain its approval while keeping her distance from woman's sphere. [19] One can only speculate as to the reasons for Morse's forgetting her early models in northwestern Iowa, but, whatever they were, any want of encouragement or stimulation was not among them.

II

By the time the Morse girl had graduated from high school in 1887 and gone off to college in Iowa City, the sisterhood's center had drawn in new women and sent out fresh lines across the state. In 1885, Mary Safford and Eleanor Gordon decided to move on 125 miles to the west to lead a new church in Sioux City and have a fresh team of women come in behind them. This move brought to Humboldt a thirty-five-year-old maverick named Marion Murdock, whom Safford and Jones had been grooming for just such an opening, and her younger sister and parish assistant, Amelia. [20]

Born and raised in Garnavillo in northeastern Iowa, the Murdock sisters had grown up in an economically comfortable home, and their broad-minded parents had given them every possible prodding toward service careers. Their mother, a free-thinking liberal who came from Universalist stock, and their father, a prominent district judge and state legislator, expected their five children, all of them daughters, to take an interest and active role in the world's affairs. They sent them to the best schools available in the area, encouraged them to read and to discuss politics at the dinner table, and tried to give them a range of experience in the public arena that would stretch both their horizons and their ambitions. Typically, during the 1870 legislative session, Marion's father arranged for her to work as a clerk so that she could see for herself how the government made its laws. [21]

The Murdock girls also enjoyed a degree of independence and latitude

MARION E. MURDOCK and CAROLINE BARTLETT
CRANE
*Associate pastors of People's Church in Kalamazoo, Michigan. Courtesy of
the Unitarian Universalist Association, Boston, Massachusetts*

that was customarily given only to boys. Their parents' flexibility was a special blessing for Marion, who was intensely averse to most of what went on in woman's traditional precinct. She much preferred weaning the calves and breaking the colts to cooking or washing clothes, and she flatly refused to learn how to sew even though she was expected to do so at school. Disdaining as well the conventions of fashion, she put off as long as she possibly could the mandatory hoops and bustles and even occasionally scandalized her younger sisters by donning a male cousin's suit so that she could ride their horses astride.[22]

Though none of Marion's sisters were quite as resistant to custom as she, it was impossible to grow up in the Murdock home without absorbing some of the feminist viewpoint. The oldest sister, Ellen, was an ardent egalitarian who collaborated with Marion in taking the press to task for "maligning the young 'Joan of Arc,'" Anna Dickinson, when this popular women's rights orator made a tour through Illinois and Iowa. What did the editor of the *North Iowa Times* have against this heroic woman, who had been "laboring for her people, her country, and her God"? The editor and his kind, they gathered, were the rigid sort who deemed it improper for *ladies* to "fish, play ball or skate," to refuse "the fashionable trivialities" that kept them from learning to think and be strong, independent human beings. They had heard and read far too much "about intellectual women outreaching their spheres" and "mistaking their vocation," the Murdock girls said. For their part, they intended to defy the tyranny of such talk.[23]

Since Marion had always been quick to claim equal rights for her sex, it was no surprise to the family when at the age of eight she announced that she was going to be a minister and started preparing right then. When she and her sisters went wading in the rocky stream back of their farm, she would run up onto the bluff and begin to preach to the small congregation below, much as Mary Safford was doing at the same time in Hamilton 150 miles to the south. Reflecting her parents' relaxed theological views and strong patriotic feeling, Marion preferred reciting poems like Whittier's "Barbara Frietchie" to preaching the fire and brimstone she heard when, for want of another, the family attended the Baptist church.[24] By the time she had reached young adulthood and heard several sermons by Jenkin Lloyd Jones, Marion had fully embraced the warm humanistic faith and strong social consciousness of Western Unitarianism. It was not until 1882, however, that the woman, who by then had been to three colleges and taught for a number of years, felt sure enough of her calling to take her first step toward ordination by entering Meadville Theological School. She was then thirty-two.

Meadville's liberal theology, Western identity, and friendly coeducational policy made it the natural seminary for women like Marion Murdock, and she expected to have a rewarding four years. The faculty and students welcomed her warmly, and she always maintained that, as one of three females in a student body of twenty, she never felt any discrimination because of her sex.[25] In other respects, however, her hopes were greatly disappointed.

The problem, she told friends, was that many faculty were intent on bridling students' radical tendencies. "Efforts are constantly being made to civilize us . . . to make us more conservative," she complained to Jenkin Lloyd Jones, who remembered a similar tug-of-war in his own student days at Meadville.[26] At one point, according to Murdock, an evangelical Unitarian lecturer, Jasper Douthit, tried to "punish" the students for their dislike of sectarian ties by trying to pressure the local Unitarian church to insist that they subscribe to a Christ-centered creed before letting them become members. Meadville's President Abiel Livermore, who was more in touch with the students, stood by his word that no doctrinal tests would be put to those who wanted to join. Yet by Murdock's account, Livermore's lectures on Systematic Theology were rooted in all the same orthodox ideas about a Jesus who was divine and authenticated by a display of miracles, and he continued to bring in new faculty who shared this "old school" theology. Murdock saw early on that she was not going to learn the more advanced thought she had hoped for, and therefore she simply resigned herself to an education in "bearing and forbearing."[27] After three years of such discipline and a summer's itinerant preaching, Marion Murdock became the first woman to finish the work for a B.D. from Meadville. With credentials in hand and her younger sister Amelia to assist her, she accepted the call to succeed Mary Safford in Humboldt.

"A slight little person with a low-pitched voice," the new pastor seemed to be "essentially mind" when she preached, taking such themes as "The Idea of God" and "Universal Religion" and developing them in a scholarly way, one listener suggested, "as a teacher of philosophy might have" done. Outside the pulpit, however, there was little of the lofty intellectual in Murdock's bearing. Parishioners spoke approvingly of her modesty and down-to-earth manner and privately smiled at her bubbly nature and constant motion.[28] With her sister Amelia performing the duties of "minister's wife," Marion managed to give Humboldt's liberals the strong leadership that they had come to expect. She continued the special Sunday evening forums that Safford had held in the church and in a typical year arranged programs on Harriet Beecher Stowe, Emerson, Victor Hugo, William Gladstone, and "Art and Religion."[29] During the week, she kept up the clubs, philanthropic activities, and sociables that doubled as fund-raisers to ease the pain of giving. The minister also drew large enough numbers on Sundays to clear the building debt within a few years, quite a feat, she told Boston, for a small town that had gone through a business depression. In fact, under Murdock's leadership, the Sunday School grew at such a pace, and the social events became so popular, that the church had to start planning for an addition even before it had paid for the sanctuary.[30]

These accomplishments had their price, however. Murdock's health began to deteriorate, and, although the people insisted that she take more time off, this was hardly possible when the parish was always on the minister's mind and followed her everywhere. There was hardly a time she could leave town without being notified of some grave illness or crisis back home. On one occasion, she wrote Jones remorsefully, "it was one of our dear little Sunday School girls," and she was obliged to go right from the train with her luggage in hand to conduct the funeral.[31] While she was away on another occasion, one lady died, and a number of others became extremely ill, two of them dying the week after her return.[32] In September 1889, the death of the Tafts' daughter, Mary, was an especially cruel blow, for she had been one of the sisterhood's protégées, a "girl of promise" as a "prospective minister."[33]

Although by the late 1880s Murdock was getting offers from other societies that could have paid her more and lightened her load, it took several years and a further decline in her health before she could break away from the family that had ordained her. Though she might better herself financially by going somewhere else, she explained of her hesitation in 1888, she "could never find dearer, better friends" than those she had made in Humboldt.[34] Nor was she able to wrench herself free the following year, even after she searched for and found a successor. "A very determined effort" had been made to persuade her to stay, she told Jones, and with such a great show of appreciation that she could not leave quite yet. Besides, "it would be a great sorrow to do so."[35]

A further inducement to staying in Humboldt was the fact that it was the favorite meeting site for the women ministers in the area. Gordon and Safford often came back from Sioux City for Iowa Unitarian Association conferences, weddings, and holidays or just to spend their vacations together and catch up on the news. The gregarious Murdock loved being a part of these gatherings and could barely contain her excitement when she wrote to tell Jones about them. "There is quite a bevy of us here at present," she bubbled one summer. They had just had a Fourth of July reunion with Mila Tupper—a young worker who had been preaching at Eagle Grove—Miss Gordon, Miss Safford, Amelia, and herself, which altogether had made for "a very talkative family" indeed.[36] At one point, the sisterhood even considered trying to institutionalize their base by converting the town's idle college into a ministers' training school staffed by proven clergy like themselves, who understood Western needs.[37] While nothing ever came of this plan, Humboldt remained a sacred retreat for these women for many years, long after Marion Murdock finally left in 1890 to work with a pastor in Kalamazoo by the name of Caroline Bartlett.

Chapter Three

A HAPPY COMPANY

A new manifestation is at hand, a new hour is come, when man and woman may regard one another as brother and sister, able both to appreciate and to prophesy to one another.
—Margaret Fuller

I

In the later 1870s, when Mary Safford and Eleanor Gordon were still back in Illinois planning their future together, another restless young woman had sometimes come out to the Gordon's orchard to join them. This was Carrie Julia Bartlett, the only daughter of a steamboat captain who had moved to Hamilton some years before and used the river town as his home port. Though six years younger than the others, Carrie had found that they had much in common. Like Safford and Gordon, she had as a young child rebelled against the religion she learned, having never been able to think that a God worth caring about could inflict pain as arbitrarily as the orthodox church suggested. She had flatly refused to swallow the teaching that unbaptized babies and heathens were sent to hell and that Jesus, for whom she felt deep affection as a human being, had been involved in anything as "impossible" as the Resurrection. She had agonized over the Crucifixion, "never could see what good it did," and rejected it wholesale along with the Atonement. Something inside her insisted that God's power make sense in everyday life, but, when she aired her objections and tried to explain them in Sunday School, she was either ignored or rebuked. Unable to silence her private revolt, she had about resigned herself to being damned when her father took her to hear Oscar Clute deliver his first Town Hall lecture. As she told it later, Clute's words had dissolved all her fears on the spot, and, from that moment on, she wanted to be a Unitarian minister.[1]

CAROLINE BARTLETT CRANE
*Civic leader, ca. 1914, in Kalamazoo, Michigan. Courtesy of the West-
ern Michigan University Archives, Kalamazoo, Michigan.*

It was a great comfort to Carrie Bartlett to share her story with her older friends, who could well understand what she had to contend with. They were able to sympathize when she explained that her father thoroughly disapproved of her daring ambition and would not permit her to mention it in his presence. His objections were understandable enough considering that the only female he had ever seen preach was an enormous, red-faced revivalist who, with a large, sweaty arm thrown across the penitents' shoulders, had knelt beside them and coaxed out their sobbing confessions. Carrie, a tall, slender girl with a glowing complexion and cascades of chestnut brown hair in which she took a good deal of pride, tried to assure her parents that she was not going to be "that kind" of preacher, but they were unmoved.[2] With no other choice, she let the discussion rest and did what she could to prepare for her goal surreptitiously. When her father sent her to nearby Carthage College, she entered the classical course and majored in Greek, "in the fond illusion" that as a minister she would find the language indispensable.[3] She also kept her dream alive by entering into her friends' plans to start a church, sensing as they did that this could well be the entering wedge that would open the field to women and ease the way for her.[4]

After graduation from college in 1879, Carrie again raised the issue of ministry and asked her father to send her to Meadville, but his views had not changed, and, as he refused to abet her ambition, she had to find other ways to get to her goal. One such avenue opened up in 1883 when the family moved to St. Paul and she took a job as a journalist. For at least several years, Bartlett had been reflecting on the kindred purposes of the press and the pulpit, both of which, as she saw it, strove to better society by raising public opinion. If this were actually so, she reasoned, the practice of the first profession would help her prepare for the second.[5]

Bartlett broke into newspaper work by free-lancing feature stories for the *Pioneer Press* and after a few months talked her way onto the staff of the *Minneapolis Tribune,* even though she made it clear that she did not want the society page and the managing editor could not envision a woman doing anything else. Over the next few years, she was able to stretch her employer's imagination by covering murder trials, fires, Indian uprisings, and political feuds—and packing a pistol when she went out on assignments late at night. This produced a portfolio good enough to land her a city editor's job when one opened up at the *Oshkosh, Wisconsin, City Times.* Looking back on the experience, Bartlett was justifiably satisfied that it had been as invaluable a preparation for preaching as she had expected. Newspaper writing changed her formal and somewhat stilted style of composition into an enviably efficient and engaging prose. It taught her how to work rapidly with all sorts of confusion around her and above all, she stressed, to know the difference between the world as it really was and purely mythical views of the human condition.[6]

For Caroline Bartlett's personal as well as professional evolution, none of her assignments as a reporter was more important than the National American Woman Suffrage Association convention held in the Universalist Church of the Redeemer in Minneapolis in October, 1885. Not that these meetings converted her to the cause of women's rights, as she liked to imply in later years when she became prominent in the movement.[7] Far from it— and quite as her editor might have expected from a reporter whose individualistic columns had already shown mild contempt for feminist politics— her write-up supported the opposition by questioning the wisdom of trying to legislate changes that would be better left to the passage of time.[8] Yet, if this assignment did not win her over politically, it did expose Bartlett to a female solidarity that she had never before encountered in such magnitude or intensity. Even more important, her interviews introduced her to several women who became major inspirators in her life. A friendship with Susan B. Anthony got its start at this convention, as did a closer relationship with the Methodist minister-turned-suffrage-leader Anna Howard Shaw, in whom the newspaper woman confided her "secret hope" of becoming ordained.[9]

In fact, Shaw's encouragement seems to have given the younger woman the extra push she needed to declare at the age of twenty-eight that she was now old enough to decide her own future. Her father reluctantly gave her his blessing, and she wrote to Oscar Clute, the Iowa Unitarian Association's field officer, to ask for directions on how to proceed and to lay out her motives and background. Bartlett's profile must by now have seemed a familiar one to Clute, for it was typical of the growing number of women who had been expressing an interest in joining the ministry. Bartlett explained that, while she had little taste for sectarian boundaries, she felt that she could identify with the Unitarians best because they did not impose creeds on either the clergy or the laity. She was attracted as well, she said, to the Unitarians' polity, which placed pastors as equal convenanted members of congregations, with special responsibilities for the society's care and direction but not any higher ecclesiastical power or authority.[10] Bartlett could not pretend, she said, to possess some supernatural influence. "Prayer to me," she explained, "is lifting our hearts up till the Divine nature overflows into them. I cannot do that for others—each must do it for himself." Her interest was putting the pulpit to better use by preaching sermons that showed people that their religious faith could be strengthened "by living a rational life." [11]

Bartlett spent the next eight months in the Dakotas, where she and her father had taken up claims of government land. She used this time to reflect on a series of issues that she felt she must try to work through herself before she could be any help to others. Why did she believe in God or in immortality? What was the Bible's importance for her? What was the basis of ethics? What should a liberal church mean to a community? Bartlett wrote out the answers to these and other questions in the form of sermons, sent them to Clute and Jones for their critiques, and arrived back in civilization not only with a clearer sense of what she believed but also with enough pulpit material to last her six months. [12] When the Iowa Unitarian Association met in Des Moines in the fall of 1887, Mary Safford, now the association's president, and a half dozen sister preachers welcomed their new colleague into their ranks, and, a few months later, just before the New Year, Carrie Bartlett accepted a call from a young church in Sioux Falls, Dakota.

II

Though barely out of its infancy, the Sioux Falls society already had a tradition of female leadership. For the group had been organized by a middle-aged missionary and mother of six named Eliza Wilkes, a woman who had been preaching in the backwoods for years with the blessings of both the Unitarians and the Universalists. When a core of thirty religious liberals approached her about starting some sort of movement in Sioux Falls, she began holding worship services in her husband's law office. Since, however, her own interest was in starting new groups, not maintaining them once they got going, she set out to find a regular minister, preferably one who was a female. A decade of looking for competent help had minimized her expectations of the male seminarians who were sent out from the East. While she had found most to be likable enough, they had been too academic and failed to understand that, to build and sustain congregations, a minister had to speak plainly and be concrete. Even less satisfactory were the young men who tried to serve up Boston's kind of theology to hungry

ELIZA TUPPER WILKES
*Courtesy of the Unitarian Universalist Association,
Boston, Massachusetts*

liberals out on the frontier. "A course at Harvard is not sufficient antidote for a lifetime in Orthodoxy," Wilkes complained to the officer sending them out. "You cannot plant 'eastern Unitarian churches' in this soil." [13]

After her many disappointments, Wilkes had been overjoyed to see the nucleus of capable women forming in Iowa and spreading out to take up the slack where the men had either failed or else refused to come. Not only were these sister ministers more idealistic and willing to work a lot harder, but, as native Westerners, they understood their parishioners' world, and, if they had no advanced education, they also had neither the supercilious airs nor the academic provinciality that had often prevented well-schooled ministers from reaching rural parishioners. With so many people asking to hear the liberal message and so few to carry it, Wilkes felt her own limitations acutely. "If only I could multiply myself," she suggested wistfully in a letter to Boston while trying to get them to understand her frustration. [14]

Carrie Bartlett's arrival in Sioux Falls in early 1887 was an answer to Eliza Wilkes's prayer. Within just a matter of months, the new pastor had anchored the group by renting the Adventists' chapel for Sundays, organized a church school and a Lady's Unity Circle, and put in motion a plan to construct a sanctuary. By the end of March, the women's concerted appeals from the pulpit had brought in the $1,200 in cash that was needed to purchase a lot and pledges of an additional $800 toward the construction costs. [15] A handsome new building of Sioux quartzite stone, replete with modern furnaces, parlors, and a suite of minister's rooms, was ready for occupancy by year's end, and "it was a happy company," as Wilkes told her colleague Jones afterward, that filled the hall when the new pastor stepped to the pulpit to preach her first sermon there. [16]

If the minister's gender was ever an issue in Sioux Falls's Unity Church, it was only because it established the norm, not because it was something exceptional. With Bartlett presiding most Sundays, unless Wilkes or Safford's group were there instead, the congregation came to think of their pulpit as female domain, and there seemed to be something amiss the first time the pastor exchanged pulpits with a male colleague. The Wilkeses' little girl Queenie had been so thoroughly unprepared and scandalized that she cried out in a whisper that everyone heard—and many repeated for years—"Look, mama! There's a *man* up there in the pulpit!" [17] Thanks to stories like this one, the distaff's hegemony during this period was to become legendary.

While the members could not have been happier with their minister's first year, Bartlett herself was both pleased and dissatisfied. She had gone to

Sioux Falls for a token salary thinking that she would have time for enough
independent study to offer "a passable substitute" for the seminary training
she lacked and with this expectation had even put off her ordination.[18] But,
as Wilkes or the others might have warned had they not all been so eager to
have her take the position, pulpit duties and parish work, to say nothing of
building campaigns, left little time for quiet meditation. As early as the fall
of 1887, Bartlett was talking about resigning after the holidays to attend a
winter school of short courses Jones might be offering in Chicago and then
staying on in the city to spend a term at the university. But Safford and
Gordon came to Wilkes's aid and talked Bartlett out of leaving, advising her
that her "unquestioned duty" lay with her infant society.[19] The call to duty
was sweetened by a congregational vote to pay her another $400 for ten
months, which practically doubled her wage and brought it to more than
what Safford had started out earning in Humboldt. The next year, however,
when given a chance to move back to civilization and take what she imagined would be a much less consuming position, she grabbed it.

This opening came in the spring of 1889, when the Western Conference
decided to try to resuscitate a moribund church in Kalamazoo and recommended that Bartlett be asked to oversee the effort for a salary of $100 a
month.[20] According to what she told newsmen initially, she was still thinking wishfully that for the first year she could limit her church work to
weekends and stay in Chicago during the week to study theology. But the
impracticality of such a plan, which the church board never approved
anyway, was made clear to her soon enough. The church had been inactive
ever since a bitter congregational quarrel had torn it apart some years before
and left it without a pastor, regular services, or a Sunday School. This left an
enormous job of putting the pieces back together, and for a compulsive
organizer like Bartlett, the challenge was irresistible. Predictably, the plans
for Chicago were shelved.[21]

Even before her fall contract went into effect, the pastor had started
repairing the damage and putting her new house in order. During the
spring and summer, she roused the dormant building and grounds committees and asked them to make the neglected property safe and presentable.
Her eye for detail noted overgrown brush and hazardous trees and the need
for storm doors, a wood slide, and new lighting fixtures for the lectern. At
the same time, she began to make renovations in the worship services to
eliminate the kind of dissonance that had grated on her the first time she
preached and the choir had sung a theology quite out of harmony with the
pulpit. She asked that any anthems or other church music be submitted to

her in advance, that she be given the privilege of editing the texts as she thought necessary, and that up-to-date Western Unitarian hymnals be purchased. In clearing out the cobwebs to make the church home more attractive, Bartlett also asked that the practice of church members paying for pews be abandoned and all the seats be unreserved and free to the general public.[22]

Since Kalamazoo was not a Sioux Falls and had never before had a female pastor, the new minister also had to uproot the old-fashioned attitudes that kept the church from making full use of its woman power. Bartlett knew from the start that there was a strong conservative element; they had threatened to boycott her services when she first preached and abandoned the plan only when curiosity got the better of them. Yet the total absence of women on the church's policy-making boards showed that even the friendlier faction held to conventional demarcations. Now, however, the combination of Bartlett's Gibson Girl beauty, powerful preaching, and awesome executive skills posed a serious challenge to the validity of the gender stereotypes.[23] Soon the pastor's appeal had reached the point where she had to hold two Sunday services, the people had turned their attention from what she looked like to what she said and did, and the congregation voted to seat two women on its board of trustees.[24]

By the time of her ordination in October 1889, Carrie Bartlett had come to feel, as her sister colleagues before her had felt, that this formal passage was more than simply another important professional step or, as a domestic contract, certainly more than the usual marriage. For, as a position that made her the mother and head of a congregation as well as her group's business manager and representative in the public arena, the minister's office established a woman's majority as a whole, mature person. Bartlett's sense of achieving this status was so strong that she now decided to change her name to Caroline, which she thought more fitting in "a profession of such responsibility and dignity." "*Carrie was more suitable for your little girl,*" she explained to her father, and it would be as inappropriate now as using just her first initials. From this point on, she told him, people would need to know that it was neither a man nor a girl, but *a woman* running the church.[25]

Chapter Four

COMING TO THE FRONT

For now the Lord hath made room for us, and we shall be fruitful in the land.
—Genesis 26:22

I

Quite unlike Mary Safford's, Eleanor Gordon's choice of career had been the expected one for single women who wanted to find respectable work away from the home in the 1870s. Since the start of the public schools fifty years earlier, so many women had flocked to the schoolrooms that females accounted for almost two-thirds of the teachers by the time Gordon joined them. Not that the field led to any great wealth or prestige. Women teachers earned only half what their male counterparts were usually paid and, though legal reforms in the 1870s paved the way for women in states like Gordon's to hold administrative posts, relatively few infiltrated these bastions of male authority.[1] Yet, even so, the teaching profession offered at least an avenue, as Catherine Beecher said, "to honourable independence and extensive usefulness" well within "the prescribed boundaries of feminine modesty."[2] Beecher, of course, had recommended the classroom as a training ground for "the great purpose of woman's life—the happy superintendence of a family," and most women who went into it did so only for a season or two to mark time until they found husbands and started preparing their nests.[3] For those like Eleanor Gordon, however, who put little stock in "prescribed boundaries" and had no intention of ever submitting themselves to the strictures of marriage, teaching was of itself one of the ways to fulfill the "great purpose" of life.

Certainly, Gordon's vocation could not have been more congenial to the kind of partnership that she and Safford had wanted to shape in Humboldt. Indeed, so closely did her activities as an educator support the pastor's, that though no such post existed officially, Gordon was almost always considered the church's assistant minister. Gordon's approach to all education, secular and religious, was evident in the way she managed the town's little eight-level public school. Students always remembered her standing guard in the stairwell at lunchtime and recess to keep them from sliding down the black walnut banisters, and their parents remembered her monitoring the curricula with the same care and humor. While there were none of the extras like music, art, and physical education, which came only many years later, Gordon kept everyone busy enough with a rigorous complement of courses, including physics, chemistry, advanced mathematics, history, and literature. Moreover, when this proved to be insufficient for her first pioneer graduates, who after completing the eighth grade asked to come back the next fall and go on, Gordon had them return and added new courses as long as there was the demand.[4]

As a "modern" educator in an age when everything from theology to social questions was thought to be governed by fixed laws and principles, Gordon insisted that her students approach whatever was studied in the scientific spirit. Instead of simply accepting what was offered to them as fact, they were expected to use their powers of observation and reason to form their own perceptions of truth. With this kind of training, attentive students like Mary Collson grew up expecting "a full and logical explanation for everything."[5] Gordon maintained that her rational method never caused any problems at school, where her faculty of five worked together harmoniously, but she was frequently called before the school board by its trinitarian members for teaching what they referred to as flagrant "Unitarianism." Generally, this meant teaching evolution or anything that smacked of it, and this, as the principal learned, could be nothing more than telling a physiology class that the thumb's position across from the other fingers was what had made all the arts of civilization possible.[6]

There were, of course, no such problems in Gordon's Sunday School, where the youngsters were molded to carry on their elders' liberal ideals. The children were studying Darwin and Emerson and reading Scripture in the light of the higher biblical criticism before they had reached the age of twelve, and most of them never heard the old theology stated "by anyone who believed it" until they were almost adults.[7] Remembering her own frustrations at being bridled when she was a child, Gordon claimed, and her

Sunday School students confirmed, that she always gave them the "perfect freedom" to question and discuss, insisting only that they use the scientific method as the ultimate basis for any interpretation.[8]

While Gordon never lost her love for the classroom or ceased to think of herself as a teacher, her partnership with Safford in Humboldt enlarged her sense of vocation. For, while the division of duties had been clear enough when they first started out, the unimagined demands of their jobs and Safford's assumption of leadership in the state conference had altered the actual distribution of labor significantly. As the pastor's outside responsibilities grew, Gordon's also increased until she realized that she had become a "Jack of all trades" who was doing just about everything ministers had to do: running a church school, preparing worship services, helping oversee clubs and church sociables, and making parish calls. The blurring of roles, though disturbing at first, gave way to a new, clearer view of her place in the larger scheme of things: she was, she decided, a teacher whose service was needed even more in the church than in the schoolhouse.[9]

From their lookout in Humboldt, Gordon and Safford had seen the vast opportunities for liberal growth in the West go undeveloped because of the dearth of leadership. Like their sister Wilkes in the Dakotas, they had watched with despair as one preacher after another had come from the East to build up their infant societies, only to be their undoing. Indeed, since their coming to Humboldt, not a single new liberal church had been firmly secured anywhere in the state, and only Davenport had been able to find, in the talent of Arthur Judy, strong enough leadership from the outside.[10] The consensus in Humboldt was that these recruits were either "too spiritually minded" to manage the business affairs of a church or, equally fatal, simply not interested in anything outside their libraries. To put it bluntly, which was Gordon's way, these men seemed to think that the minister's job meant merely presenting "a more or less original" sermon for Sunday; the parish visits, Sunday School, and social groups "were all a great bore" and treated accordingly. In her Hamilton days, Gordon had been dissuaded from any thoughts of a pulpit career because she had neither the "academic prestige" of women like Murdock nor any great speaking ability like Safford's. But, after her own competence had been put to the test in the field and she saw that a Harvard degree sometimes did little good and often much harm, she was ready to move to "the larger school, the church," and "could see no way out of it."[11]

Gordon's transition from teaching to ministry was carried out with the same team awareness that had governed the sisterhood's plans from the very start. When the Sioux City movement called Safford as minister in 1885, she requested that Gordon accompany her as her parish assistant with the understanding that she be given enough free time to study to prepare to go on to theological school. Gordon, more patient than Caroline Bartlett, accepted the fact that she would have to wait for that schooling until the new church was strong enough for her colleague to handle alone. It would be "very poor economy to say the least," she figured, thinking of Safford's delicate health, "to injure a *certain* good worker for a *possible* good one." [12] But her strong desire for more education made her restless, despite all the parish distractions, and the questions of where to enroll and how to prepare were never far from her thoughts.

Gordon was naturally writing to Jones for advice about how to proceed. "Being 'considerably smattered' in many things but superficial in most of them, as teachers are obliged to be," she explained, she was finding it hard to know where to start. Should she plan with an eye to entering Meadville and study Latin and Greek? Or should she forget about languages and just read philosophy, literature, and history? [13] Eager to help, Jones suggested that the two of them might start a winter school with a program of short, intensive courses for Western workers who had little direct access to campus scholarship. Gordon was delighted by the idea and immediately started sketching out possible blueprints for such a program until a well-run, affordable institute had taken shape in her mind's eye. Their school might include an extension course of readings for study at home, a month-long summer school "in some *dead* town, where board would be cheap," and a two-week follow-up session in winter. If a program like this added just one good minister to the clerical pool every term, it would be doing just about half what Meadville was currently able to do, Gordon thought. [14] Gordon tried to interest her friends, but could not find takers the first year to justify even a winter school, and, by the time Jones announced, on short notice, that he would be opening it at the start of 1888, when Bartlett had thought she might go, Gordon was already locked into other commitments and could not attend.

But the problem was not only getting away to Chicago for several weeks during the winter. Even at home in the parish, it was a feat to get off alone long enough to be able to study in any kind of satisfactory way, so unrelenting were the demands created by the church's prosperity. [15] With the congregation having grown from a nucleus of twenty-six to an active member-

ship pushing two hundred within the first eighteen months or so, Gordon
had to slip off to her secret hideaway on the attic stairs of the parsonage to
get some reprieve from the constant requests for assistance.[16] By the end of
the year, she knew that she would never get focused until she could take a
leave of absence. Other factors had also begun to argue for speeding up plans
for sabbaticals. As Safford already had been ill a good deal and was obviously
in need of a rest, the women agreed to ask the people to grant them a half
year's vacation in tandem. They would travel a bit and then settle down in
Ithaca, New York, where Gordon would take classes at Cornell University,
and Safford would visit with friends and relax.[17]

If there had ever been any doubt about the leadership's need for a rest,
there was none by the time the two women took off for the East. In addition
to all their regular work, the women had had to make special arrangements
so that things could keep running smoothly without them. On top of
everything else, with less than eight weeks before the parsonage closed, the
congregation was offered an irresistible purchase price for its land, and the
congregation suddenly found itself planning to build a new church. Incapable of delegating responsibilities of this magnitude, Safford now had to
manage the sale, consult with the architects, and oversee the negotiations
with builders. She and Gordon had had to stretch the hours to vacate the
church, store the furniture, lay the new cornerstone, and pack their bags,
and they left the city exhausted.[18] As parishioners feared, the strain caught
up with them after they reached Boston, where they had planned to attend
the Unitarians' annual meetings. Safford suffered a total collapse and was
ordered to rest for at least six months, and Gordon had no choice but to stay
where they were and make the best of things.

Like the others of her group, when they made their first pilgrimages to
the liberals' Mecca, Gordon was surprised and disappointed by the denominational atmosphere. As she wrote Jones, the climate seemed awfully
shallow and "lifeless" to "a wild and woolly Westerner" who was used to the
storms and "*intensity* of the west," and, although she supposed that they
were "earnest" enough, she even had doubts about that. For they were likely
"to joke at . . . devotional meetings" and raised no objections to anything
that was going on around them. What *was* going on was a series of Channing Hall papers that had seemed so dull to her that she could hardly
imagine their reaching the people who came to learn something. Indeed,
after hearing the much revered Harvard professor Andrew Peabody lecture,
she honestly doubted that he had read anything written within the last

century. What these Easterners needed were speakers who knew how to talk "to people, not at them, nor over them." Yet an elite group of "a half dozen men" were asked to do all the talking, while the young energetic ministers, teachers, and "above all, the women"—who could have prepared these basic remarks just as well or better—were never invited to. In fact, "there was a *masculine* air about all the addresses that seemed queer to a western woman" and that made it sound almost sarcastic when a non-Unitarian speaker congratulated his Unitarian brothers on having women with them in their ministry.[19] The same "narrowness" kept Gordon from spending much time at the Harvard campus, where it riled her to think that, with a mere twenty seminarians for almost as many faculty, she as a female was not allowed to enroll. Rather than be reminded, she chose to stay out of the classrooms until she could get to Ithaca, where progressive trustees had the vision to open their doors to both men and women.

Gordon was finally able to take advantage of this more enlightened policy in January 1889, when her friend was pronounced strong enough to be left on her own. In the thrill of beginning at last what she had been waiting for for so long, she initially signed up for twenty-one lectures a week and then, regaining her senses, cut her load to a manageable selection of history, ethics, economics, and Shakespeare, in which she immersed herself for four months. From the moment she got to the Cornell campus, she felt that she was where she belonged, though she was aware that the other students regarded her, a woman approaching forty, as being totally out of place. She could hardly take notes fast enough—though frequently what she got down was written too fast to make sense when she tried to reread it—and she always had the impression that the instructors were talking directly to her as the only one old enough really to understand.[20]

Gordon returned to Sioux City at the end of the term for her ordination, which culminated a week of festive activities at the church. The parish had hosted the Iowa Unitarians' conference and used the occasion to dedicate its new sanctuary, and friends and visitors came from all over to join in the celebrations. But, if a representative from Boston was in attendance, he was not asked to take part in the ordination. Gordon could not forget how most of the clergy back East had looked with "bold horror" at women who had the nerve to encroach on their exclusive offices, and she chose only Western workers to represent her church and its ministry. Brother Jones was there from Chicago to extend the "Right Hand of Fellowship," while H. H. Hunting came in from Des Moines to deliver the "Charge." Mary Safford, whose partnership with the new pastor had been fused long before it was ever official, delivered her sister's "Prayer of Ordination."[21]

II

The remarkable presence of eight other female ministers at Gordon's ordination made it more than a personal milestone for her. For those who were there, it confirmed that a clerical sisterhood had really emerged and was growing. By now the once lone trailblazer Wilkes had been joined in the Dakotas by Bartlett and a woman named Helen Grace Putnam, who was filling the pulpit in Huron and circulating throughout the area.[22] Wilkes's sister, Mila Tupper, was also preparing for ministry and helping out with the embryo church in Luverne, Minnesota, while Anna Jane Norris and Mary Leggett had been working the soil in Nebraska.[23] In Iowa, Murdock, Hultin, Safford, and Gordon had taken command of their state's denominational work and already had several younger women in apprenticeships. Indeed, several months after Gordon's ordination, three other women received their credentials within a week's time, and the female ministry seemed to be well on its way. "Just think of it," Putnam exclaimed to Jones. "Surely we are coming to the front."[24]

While the female ministry did become even more noticeable in the following decade, its sense of collective strength was never to find any basis in numbers. If they felt like a large and powerful group when ten of them got together, it was because these women remained a tiny and spread-out dissenting minority who wrestled daily with terrible feelings of loneliness and inadequacy. Anna Norris, overwhelmed by the stress of working the frontier alone, so longed for a sister to share the load that she came to resent those like Ida Hultin, who seemed to have little interest in forming the partnerships that most full-time ministers needed.[25] But even women who did work in pairs spoke frequently of the kinds of exile imposed on them by their calling. Florence Buck, who came into the ranks in the early 1890s through her fast friendship with Marion Murdock, began with how "often lonely" her profession could be when asked to say a few words about it to colleagues in 1904.[26] Marie Jenney, who became Safford's assistant in 1896, and Jenney's hometown acquaintance Elizabeth Padgham, who also came in under Safford's eye, both found the Iowa network to be a haven of understanding that accepted them professionally after other valued communities failed to do so. Not only had Padgham's father and sister frowned on her choice of career, but her Smith College chums had failed to affirm her in it.

E. ELIZABETH PADGHAM
Pastor of the Church of Our Father, Rutherford, New Jersey. Courtesy of the Unitarian Universalist Association, Boston, Massachusetts

Never thinking that she could be serious about her announced ambition, and therefore happy to humor her, they had elected her as their class chaplain; but, when they realized that she was in earnest and had actually made her way into a pulpit, they tried to persuade her to give up her "idiotic career and come home and have a good time."[27]

The consequent need for a broader affirming community strengthened the Safford sisterhood's nonsectarian impulse. To their way of thinking, the abstract distinctions between Unitarians and most of the other non-evangelicals were but nuances in a culture that was overwhelmingly ortho-dox trinitarian, and liberals could hardly afford to let their differences come between them. To be sure, there were one or two groups with whom they could not form working alliances. The Quakers, for one, were close allies in social concerns and open to female leaders, as their three hundred female ministers witnessed heroically, but they also had ideas of their own about ordination and salaries that more or less precluded any professional coali-tion.[28] Christian Science, also a theologically unitarian sect that gave women visible and often high-paying leadership opportunities, was neither itself disposed to interdenominational mixing nor considered to be a legiti-mate and desirable connection.[29] On the other hand, the Unitarian sisters actively sought out relations with the freer Congregational groups whom they called "Liberal Independents" and especially courted the Universalists, who had been first to give women, their own Eliza Wilkes among them, full authorization as liberal ministers. To be sure, Safford's cohort did not care at all for the trinitarian character of the Universalists' "expositions," and the "business about the leadership of Jesus Christ" was "a stumbling block" when they and the Universalist sisters tried to speak with one voice. But still it was "too much to claim all the mental clearness and courage for the Unitarians," and they just needed the wisdom to see and accept it.[30]

Yet even the most inclusive groups of women in ministry could barely find enough members to stay alive, much less offer the members they had sufficient community. This was obvious in the congenital weakness of Julia Ward Howe's Woman's Ministerial Conference, which simply did not have a basis for more than a letterhead organization. The conference's own research in 1892 turned up fewer than seventy ordained women altogether, not counting the Quakers, a minuscule pool compared to the 101,640 Protes-tant clergy who had been listed in the government census two years ear-lier.[31] They could find only fifteen among the Methodists and Congrega-tionalists combined, sixteen among the Unitarians, and twice that number among the Universalists, though these, one historian noted, were seldom called from outside a parish to pastor a church.[32] Any really sustaining experiences of community had to come from the actual work in the field, where interfaith reciprocities, pulpit exchanges, and joint-service ventures brought women together. This was the kind of interlacing that drew a lonely pastor into what Marie Jenney described as "a wide spread web," whose "little centers" were fastened by women and joined by a common thread spun out of their "service and sympathy."[33]

Anna Shaw, who had never relinquished her early identity as a minister, expressed the profound satisfaction that came from being a part of the "wide spread web" after spending a Sunday in Grand Rapids with Caroline Bart-lett and Mila Tupper. It had been "a day in a lifetime," she wrote to a friend afterward, "the best and fullest Sunday" that she had ever spent. Tupper's Unitarian church, where the three shared the platform, had been just as busy as "a well-worked Methodist church," and, what was even more impressive at a time when male attendance was at an all-time low in the Protestant churches, there had been "a larger proportion of fine-looking, intelligent men in the congregation" than Shaw had ever seen in a sanctu-ary. "I was almost in seventh heaven when we all three ascended the pulpit of this woman minister's church," she wrote. "Never were there three people who rejoiced more in each other's successes."[34]

Part Two

A DOMESTIC MINISTRY

Everybody knows that, beyond almost any other, the minister is one who lives at home.
—Frances Willard

Chapter Five

TENDING CHURCH FAMILIES

The influence of the two most exalted possible vocations—that of a mother and a minister—combined in one personality ought . . . immeasurably to spiritualize and exalt the nature of her children.
—Frances Willard

The clergy's image and role had been linked to the female world for many years before the nucleus of a female ministry ever began to take form. Ever since America's dominant culture deserted the church for the marketplace, religious institutions, seeming the more expendable, had been left to the ladies as their domain. The men who presided, dependent on their clientele's good opinion, told them that their homely duties and the pastor's work were both divine callings and emphasized how much the two had in common. Preachers declared that those who raised families were occupied with what one minister called "the preamble to both ethics and religion," a sacred endeavor that should be considered a "rare and precious preparation for the ministry." [1] Of course, these assertions were not as a rule intended to be more than flattering rhetoric. Most preachers, already anxious enough about their vocation's loss of virility to be desperately seeking "a manlier ministry," were not about to invite the "weaker sex" in to make matters worse. Indeed, the vast majority were appalled when a few of their sisters took them literally and actually got ordained. Only the rare brother feminists like Jenkin Lloyd Jones, William Channing Gannett, Oscar Clute, Jabez Sunderland, and Newton Mann urged the women to draw the metaphors' full implications and act on them. This meant not only entering pulpits as men did but really implementing, as few clergy ever had, the idea that ministry at its best was homemaking for a church family.

Though unorthodox in their ambitions, the small band of women who rose to the challenge did not need their brothers' persuasion to recast their

63

work in terms of womanly nurture. Like most of their feminist generation, they had put the combative liberalism of prewar reformers behind them and taken to crusading for women's rights in the interest of healing and harmonizing society. Although they sought to dispel the perception of domestic competence as some sort of genetic tag carried only by their sex and insisted that men, if just given the chance, could also develop the homely skills, they did not suggest either that women ought to abandon the family responsibilities, only that they ramify the accepted female agenda. In describing their practice of ministry, they spoke of themselves as mothers of congregations who were making good homes for their families by using not only their sympathies but also their mental powers, business acumen, and understanding of world affairs beyond the kitchen and the nursery. If the conception of ministry as a religious housewifery made the male clergy worry about being lesser men, it offered their sisters a chance to aggrandize their womanhood by elevating the sphere that had been theirs historically.

Indeed, it was precisely because they did recast the minister's role within the familiar, nonthreatening structure of domesticity that these women, who never broke through the hostilities at the top institutional levels, were able to win the acceptance of their parishioners at the grass roots. While they could expect to meet with a certain amount of resistance when they first arrived, they found that this quickly dissolved once they showed that they could do "a man's job" and, as crucially, that they could do it without seeming less womanly.[2] Their approach's appeal can be judged well enough from their drawing and holding power at a time when liberal societies back East were languishing and the clergy in general had lost the confidence of the laity. The women had the attendance figures and hefty offertories to back up their boasts of having won loyal constituencies—with unusual numbers of men coming out, as Anna Howard Shaw had noticed the day that she visited Bartlett and Tupper's societies.[3] What was even more telling, they bragged, was that, once their societies had the benefit of good female leadership, they came to prefer the woman's touch and looked for another woman when they had to bring in a new minister.[4]

In one sense, the claim to domesticity was primarily figurative since the women in Safford's ecclesia had little time or inclination to engage in the mundane tasks that occupied most of their homemaking sisters. They wrote their sermons and speeches, led Unity Clubs, kept up the church correspondence, made their parish rounds, and tried to find girls who could do their cooking and sewing and keep the parsonage presentable. It was only because they did make such arrangements that they could honestly say, as they did, that their church and home duties were rarely in conflict.[5]

Indeed, even simple domestic tasks were as foreign to some of the women ministers as they were to the men in their congregations. Elizabeth Padgham had come from a middle-class home that had always kept maids, and, when she took up a broom to clean out the church when she started in Iowa, it was "the first sweeping" she had done in her life.[6] In the same way, though Caroline Bartlett encouraged her lay sisters' domesticity, at age thirty-two she herself knew so little about what to do with a thimble or a stove that having managed to mend a few things and put her supper together *"all alone"* was really something remarkable enough to write her father about.[7] But even for Mary Safford, who as a girl had done her share of the housework, getting down on her hands and knees to scrub floors was so rare in her life as a minister that, when she once did so during a summer retreat, she joked at the incongruity. Her claim that to work as pastor meant having "to preach and sweep . . . pay bills and wait on tables" was nothing more than a bit of lighthearted posturing.[8] In short, as one devoted parishioner later recalled of Eleanor Gordon, who gave her her very first cookbook when she was a girl, while they were quick to appreciate others' abilities in the kitchen or sewing room, as a rule these pastors "would have no part of it" themselves.[9]

The reality of what it was like to try to meet the needs of the church as well as those of the parsonage was conveyed by a letter that Marion Murdock's sister Amelia wrote to her mother in 1889 while she was in Humboldt working as parish assistant. With Marion out of town on church business, Amelia had been left with the care of the pulpit and people as well as the house and was overwhelmed by it all. That afternoon she had rushed home right after her visits with several sick families to start taking up rugs, only to be called away again by a woman with a newborn baby. "She had to have me last night at 5 o'clock with the matting in the dining room one third down and I had to finish the best way I could," Amelia wrote frantically. To make matters worse, she still had to set up two services for the coming Sunday and was in line to deliver the pulpit paper the following week. With all that to finish and housecleaning too, she had come to see, as her sister did, that "the two kinds of work do not go well together."[10] Obviously, a display of practical domesticity was neither feasible nor requisite for the successful female minister. Parish assistants performing the functions of ministers' wives could take up this slack. The essential element was the pastor's consistent promotion of values and forms that girded up the home and family life.

For most women in the ministry generally and almost all Safford's cohort, the same thing applied to marriage and motherhood. For, while more than half the women who were ordained in the nineteenth century did marry and sometimes remained active in the field without losing effectiveness, the rest did not marry, having observed that this step did tend to abbreviate a woman's ministry or at least compromise its professional character.[11] Older feminists warned them darkly of the costs of conjugal relationships and did not try to mask their disapproval when their advice was ignored. Marriage and maternity, "a profession to themselves," were "incompatible with what the world calls a career!!" was Susan B. Anthony's word of congratulation to the newlywed Caroline Bartlett Crane in 1897. "Either the home or the Profession—or most likely *both* suffer," she predicted.[12] Anna Shaw felt the same pangs of disappointment when she heard that the Cranes had adopted two babies, which she was afraid would keep her protégée from going on with "the things that so much needed to be done."[13]

As Shaw feared and Crane herself came to concede, if one attempted to be "a first-class mother," it interfered "considerably with almost any kind of career—even with a career of authorship within the four walls of a home."[14] With a family, moreover, she learned how elusive the ideal of parenthood was and how draining the actual experience, especially when there was more than one child to demand a mother's attention. While either one of the children would have been perfect without the other, she once complained to her husband, the two of them fought constantly when they were together, and it was "so wearing to work so hard" and still have these problems to deal with.[15] But then things were not any easier when she went out of town and left them at home, for then they were still never far from her thoughts, and the distance between them made her worry more. As a case in point, Crane was once in Chicago attending a suffrage banquet when a messenger entered the hall to page a Dr. Rayne or Payne in connection with a crisis at home. Uncertain about the name and fearing that the call might be theirs, she and two other women had torn from the room. As it turned out, the message was not for any of them. But, "even so," Crane later wrote privately, all three had "felt like starting right home."[16]

Such private confessions were not the sort of thing most career women wanted preserved for posterity or publicized, but Crane's are not the only ones of this sort to have come to light. Margaret Olmstead, who also aspired to being a first-class mother as well as a good pastor, ended up feeling defeated on every front. Writing to Safford and Gordon in strictest confidence, she said that, after attempting to "do it all," she was forced to admit that she had not only neglected her son but been "a failure in the ministry" and unworthy of the trust her sisters had placed in her. "Some women could manage a house, a family and a church all at once successfully, but I can't," she wrote apologetically when she bowed out in 1907.[17]

Even before Olmstead's resignation, her unmarried colleagues had been confirmed in their personal view that marriage and ministry were a bad mix and that an intelligent woman in any field probably did better if she stayed single. Not only had Caroline Bartlett lost a secure place in the profession by getting married and leaving her pastorate soon afterward in hopes of starting a family, but Marie Jenney's marriage to Frederick Howe had taken her out of the ministry without delivering any of the imagined emotional compensations. As ministers, women like Safford and Gordon had also seen their share of bad marriages among the lay people in their congregations. Yet, however unappealing the institution was to them personally, and however discouraged they were by its resistance to reform, these pastors were hardly prepared to abandon the ideal of happy married life.

To the contrary, as they conceived it, their role was in part to preserve and uplift the institution of marriage by changing the faulty assumptions that people brought to it. According to Safford, women ministers had a special responsibility for discarding the relics of an earlier, less evolved era when their foremothers were denied the stature of full human beings by being transferred from the guardianship of their fathers to that of their husbands. To right these inherited wrongs, they as the daughters must press for reform. Beginning with changing the rituals that planted these obnoxious ideas, they excised the word *obey* from the wedding service, pointing out that it was demeaning for any adult person to be expected to pledge blind obedience and agree to be given away like a piece of property.[18]

None of this meant that the marriage service had to be a somber affair, and the record shows that it was not. It sometimes became almost recklessly playful, as the time when Caroline Bartlett, with Jenkin Lloyd Jones's collusion, used her own wedding to pull a mild practical joke on her congregation, who came to the church knowing nothing of her plans, their invitations having said only that there would be a musical entertainment.[19] There was little danger of the people forgetting how seriously their pastors viewed marriage when they were reminded on countless other occasions. All the pastors had somewhere or other in their repertories a sermon on what a marriage ought to be. The thesis, as summed up by one woman who heard it preached by Eleanor Gordon—and gave it credit for her happy marriage of almost seventy years—was "simply that to work well, a marriage must be a matter of teamwork with neither the husband nor wife running over the other." In this, a "marriage of equals," they stressed, the wife was treated as a trusted partner and counselor and kept informed about every aspect of the family's business.[20] Such talk as this, Gordon acknowledged in her memoirs, was "rank heresy" at the time, and it put the pastor on the defensive for weeks afterward. But she and her colleagues persisted in pleading for marriage reform, often enlisting Ibsen's *A Doll's House* to bear their brief that, once women were respected as people in their own right and not treated as men's subordinates or playthings, "wifehood and motherhood would take care of themselves."[21]

As domestic reformers concerned with the uplift not only of marriage but of the whole family, the pastors also contributed to the popular promotion of the home as a "sacred canopy" or, as Marion Murdock poetized, "the crown of earth without the cross," a refuge where people took care of each other.[22] The ministers' own devotion to their parents and kin served their congregants as a model of filial devotion. Parishioners spoke admiringly of how Miss Safford brought her aged mother to live in Sioux City "as part of the family at the parsonage,"[23] and they nodded approvingly when they learned that Miss Gordon sent part of her small paycheck back to her invalid sisters in Illinois. While the pulpit's example was obviously an inspiration to many, however, the preachers did not rely on it to instill the values that strengthened the home.

To encourage and honor parental devotion, the ministers held "dedications" of babies and children, a tradition "too often neglected" by men in the ministry, they said. Here as in the weddings, language and symbolism deemed inappropriate were removed and replaced with forms that better advanced the liberal perspective. Instead of having godfathers and godmothers promise "impossible things," the ministers spoke to the parents directly and had them pledge to give their children the best homes they possibly could. For ritual, they placed white roses in the little ones' hands, sprinkled a few drops of water on their heads, and prayed that each would feel God's love through the love expressed by their families at home and at church.[24] The sisterhood also used *Old and New,* their Iowa Conference monthly, to reiterate the importance of putting the needs of one's family first. In a typical issue, one article cautioned the readers against getting so caught up in serving the world that they let their own homes become the "foreign missionary fields" that other people ended up looking after; another, a reprint of one of Safford's sermons, repeated the warning that members who thought only of their own interests were harming not only themselves but the family as a unit.[25]

If they found that a parishioner still missed the point and was shirking domestic duties, the pastors could speak even more directly. When their protégée Mary Collson, for instance, went off to Chicago to work for the Juvenile Court, which paid even less than the small-town pastorates she had left in the lurch, Gordon angrily dashed off a letter to Jane Addams at the settlement and another to Jones at his church across town to solicit their help in reminding the new resident of her first obligations. In Gordon's opinion, a woman who still carried $600 in college debts and whose mother was living as a "dependent in the home of an undesirable son-in-law" had "no business" offering herself "on the alter of humanity" until she had paid off what she owed and provided a home for her mother.[26]

Like Collson, young Nora McNeill learned what it was like to be lectured to privately about the meaning of family responsibility. Gordon was boarding with the McNeills, who were among the charter members of her Orlando church, when Nora's mother had to be hospitalized for a serious illness. Nora's father, ridden with guilt and overwhelmed by the prospect of having to care for the family alone, finally went to the pastor in desperation. The next morning, Gordon called Nora, just barely a teenager, up to her room and described what had happened the night before. Nora's father, whom she had always seen as "a man's man in every way," had not only told her that he was afraid and felt unable to manage his home but had actually broken down and wept openly right on the minister's shoulder. Explaining that she had been faced with a similar crisis when she was a girl, Gordon told Nora frankly that she, too, would have to step into her mother's place now because that was where her father and sisters needed her. The girl had a natural talent for homemaking, but she was angry and terrified that the pastor "would do this" to her, and she burst into tears. "But firm as the Rock of Ages," Nora later remembered, "Miss Gordon just went to her bureau and took out a great, white handkerchief and dried my cheeks; and I went on ahead and did as she said, though I sure didn't like it one bit."[27]

At no time were the ministers more attentive to the importance of family ties than when they conducted a funeral or a memorial service, and at no time more thankful to have an evangel of hope that presented those ties as insoluble. By rejecting the concepts of hell and damnation and stressing the ongoing progress of every soul, their religion made something akin to "salvation" accessible to everyone. It offered the consolation that the bereaved and their loved ones would be reunited and go on together "enfolded by the Infinite Love" that they shared on earth.[28] A letter that Wilkes wrote to Jenkin Lloyd Jones in the winter of 1888 shortly after conducting a funeral for a woman who was an agnostic spoke eloquently of the "glorious work" of bringing these "glad tidings" to families that had been broken by death. Wilkes had been called from Sioux Falls to Rock Rapids, there being no other minister within reach who "could be trusted to conduct the service," they told her, "without insulting the dead or wounding the living." When she arrived, the relatives filled her in on the details, which were familiar. "She was what you'd call an infidel," the woman's husband explained, for though she had read her Bible a good deal, "she said she *didn't know* anything about the other life" and "couldn't make out as there was any hereafter." Her idea of religion was that she would just *"do the best she knew"* and "guessed it would be all right," but "this had not satisfied the neighbors." Indeed, when the time for the service arrived, the townspeople were out in force expecting to hear something quite different from the message the minister brought. Wilkes "was glad," she told Jones afterwards, "to be where, by an open grave," she could proclaim their gospel.[29]

Florence Buck later echoed these sentiments when she told the Women's Ministerial Conference in 1904 about a funeral that she had preached in Wisconsin. One of her church's trustees had approached her hesitantly about doing it, awkwardly telling her that the deceased had been "honest and upright" but had "died of drink owing to an inherited tendency." The family was asking for nothing more than a private service in the undertaker's rooms, but Buck had insisted that it be held openly and with all due ceremony in her church. The arrangements were made, and, when the music commenced and the minister moved to the front, she saw that the sanctuary was packed with people of every sort, including the Bartenders' Union, who were sitting together in a block. "I looked into the faces of those men," Buck recalled, "and it was evident that some of them had been 'bracing up' for the occasion, and that the bracing up had not been effectual." Many of them were very young, and, as she spoke to them about character, discipline, hope, and love, she felt that this chance to reach floundering souls justified all the struggle of her ministry. The next day, the word went around that the bartenders, fully expecting to be sent to hell, had been amazed that the preacher had instead talked to them just "like a mother." "It was an opportunity that I would not have given up to preach before the President and Senate of the United States," Buck told her sisters.[30]

FLORENCE BUCK
Courtesy of the Unitarian Universalist Association, Boston, Massachusetts

The pastors' maternal aura was a powerful asset at a time when a cult of holy motherhood was flourishing in the culture at large. In her ideal presentation, the motherly figure had an elemental wisdom that gave her perfect understanding of her children and infinite sympathy. The secular culture was joined by the pulpit in spreading this ideology. Liberal as well as orthodox clergymen were effusive in praising motherhood, declaring that they knew of "no other word so sweet, so dear, so holy, so persuasive, so commanding." A woman who sacrificed "everything to the care and training of her children" displayed "a pure heroism" and the essence of religious shepherding.[31] In the popular mind, this sort of talk helped to legitimate a woman's guardianship of a church, the most sacred of blessed households.

But the clergywomen's motherly aura was more than a figment of popular rhetoric. In a day when parish calls were fast going out of vogue among the male clergy, the sister ministers still made these visits faithfully. Their priorities and approach, they told Marie Jenney when she conducted a survey, gave them a knowledge of intimate family needs that let them "get close to home and heartlife in a way men knew little about."[32] This claim was often corroborated by their parishioners' testimonies, which spoke of the ministers coming to them at all hours and helping in ways men could not. From all accounts, the ministers' motherly image played prominently in inspiring the parishioners' trust and respect. Elizabeth Padgham, whose twenty-two years with the Rutherford church in New Jersey was the longest of any woman's settlement and one that outdistanced most of the men's, found that people of all ages, sexes, and even religious persuasions came to her with "all their perplexities," making her something of a "minister-counselor-at-large" in the community. As she analyzed it, the men saw in her a wise and understanding parent to whom they could take all their troubles—many of which they would have been loath to reveal to another man—as easily as they had gone to their mothers as little boys. The women, on the other hand, came to her just as "naturally," but out of a need for a wise and understanding adviser they could talk to about uniquely "female problems" without embarrassment.[33]

The frequency with which these mothers of churches spoke of the loving devotion that they had received from their own mothers when they were girls suggests that their domestication of ministry was in part "a reproduction of motherhood" rooted in those early psychic experiences."[34] More clearly still, the sisters' nurturant style of ministry was an expression of their theological struggle to make a place for the female element in a male-skewed system. This entailed more than just putting women in pulpits. It meant reinstating the feminine facet of the Mother-Father God. Their expression of the maternal aspect of the divine carried with it the fundamental idea that humans felt God most immediately as the binding force that held them together and made their relationships possible.[35] As Safford summed it up in a talk to her colleagues on liberal religious leadership, their mission as pastors and feminists must be a ministry that emerged from an understanding of God as the harmonizing power that worked "toward a larger state of love" in communities, families, and friendships.[36]

Chapter Six

SPECIAL FRIENDSHIPS

Friendship is a single soul dwelling in two bodies.
—Aristotle

I

Church households provided the women who ran them with loyal, extended families, to whom they often became so attached that they actually felt like real kin.[1] Few were able to leave a parish home without the terrible pain of their hearts being pulled "by the roots," a wrenching that seemed to get worse, Gordon said, every time she went through it.[2] Yet, close as they were to their parish families, and much as they valued the people's affection, the ministers also required the intimacy of more narrowly focused relationships. Most of the women established these closer quarters with other women, sometimes keeping house as couples, sometimes sharing pastorates, sometimes admitting each other to their lives more as mothers or daughters than as sisters. A few elected to live with men, though none agreed to anything like the marriages most women had. Whether they formed their special relationships with their own or the opposite sex, they found their alliances most fulfilling and helpful in anchoring their public lives when they and their partners were both committed to the advancement of liberal religion.

The salutary effect of breaking the rules to restructure conventional home life was well illustrated by the marriage of Eliza Tupper to William Wilkes, a prosperous lawyer whose backing of his wife's ministry was unqualified and constant. While the record is sparse, it is evident that William had endorsed Eliza's decision to seek ordination soon after they married and from then on used his every resource to help advance her calling. He put his law offices at her disposal for organizational meetings and services, served as

74

the president of the church board, and underwrote the pastor's expenses, which included a maid and tutors for the couple's six children. Even when the family's income was cut drastically during the economic depression of the 1890s, William kept the domestic help for his wife and did his best to comply with her wish that the youngest children be sent to a boarding school run by their friend Jones's sister in Chicago.[3] One learns from Eliza's letters to Jones that even with William's abundant help it was hard to keep the demands of a home and an outside profession from colliding, but it is clear, too, that the couple's respect for each other and shared religious devotion enabled them to work through their problems with remarkable courage and grace.[4]

Celia Parker and her dentist husband, J. H. Woolley, also enjoyed a relationship that their close friends liked to cite as a model marriage. The Woolleys were both Unitarians of the radical cut and had made adjustments for Celia's involvement in church work long before she became a parish minister in her middle age. A deceptively mild-mannered woman with enormous determination, Celia was part of the Western Conference's lay leadership for many years and one of Jenkin Lloyd Jones's closest associates on the *Unity* staff. Her husband, a man whose abilities ran to the sciences but not to writing or speaking, confided to Jones that he was not only enormously proud but frankly in awe of his talented wife, a woman "remarkable in dispatch of letters," "quick in decisions," "excellent in judgment," and capable of a "brainy love" that "kept the . . . whole household in harmony."[5] Though Celia's decision to enter the ministry, like her persistence in voicing unpopular views about race and government, had caused the dentist an awkward exchange with many conservative clients and neighbors, he had always felt bound to respect, as he put it, "the dear one's individuality" and stand behind her acts of conscience. So it was that, when she resigned from her pastorate on Chicago's wealthy North Side and then said that she wanted to start a new kind of ministry in the city's black district, he helped her. He obligingly sold their fine private residence and accompanied her to their new home upstairs in the Frederick Douglass settlement house on Chicago's South Side, where they spent their last years together. "To have lived with her 49 years," he explained shortly after her death in 1918, "was a constant inspiration" and moral enrichment; for he always felt that, by doing his best to help her as a minister, he was "furthering what was best in a broader humanity."[6]

For Caroline Bartlett, as for Eliza Wilkes and Celia Woolley, the solid domestic foundation of marriage to a man who gave her respect and free rein was on balance much more of a help than a hindrance to her professionally. Augustus Warren Crane had just finished medical school and was trying to set up a practice in Kalamazoo when he first heard the woman at People's Church preach, and he started attending church regularly. The two fell passionately in love, and for months the minister agonized over the wisdom of getting married, though she felt from the start that, if she did, Warren would be the right man. He was bright and knowledgeable but also gentle and sensitive, and every bit as romantic as she.[7] Moreover, as the city's consulting bacteriologist and later a pioneer radiologist, he was also able to use his influence to open doors to the jealously guarded male world of medical science that helped her forge a second career in public health as few women could do.[8]

Then, too, the fact that Warren was ten years the minister's junior put the relationship on an easier footing for both of them. For the more retiring scientist, having an extroverted wife who was older and always to some extent wrapped in the aura of being "his minister" spared him of having to posture as the dominating patriarch. Comfortable with his own career and ample abilities, he was content to yield center stage and let his wife manage the family's affairs, including the financial end of his medical practice.[9] For Caroline, who much preferred giving orders to taking them, her seniority gave her the edge that she needed in order to feel in charge of her life and free from the male authority her father had held over her all too long. Warren pledged that he would not try to tame his wife and keep her tied down with domestic duties, and, even after they had adopted two babies at Caroline's urging, he kept his promise never to clip her wings.[10] It is plain from the letters she wrote to him daily when one or the other had taken flight that her love remained deep and unqualified by any regrets about marriage because the relationship gave her the best of both the private and public worlds.

If the marriage of Caroline Bartlett had raised some eyebrows because of her husband's youth, the marriage of Rowena Morse to the elderly widower Newton Mann raised more: she was forty-one and he seventy-six when they exchanged vows in 1912. Tongues also wagged about the couple's long friendship and rumored romance going back fifteen years to a time when Newton's first wife was still living.[11] A retired Unitarian minister, he had been Rowena's pastor in Omaha when they first met and had been the catalyst in her decision to prepare for the ministry. He had written her passionate love poems, and one can only conjecture how fully the young woman answered the feelings behind them or how much the passion had cooled in the intervening years. By the time the two married, however, the couple's relations had certainly become more relaxed, though they were hardly platonic either, to judge from the lusty impression Rowena left with a young, frankly startled parishioner to whom the pastor confided her active sexuality.[12] Clearly, the marriage provided her with intellectual stimulation and a domestic life that was free of family responsibilities that would have cramped her professional style. Newton's children were grown, and he himself prepared his meals and made no real demands on the woman he lived with. His husbandly role was essentially one of a doting and fatherly mentor, whom the church ladies recognized as "a darling old man" who "obviously worshipped his wife and would never have thought of telling her what to do." As he once told a colleague who asked him for their joint opinion, "The Dr. [would] speak for herself."[13]

At forty-one, Rowena Morse Mann was a most commanding presence. Admired by her parishioners at Chicago's Third Unitarian Church for her "masculine" grasp of affairs and way of conducting herself "with all the authority of a man," she seemed the very embodiment of self-possession.[14] She was, in fact, just as amused as anyone by her husband's protective attitude and laughingly wrote her mother, "He is a hundred times worse than you ever were about having me out at night alone, and so goes to all these church affairs and everything else with me. Some of these things are not very entertaining. But he says it is easier to be bored than worried."[15] It was Newton's concern for her welfare as a beleaguered professional that she most valued and actively encouraged. She was happy to have Newton earmark large contributions to her church treasury to remove the indignity of her having to work for a token wage, and, after the neighborhood changed and the church lost its clientele and folded, she had Newton write to the American Unitarian Association (AUA) and several societies in her behalf to help her find another pulpit.[16] Whatever the ungenerous thoughts of the A.U.A. high command or the reservations of colleagues like Safford and Gordon—who did not consider Rowena sincere in her relationships generally—from the couple's perspective the marriage turned out to be an ideal arrangement, one that followed its own rules, not others', and therefore enriched them both.

The marriage that troubled the sisters much more was Marie Jenney's to Frederick Howe. Indeed, as Fred later remembered, the older women had put up "a large protest" when their "Little Minister," who was at the time Safford's associate pastor in Des Moines, broke the news that she was going to leave the ministry and be married to him.[17] Although they had all wished her well and Safford herself had performed the service in the spring of 1904, they had had deep misgivings, and not without cause.[18] They knew Marie to be the most radical feminist in their group, an outspoken individualist who had come by her fierce independence through a family tradition of strong-minded women. Her mother was a pioneer suffrage crusader in New York State and a sister a law school graduate who practiced in the family firm.[19] In the interest of her own career, Marie had put off her suitor for years and had seemed to be getting more independent and radical as the years passed. As an ardent "disciple" of Charlotte Perkins Stetson (later Gilman), whose *Women and Economics* had crystallized "her most cherished convictions," Marie preached that women should be self-supportive and economically free and that they must be released from the domestic structures that stood between them and this freedom.[20] Her sincerity and public promotion of this belief made it all the more shocking that she would agree to marry a man like Fred Howe, who clung stubbornly to the conventions of home life that she found the most obnoxious. While Fred was an idealistic attorney who defended society's poor and powerless people against the forces of oppression and exploitation outside the home, he admitted to thinking that wives were household "conveniences" that men acquired to cook and clean and keep them content; wives were told to get by on as little as possible and were to ask for what money they got.[21]

More ironically still, it had been Marie's reading of Stetson's indictment of such attitudes that made her believe that her marriage to Fred might actually work after all. *Women and Economics,* as she wrote the author gratefully, had persuaded her that "the nature of men as husbands" could be altered radically as the institutions that molded their roles were changed by society, in other words, that there was hope of reforming Fred's views after all.[22] At the same time, Marie indicated, she was dissatisfied with how the church home was structured. She believed, she said, that it would be better to have "separate churches" for men and women where the former could learn the virtues of self-sacrifice and gentleness and the latter self-reliance and intellectual development. When she married Fred five years later and left the church ministry for the separate female communities of the suffrage movement and radical feminism—eventually forming the Heterodoxy Club in New York's Greenwich Village as a sanctuary apart from the patriarchy—it was with the belief that through these new ministries she would transform society's attitudes and solve her personal domestic problems in the process.

Eventually, Fred changed his views about what Marie's role would be as a wife, but the marriage did not bring the happiness she had hoped for. After losing her first baby, an infant son, she who doted on children was to remain childless, and Fred, quite possibly as a result of this loss, was less able than ever to fill the void that Marie had felt since first marrying him.[23] Indeed, as friends saw it, the marriage's "letdown" for her was that once Fred had made his catch, he seemed to forget all about her.[24] Marie told close friends like Fola La Follette how her loneliness during his constant trips quite literally made her sick for days.[25] But, while Marie's sense of abandonment was all too clear to others, Fred continued to go off without her, seemingly too engrossed in the great humanitarian problems abroad to notice the problems he had in his home. The problem was not just Fred's physical absence, however, but also his emotional distance, as the journalist and family friend Hutchins Hapgood pointed out. Fred was "dominantly a mental person" who could not understand his wife's need for love and affection, whereas "she could not understand how he could be so good and kind and yet so aloof."[26] Though their marriage was never dissolved and lasted some thirty years, it was what their friends recognized as a case of "domestic sterility." Ironically, as if to confirm this, Fred never mentioned a home life at all when he first wrote his autobiography. Only after Marie read the draft and commented on the omission did he dash off a few extra pages about the courtship and marriage.[27]

It was not until after the Howes had lived in New York for a number of years and Marie had met Rose Young, a sister feminist and one of the Heterodites, that she found the domestic intimacy and locus for her deepest affections that she had initially hoped to find with Fred. A writer and onetime editor of the *Woman Citizen,* Rose was about the same age as Marie, domestically independent, and able to give the relationship her undivided attention. Certainly by the mid-1920s, and possibly earlier, she had replaced Fred as Marie's primary partner. When Marie's biography of George Sand, subtitled *A Search for Love,* appeared in 1927, friends were not surprised that it was dedicated to Rose, not to the man whose interests and comprehension—as his wife still often complained—ran to banking, not to matters of the heart.[28] When Marie died in 1934, it was not her husband's needs but Rose's grief that most concerned their family and friends. Rose was the one consulted about the memorial service and the one who virtually closed the house and sent the news to old acquaintances, sometimes enclosing a scarf of Marie's or some other token as she would have wished.[29] Disappointed by a church that was liberal in all things except its relations between men and women, and let down again by a husband whose love proved as selfish as the church's, Marie Jenney Howe had returned to a female community of radical feminists. There, supported by her magnanimous family of Heterodoxy, the disillusioned minister finally found solid ground for her pulpit and a home in which the love she had searched for could flourish.[30]

II

In the judgment of women like Safford and Gordon, the female pastor was best off avoiding marriage entirely and not inviting its conflicts and disappointments. Love had its price in any committed relationship, Gordon said, but, given the usual structure of heterosexual partnerships, the married minister was likely to have extraordinary problems.[31] In explaining why they themselves chose not to marry, they cited competing demands of homes and congregations and spoke skeptically about the commitment of women who split their attention as if they had part-time jobs. Both occupations, said Gordon, were too sacred to be shortchanged in this way, and any woman who really was fit for the pastor's profession should understand this. Ordination implied a pledge of undivided loyalty to the church, and the pastor should have the integrity to want to keep her contract "inviolate."[32]

Nor could this dissenting group see that a marriage's drain on a woman's commitment to ministry was offset by any great benefits to society. Although they promoted the family ideal, they did not intend to let people think that the race's survival depended on everyone's having large broods of offspring. One needed to think only of the immigrant populations in the slums to realize that reproduction often "contributed nothing to human well-being," but just added to the weight of human suffering, Safford said. The quality of a state rested ultimately on the character of its citizens, not on their marital status. Unmarried people were "not ashamed to be in the company of Jesus and Paul, Herbert Spencer and Dorothea Dix." To the contrary, whether supporting their aged parents, teaching large families' neglected children, or giving their lives to upgrade the quality of home life generally, bachelor men and women took pride in doing as much as anyone to strengthen society's warp and fabric. As their ordinations symbolized, the women ministers frequently chose to renounce conventional matrimony in order to wed a vocation that nurtured a higher concept of family life.[33] Whatever their fondness for children, women like Safford and Gordon had no illusions about biological motherhood being the only or ultimate avenue to a woman's salvation.

In fact when defending their vows of chastity privately, these women were even less generous in their estimates of what marriage held out for females with talent and broader ambitions. Marie Jenney's marriage had certainly done little to recommend the institution, but there were many others as well that confirmed the unmarrieds in their decision. It pained them to see noble women with great potential transformed into "patient Griseldas" who put up with being abused and "buried alive" by unworthy brutes of men. One of the singles who tried to get at the reasons for this mystifying submission disclosed in her journal that she had asked one battered wife if the presumed "compensation of the married life, i.e., sex satisfactions," was "great enough to make up for all else." After being assured that they did not, she felt more "thankful" than ever that she had not taken "the risk of marriage" herself.[34] For these satisfied single women it was therefore as baffling as it was infuriating when Freud and his followers started interpreting lives like theirs as inadequate or empty because they were celibate and dismissed their family feeling, religious devotion, and cultural interests as nothing more than camouflaged libido. If Jesus could be the virile and vital personality that he was without having sex with all the females around him to maintain his manhood, they said, they themselves could surely refuse to bow before the imperious claims of sex and be no lesser women for doing so.[35]

Intent on treating the ministry as a full-time career and shunning conventional marriage, the core of Safford and Gordon's ecclesia sought the stabilizing centers for their emotional lives in friendships with other women. In an age before the modern psychosexual perspectives had made female intimacy seem either nonexistent or socially aberrant, these women frankly regarded the deep emotional bonding of females as the most sustaining of any relationships. Their sermons and publications paid tribute to the beautiful, uplifting friendships like that of Maria Hare and Lucy Stanley, who "fell in love with each other when they were seven, and were just as much in love when they were seventy." Bound together by emotional ties that their society respected and even deemed fully compatible with conventional married lives, Hare and Stanley exchanged long letters from youth to old age and "had gay times and sorrowful times, as people do, but never ceased to be devoted and true through everything."[36]

In their female friendships, the ministers did not deny their capacity for a deep or erotic love or refrain from expressing their feelings in physical, if not fully sexual, ways.[37] But the governing mode of relationship or dynamic seems to have been a professional domesticity that they themselves thought

of as more "sisterly" than "romantic," more suggestive of the shared vocation than the "Boston marriage." What they obviously valued most was the
wonderful paradox that their relationships—unlike the usual heterosexual
marriages—could develop within an environment that embraced both the
male and the female domains. As inhabitants of the womanly world of
nurture and caretaking as well as that of business and public service, the
couples were able to get close in ways impossible for men and women whose
marriages sharply carved out and segregated male and female space. For
women who lived together in the parsonages, neither realm was off limits,
and they could develop a greater intimacy by sharing the full range of their
concerns, from the most personal problems of health and family finances to
theological controversies and denominational politics. They traveled
together as friends and colleagues, nursed each other through illnesses,
pooled their skills to revive failing congregations, and marched side by side
for suffrage. At the end, when death divided them, they wrote their sisters'
memorials and bravely delivered the benedictions.

Marion Murdock and Florence Buck appear to have met in the spring or
summer of 1890, shortly before Murdock took up her new work in Kalamazoo as Bartlett's associate.[38] Buck was a science teacher and principal who
attended Murdock's new church, and, at thirty, she was the younger by ten
years. The two women came from similar backgrounds and liked each other
immediately. Both had been born and raised in the Midwest, the one in
Iowa and the other in Michigan. Both had worked hard to get good educa-
tions and had stubbornly refused to accept as their fate the domestic drudgery that custom cut out for their sex. They shared a deep love of nature and
expressed it in complementary ways, the older woman with a poet's adora-
tion and the younger with the scientist's respect. A photograph of them
sitting with Caroline Bartlett in her study, Buck cradling a guitar, Murdock holding a hymnal in her lap, and next to them a table on which one of
the group has rested her violin, shows that a mutual love of music gave yet
another dimension to their experience as a female ensemble.

It was natural in the friendship's early stages that Marion take on the role
of older sister and mentor to Florence, who had been raised in the Methodist
faith and sent to a Baptist college and was still a relative novice in liberal
theology. Especially after deciding, as Eleanor Gordon had, that there was
more need for her in the pulpits and parishes than in the classrooms, the
younger woman turned to her minister friend for instruction and guidance.
But, in other respects, it was Marion who was the more dependent. Having
succeeded in learning practically nothing about domesticity, she relied on

her friend's competence in the home to keep them fed and presentable, and, when serious and persistent medical problems sent her to bed, she gratefully gave herself over to Florence's care and calming influence.

By the spring of 1891, the two women had become so close that they were considered a couple, and, when Bartlett announced that she wanted to take a year off to travel abroad, it seemed natural for the church to ask Murdock and Buck if they would fill in as a team.[39] The chance for Buck to serve an apprenticeship and be ordained quickly was awfully tempting— and all the harder to refuse when a friend's sabbatical lay in the balance. However, the women decided that Buck would do better to go directly to Meadville and not put down roots that might keep her from getting the same formal training her male colleagues had. Murdock would go along, take some graduate courses, and give her friend moral support.

From the time they left Kalamazoo in the summer of 1891, Murdock and Buck were virtually inseparable. The year of study at Meadville was followed by another in England, at Oxford University's Manchester College. When they returned to the States, they embarked on a six-year joint pastorate in Cleveland's Unity Church, where together they built up a flourishing movement. There was a second trip abroad in 1899 and then a half-dozen years when, by serving two churches that straddled the line that divided Wisconsin from Illinois, the two continued to keep house together though working in separate states. Marion's physical problems compelled her to leave her pastorate in Geneva, Illinois, in 1906, and Florence resigned from hers in Kenosha, Wisconsin, in 1910. After a year or so missionizing in California, they retraced their steps and continued on to Boston, where Buck went to work for the AUA as associate secretary for religious education, a newly created job that gave her and Marion a regular income.[40]

Chroniclers often caught sight of these women together at functions in public places: at All Souls Church in Chicago, where Buck was ordained, with Marion helping confer the credentials, in 1893; at Meadville the following summer, when Buck received her divinity degree; in Geneva, Illinois, as participants in Rowena Morse's ordination in 1906; and increasingly, at the funerals of old friends. Out of public view, however, the women kept their private life to themselves, though, after Florence's untimely death of typhoid fever in 1925, Marion did share a little of the relationship's intimate side with their friends. "In my daily visits to the hospital, sitting near her," Murdock wrote, "she spoke little of herself or her suffering," showing only the "same thoughtful regard for others that I had known so well through the five and thirty years of our happy companionship." It had been a partnership, said Marion, with a courageous and generous soul whose "heroic" religion had brought out the best in both of them. To the end, her sister and colleague had been an "inspiring and beautiful" friend who had given her the happiest of homes.[41]

Even among women with as much sympathy and common ground as the Western ministers, it was rare to find a relationship as placid as Buck and Murdock's. More typical was the friendship between Mary Safford and Eleanor Gordon, which bore all the common and unavoidable tangles of close sisterhood and yet survived because of the trust and devotion that accrued to it through its long history of shared struggles. It was natural that as girls and young women who shared a dream and had different abilities, they would pool their complementary strengths. Mary provided the pulpit appeal and performed miracles raising money, while Eleanor, slower to seek ordination and less charismatic a preacher, labored steadily in the background, tending to the Sunday School and endless parish tasks. For years this arrangement was highly productive and seen by the church people as a model of cooperative enterprise, but, as the two women got older, the relationship's structure ceased to fit comfortably.

Gordon plainly felt the strain most, for it was she who labored in the shadow of a charismatic sister who had captured the fancy and token support, if not the genuine backing, of the denomination's male establishment. Typical of the gallantry extended to Mary Safford was that of Rev. George Badger, then editor of the *Unitarian*, when he wrote of her as a "winsome personality of grace and charm," a woman who was "delightful in social converse," "vivacious," and "sensitively refined." Altogether, he assured his readers, she was "preeminently feminine," though only "in the right and not the wrong sense of the word."[42] Gordon, rugged and blunt, had no interest in competing to please the male taste for the "feminine," but once she had built up a record of leadership that was as strong as her friend's, she was no longer willing to be dismissed as Safford's subordinate either.

Even without being privy to what the Boston men wrote to each other in confidence, Gordon knew what they were saying about the partnership: Miss Safford, with her "clear head and broad sympathies," had done all the work, while she, the sidekick, "shone largely by reflected light."[43] AUA secretary George Batchelor offered one colleague his view that Safford's services were by far the more highly valued in the movement. Miss Gordon, who by her own admission had "no time to be sweet" to her friends, much less to officious bureaucrats, had not impressed Batchelor as the "attractive personality" that her associate was, and at least in the circles in which he traveled—which were far from the parishes that she served—she had not engendered the kind of personal "attachment" and "respect for her administrative ability" that was "everywhere expressed for Miss Safford." [44]

Even Jenkin Lloyd Jones, who as her close brother in ministry should have known better, was now and then guilty of putting a credit due Gordon into Safford's account. A casual reference he once made in *Unity* to *Old and New* as Safford's publication made Gordon so furious that she lashed out, "Why it should be called her organ is more than I can see. Mr. Judy and I do nearly all the writing." While Safford may have raised most of the money to keep the paper going, she wrote virtually nothing but her reports as an officer of the Iowa Conference. [45] What really bothered Gordon was that, with her partner's unstable health and business trips, she was doing not only her own work but much of Safford's as well and not getting adequate credit for any of it.

While an unshakable sense of duty and affection brought Gordon back to Safford's side whenever there was a crisis, by the mid-1890s the conflict between her partner's needs and her own had convinced her that she would do best leading congregations by herself, and so she took pastorates of her own in Iowa City and Fargo. Although it was terribly lonely for her, this seemed a fair price for her self-esteem, and she paid it willingly, having learned that working relationships built on old loyalties and shared ideals could cost more.

In contrast to the Buck-Murdock friendship, whose surface calm was so constant that even good friends sometimes wondered just how the two "really felt" about each other, those who were closest to Safford and Gordon had at least strong intimations of the disturbances in their relationship. [46] They could readily see the toll it took on Gordon and understand why her strongest emotional ties were not to Safford but to a married Sioux City church friend named Caroline Groninger Gore. They knew Mary Safford as a woman with enormous powers of attraction, not the least of which were her generosity and capacity for showing gratitude for friendship and kindness. Yet insiders also knew that she had a sharp tongue, a strong will, and a sense of entitlement to having things on her own terms. [47] The tension that this created was contained or diffused enough over the years by Gordon's compromises that it was 1912, when Safford was already semiretired, before it erupted in public and exposed the darker side of the women's relationship.

The rift developed in Florida, where the women, now in their sixties, found themselves in competition for the leadership of a new church. A group of former Sioux City parishioners had settled in Orlando and convinced Safford to use some of her inheritance to buy property there, retire with them, and take up citrus growing. Gordon, who had no inheritance or plans to settle in Florida, had intended to try church development on the West Coast. But, during a visit there, her best friend Caroline Gore, with whom she was staying, asked her to hold a few Sunday services in her home, and before long there was serious talk about starting a new society. Gordon insisted that Safford, who already lived in Orlando, should have the first chance to organize locally and lead the new movement, but Safford, when asked, said that she was not interested.[48] She could not realistically farm and look after a church as well, she told Gordon, assuring her that, if she wanted to preach in Orlando, the field would be open as far as she was concerned.[49] Yet no sooner had Gordon taken the woman at her word and moved in to organize than Safford's interest in taking the helm was instinctively aroused. When a core of liberals met to develop a workable plan, both were there with the expectation of being given the pulpit. Nora McNeill remembered how shaken her mother had been after witnessing the "awful set-to" that had followed.[50]

The substantive issue that pitted the two against each other was whether to ask the AUA for financial help, with Safford, as always, opposing such an appeal as damaging to their autonomy and Gordon adamant that without it there would be no church for either of them to lead. But, as Gordon acknowledged in her account of it for posterity, it was not the bad feelings between them and Boston but "the personal element" between her and her former associate "that made the situation difficult." When, "after a tense and very unpleasant hour," Gordon was asked to return the next year as the minister, Safford, a lifelong champion of the free church and liberal expansion, refused to have anything more to do with the movement in Orlando.[51] Outside the church, the women's tightly integrated circle of friends made it hard for them to avoid each other socially and kept the split from destroying their relationship altogether. But the break never healed entirely. Safford rarely if ever set foot in the Unity Chapel that Boston helped pay for and Gordon led, and she never went with the rest of her crowd to the Round Table Society, whose programs were listed as part of Gordon's church calendar. Not until 1922, when her rival was no longer serving as minister, did Safford sign the church's membership book.[52]

If Gordon ever worked through her own anger at her old friend's desertion, it took at least as long. The wound was still tender in 1927, when AUA president Samuel Eliot, writing in the *Christian Register,* happened to make a reference to Safford and Gordon as "colleagues in the Orlando Church" when the movement was first getting under way. Simply reading this casual phrase was enough to arouse the old resentment, and Gordon dashed off a letter to set the record straight. The offender was so confounded that he hardly knew how to apologize, except to suggest feebly, "surely you and Miss Safford were colleagues in the old days in Iowa and that is what I had in mind."[53] Even a close friend who had known both women for years and knew of the Florida trouble was "hurt and surprised" when she visited Gordon after Safford's death in the late 1920s and saw "the intense feeling" when she spoke of the relationship. Gordon's "complex" about her, "her bringing up this and that in bitterness and accusation," seemed to this visitor "too settled" ever to be resolved.[54]

With her need to dominate, it was not surprising that Mary Safford formed her most satisfactory friendships with women who were a good deal younger than she and inclined to relate to her more like dutiful daughters than competitive sisters. Adele Fuchs was one of two women who assumed such a role in Safford's story, and being a bright, articulate diarist and one of the inner circle, she serves as an invaluable chronicler and perceptive analyst of those aspects of her mentor's life that were usually hidden from public view. If the older woman was looking for a daughter when she met Adele, she could not have found a more willing one. Almost twenty years younger than Safford, Adele was the youngest of five children born to German immigrants who had settled in the Midwest in the 1850s. Her diaries and a memoir explain that she and her brothers had soon lost the happy and stable home life their parents had dreamed of giving them. When Adele was just ten or eleven, Matilda Fuchs had slipped into a deep and progressive mental illness, and the girl had had to become "a little mother" to the woman whose mothering she herself needed and yearned for. The loss became absolute a few years later when the woman was institutionalized and soon afterward took her own life.

Meanwhile, Adele's father had not performed any better in his role as provider and protector of the family and home. A gifted idealist, whose ill-advised business investments and political contributions depleted his earnings as a college professor and physician, he finally had to entrust the care of his daughter to various friends. Within a year of his wife's tragic death and before regaining his financial footing, he, too, had died suddenly, and Adele ended up as the ward of a foster family in Chicago with whom she lived until her graduation from high school in the early 1880s. That was when she moved to Sioux City, where her older brothers had jobs.[55]

One of the very first people Adele came to know in Sioux City was Caroline Groninger, later Mrs. Gore, a sympathetic and generous soul who promptly became her "patron saint." The Groningers took the young woman into their home, helped her find a job teaching, and introduced her to the Unitarian church that Safford and Gordon had recently come into town to organize. It was in this church, as Fuchs wrote in her memoirs, that she first gleaned a religious perspective that had a real meaning for her; and it was here that she first saw and heard the woman who was to affect her life most profoundly, the one who would give her "the greatest joy and greatest sorrow," who would be a constant "guide and helper," but who would also hurt her "more deeply than anyone else."[56]

The senior minister had begun to occupy the center of her parishioner's life by the spring of 1889, when Fuchs signed the church's Bond of Union and became an official member. Fuchs's journal notations during this time showed that the friendship was deepening month by month and growing in its importance for both women. "Meant a lot to me," the younger wrote discreetly of Safford and Gordon's keeping her company when the Groningers went off to Florida for a month in March 1889. In April, she "cultivated Miss S's friendship" further and then was treated to "three pleasant days" in June with the minister at Storm Lake, the site of other emotionally stirring retreats in the months that followed. When later that summer the minister suddenly "underwent a severe operation" for an unspecified problem, Fuchs spent the critical days as her live-in nurse, a role she would fill many times in the future. From then on she appears to have been a frequent overnight guest at the parsonage. In February 1890, Safford gave Fuchs a picture of herself as a birthday gift; in July, she took her to Hamilton to meet her mother and relatives; and, in the fall, with Gordon's hearty approval, she invited Adele to move in as their housemate. At Christmas, the young woman "decorated a little Xmas tree" for her new family and "was bountifully remembered" by them. Fuchs was overjoyed at having a "new home" in which she was more than a guest. She boasted privately of furnishing her "own room completely" from her own earnings and noted "a feeling of rest there" that was a great help in calming her spirit.[57] The bond between the women was strengthened over the next few years. A trip abroad in 1892 gave Adele the chance to have her friend meet her German relatives, and back in the states the two visited sites where Safford's ancestors had settled. They also shared the care of Safford's mother, who suffered a stroke shortly after coming to live with them in Sioux City in 1891.

The letters that Safford and Fuchs wrote to each other in the late 1890s leave no doubt about the mutual dependency that developed between them. At the very least, the orphaned child found in the older woman a loving mother and spiritual mentor who filled a great emptiness in her life. As grown daughters do, Fuchs also performed a share of the mothering in the relationship, but she was always essentially Safford's disciple, and, while she could kiss and embrace her, she never, not even in her old age or in the privacy of her diary, felt the parity to call the minister by her Christian name. Fuchs was shaken "to the very depths" by her feelings and often had a hard time controlling them. She kept Safford's picture at her bedside and "dreamed of her every night." The dynamic between them becomes even clearer when one reads in Fuchs's late journals that she had been even more captivated in some ways by Safford's assistant, Marie Jenney, who was Fuchs's own age, unusually beautiful, and deeply empathic.[58] Marie, however, had neither enough seniority nor the need to be loved as a mother that Safford had, and, without an object to fix on, Adele's feelings for her relaxed.

The senior minister also was stirred powerfully by the currents of an emotion that surprised her as much as it did Adele. She pledged an unconditional love and asked to be loved in return "through *everything,* even to death."[59] Yet, at the same time, the pastor was pulled in another direction by her other passion, the church. As much as she longed for a permanent home with a daughter, she also recognized that what she felt for Adele was much more complicated and that its intensity sapped the vigor that she had to have for her work. She rebuked herself for having become so dependent and distracted and struggled to regain her self-possession. Determined to put the encroaching relationship on what she saw as a higher ground, she urged her young friend, who had shown some interest in studying to become a physician, as her father had been, to start her training now and go off to school. She told her to "be brave" and hold fast to her ideals and spoke of "the better love" that strove for a larger good and demanded great sacrifices from friends, including sometimes the comforts of stable domestic companionship. Fuchs, unhappy and troubled by the distance her friend now was putting between them, nevertheless agreed that it might be best and left "with a broken heart and courage."[60]

In one of the first blows that taught Fuchs to brace herself for a future of cruel disappointments, Safford decided without any warning to move to the church in Des Moines just as the new doctor was about to return from her studies abroad to set up a practice in Sioux City. "You begin to seem like a 'will-o-the-wisp' and I the poor mortal that chases it," Fuchs protested.[61] "You are apt now to feel that my love for you is weak or else I would feel more inspired for the things you are working for," she acknowledged, but she pointed out also that it was much easier to sublimate the personal realm when one was involved in the "greater things" of a full-time parish ministry. "Now I am lonely," she wrote in self-pity and anger, "and you absorbed in your work are going on."[62] Safford kept up a regular and emotional correspondence with Fuchs for the rest of her life, but she also continued to torment her friend by her evasive behavior, showing plainly enough that the warfare between her two passions was never resolved. Fearing the fuller commitment of sharing a home even while yearning for it, she kept up her game of cat and mouse to the end.

Yet, however absorbing the minister's nurture of a congregation that loved her, it was never enough to satisfy her hunger for a more intimate family life. Safford's nesting impulses were reawakened almost as soon as she moved to Des Moines, when a bright young woman named Helen Wilson started attending the church. In some respects, Helen was a replica of the orphaned Adele, whom the minister had taken under her wing some fifteen years earlier. She was barely out of her teens and without a real home, apparently having been left adrift by the recent death of a widowed mother. But Helen's nature was less intense than Adele's, and the less potent mix of their personalities and the greater age difference of thirty-two years gave a clearer definition and integrity to their respective roles as the guiding, nurturing mother and the dutiful daughter. Where Safford's maternal attachment to Adele had turned out to be far more ambiguous and disruptive than she had ever expected, her relationship to Helen evolved as a simpler connection born out of sympathy and nourished by the parental satisfaction of passing one's ideals and values on to a new generation. Indeed, though there is no record of any official stamp being put on it, those who knew them in Des Moines and Orlando always spoke of Helen as Safford's "adopted" daughter.[63] The causes of liberal religion and feminist politics placed the two in a working relationship that enabled them both to even a score with the past. Like Safford, Helen had grown up in a fatherless home and witnessed the struggle of women who were left to raise their families alone in a sexist society, and she was easily guided into the suffrage work that was fast becoming the minister's chief reform interest. When Safford went abroad in 1909 to study the women's rights movement in England, Helen accompanied her as a matter of course. As the pastor's right hand in the church work as well, Helen served as administrative assistant for the Iowa Conference and took over much of the paperwork after Safford fell ill in 1904.[64]

With the passage of time, the bonding with Helen brought Safford the nearly complete experience of becoming a family matriarch. After the pastor retired and the two of them moved down to Florida, Helen married and soon had a baby girl. The child was christened Helen Mary and called by her grandmother's name, and for a number of years the minister knew the joys of having her own growing family and, in her namesake, a share in posterity. Sadly, Safford also came to know the depths of a mother's grief when Helen Wilson died of tuberculosis in 1926.

Yet Helen Wilson never replaced Adele Fuchs in Mary Safford's life any more than Caroline Groninger took Safford's place in Eleanor Gordon's. For, in the world of social relations to which the female clergy belonged, women's friendships rarely existed as isolated dyads but developed within highly integrated networks of relationships. This was nowhere more visible than for these pastors, whose private domesticity, always conjoined to the public realm of their congregational stewardships, came to be an anchor and reference point for their larger family lives.

Chapter Seven

THE PASTOR AS TEACHER

The teacher who is worthy {of} the name works as GOD works—is in reality . . . finishing God's work, is working for eternity, shaping and moulding divine material.
—Rev. Eleanor E. Gordon

Almost all the sister pastors had taught school or been private tutors before moving into the ministry and thus were able to bring to their new vocation a practical understanding of teaching's importance in raising strong, secure families. Some of them felt that they would forever be teachers first and foremost and that, as Gordon said, they had not really left the school for the church but only moved on to a larger schoolroom with a broader range of students.[1] Certainly, in a consciously intellectual movement like theirs, in which edification replaced conversion as the pulpit's stock in trade, there was nothing unique about pastors seeing themselves in the roles of educators, but there were important differences between what this seems to have meant to most clergy and what it meant to the Western sisterhood. While most of their brothers, especially those in the older, more citified parishes, were satisfied with being pulpit professors on Sundays, the women believed in making the church a learning place all through the week.[2] Thus their male counterparts would usually leave the Sunday School work to their wives and other church ladies, while the clergywomen involved themselves directly in this area. And, whereas the more diligent of their brothers might lead groups in reading the "masterworks" written by men, the women expanded the cultural canon, turning their clubs into forums that also made room for a female perspective. Earlier in the century, the Beecher sisters, Catherine and Harriet, had envisioned a home that was also a church as well as a schoolhouse.[3] The Western women's approach to the ministry made this inspired idea concrete.

To be sure, the ministers' gender was not the only determining factor in how they interpreted the teaching responsibilities of their office. Geography also had much to do with it since, in the larger and older parishes that were in cultural centers, there was less call for the church to provide educational opportunities than there was in the Western parishes far from the cities and large universities.[4] In the early 1870s, when he was the pastor in Janesville, Wisconsin, Jenkin Lloyd Jones had been one of the first to establish a model for meeting these small-town needs. To raise the quality of his society's parish life above the chatter and idle gossip of congregational suppers and sewing bees, he and his wife Susan had undertaken to modernize the Sunday School program and introduce cultural clubs for adult education. Jones intended his program to be an alternative to the rigid and doctrinal teaching approach used back East, a method centered on catechistic question-and-answer memorization and didactic story lessons. As the secretary and editor of the Western Unitarian Sunday School Society, Jones recommended a system that would engage the children in discovery through carefully guided class discussion. His curriculum began with a study of the differences between legend, myth, the scientific method, and fact. It moved on to a modern scientific account of the earth's formation and the rise of man and civilization and then took up religion and morality. A unit on "The Great Teachers" introduced the students to Zoroaster, Buddha, Confucius, Socrates, Mohammed, Abraham, Moses, and Jesus and led into a series of lessons on the Bible.[5] Jones's designs for constructing church homes that expressed this commitment to education became the blueprints that his younger sisters followed in their ministries.

Like their mentor, the women considered the teaching arms of the church to be crucial enough to administer personally as far as they could. Elizabeth Padgham, donning the hat of the Sunday School superintendent before slipping into her robe for Sunday morning services, took this part of her work so seriously that she had her teachers give written tests to keep track of the students' progress.[6] Eleanor Gordon, who always thought of herself as "more of a teacher than preacher," met with her Sunday School teachers at midweek to plan the curriculum and calculated that she spent as much time preparing for these meetings as she did for her Sunday sermons.[7] The outlines for Bible study that Murdock and Buck produced in the Cleveland parish for publication in *Old and New* in the mid-1890s, and Caroline Bartlett Crane's year-long Sunday School course on "Good Citizenship" that was published by the Western Unitarian Conference several years later, further testified to their conviction that mothers of congregations were obliged to see that the young were well taught.

The ministers warmly embraced the emerging kindergarten concept, frequently instituting their own preschool programs based on the childhood development theories advanced by G. Stanley Hall and his followers. These theories viewed early child care not just as tending to physical needs but also as cultivating newly awakened intelligences, which required a scientifically schooled parenting.[8] Advocates of the kindergarten romanticized motherhood into an awesome profession that required a woman to be "a physician, an artist, a teacher, a poet," and even "a priest."[9] As a way of rearing young children while helping their mothers develop themselves as well, the kindergarten experience recommended itself to progressive ministers as a holistic approach to improving the quality of family life. Caroline Bartlett, who started a program at People's Church in Kalamazoo, found that, despite the youngsters' great charm, her deepest interest was working with parents. Every other week in the early evenings, she had family programs to let the fathers see what their children did during the day, and, once a month, she held afternoon meetings exclusively for the mothers. During these daytime get-togethers, "hard-worked and often tired women" sat "on the circle" drinking tea and talking about how they "could do the best for their little children with the time and the strength that they had." As the minister watched how the kindergarten created a desperately needed support group for many an anxious and isolated woman in Kalamazoo she came to believe that it was among the most worthwhile projects the church ever fostered.[10]

In addressing the older people's educational needs, the pastors again followed Jones, using his Janesville Mutual Improvement Club as the pattern for their own adult study groups. In the early 1880s, when Safford was just starting out in Humboldt and coined the name *Unity Club* as her hallmark, she had her people present and discuss papers on a vast sweep of topics from Unitarian history, world religions, art, and literature to politics, economics, and such speculations as "The Relation of Disease to Morality."[11] Safford's successor, Murdock, had given Humboldt more of the same, and, by the 1890s, Unity Clubs were meeting in women's parishes throughout the Western Conference. Frequently challenged about the secular character of these cultural programs, the pastors declared that a minister who had the insight and courage could turn the most worldly topic into an instrument for deepening her people's religious life.[12]

While this interpretation of the church's teaching mission was held by all the West's more progressive clergy, not just the female contingent, the women's implementation of these ideas through their domestic feminism put a highly original mark on their work as religious educators. In Unity Clubs led by these female pastors, the woman's perspective was no longer slighted. The scholars discussed the literary works of both male and female authors and talked about matters of social relations not normally broached in mixed company. The ministers kept their clubs informed about the latest sociological thought that challenged the cult of True Womanhood and attacked the oppressive, gender-based fragmentation of society. Whenever Unity scholars decided to take up some facet of economics, politics, or social organization, the pastors made sure that the "modern view" was well represented by having as guest speakers some of its best-known advocates, people like Jane Addams, Mary Livermore, and Carrie Chapman Catt. Jenkin Lloyd Jones, of course, was also called on constantly to demolish the obsolete attitudes that enslaved both sexes and weakened the home and society. His lecture on Ibsen's *A Doll's House* always ruffled some feathers but made an eloquent case, Gordon thought, for "Womanhood first, then wifehood," and for the kind of enlightened relations the Unity Club was created to teach.[13]

This vision of church education brought even more radical changes to the ladies' groups, which the ministers saw were retarding instead of promoting their sisters' development, exploiting their dedication when they should have been advancing their interests. In the patriarchal church these circles encouraged their members to accept the demeaning identity of selfless servants whose talents were equal only to serving church suppers and cleaning up afterward. Such activity offered the distaff nothing but "drudgery," said Marie Jenney Howe, who doubted that more than one in a hundred women really liked sewing as much as the typical clergyman seemed to think.[14] The clergywomen attempted to change the alliances into groups based on self-affirmation, not self-denial.

In this attempt to address their lay sisters' need for fuller expression, personal growth, and useful involvement in public affairs, the sisterhood's strategies followed the thrust of the women's club movement nationally. From the time Sorosis, the first club, was founded in 1868 as a protest against the "demoralizing waste" of women's time in the churches, intelligent women had been creating their own associations for self-improvement, social reform, and the practice of what they deemed the higher qualities of an enlightened womanhood. They sought to enforce parliamentary methods and disciplined organization and patterns of interaction that fostered respect and mutual growth among members.[15] The feminist ministers had their church groups join the state Federations of Women's Clubs to align them with others whose goals were the same.

Since the pastors routinely belonged to the clubs and could have the presidency when they wanted it, they were uniquely positioned to set a new tone and steer the groups onto this higher road. The minutes of the Ladies' Society at People's Church in Kalamazoo show that, when Bartlett took over the group's leadership when she first came as minister, she let it be known that she really meant business and hoped to be seeing some changes. She expected her sisters to be more faithful and punctual in their attendance and not come out just "to have a good time," though she thought they might have that as well; she wanted the group to be motivated by a genuine interest in personal growth and more purposeful undertakings in the church and community.[16]

In the interest of teaching a new set of values on which to build a sense of worth, the clergy also confronted the clubwomen with their enslavement to fashion and their practice of making their meetings a showplace for misplaced investments and vanity. "Fancy telling Susan B. Anthony, or Clara Barton or Jane Addams that their first duty is to be beautiful!" Celia Woolley chided her sisters after seeing the excess of finery at a Federation of Women's Clubs meeting in 1898.[17] In striving to free their groups from such bondage, the pastors again called on their brother Jones, who was able to captivate the ladies while taking them to task for losing sight of what really mattered and building a market for needless goods just to make themselves conspicuous.[18]

Once a club's consciousness had begun to evolve, the ministers prodded their sisters still farther, in some cases even asking them to put their club work ahead of everything else in the church except the Sunday School and the worship services. Not just the pure socializing but even the fund-raising projects that helped pay the bills must be made subordinate to their own organization, said Eleanor Gordon. If the church was intended "to quicken the life of the spirit," Gordon advised, then her sisters should never become so immersed in making money for its operation that they had no energy left for their own special group.[19] Ironically, in Des Moines the women were so agreeable to this advice that they ended up at least one year with practically nothing in their treasury and had to cover their debts with Sunday School funds. The minister, nonetheless confident in the order of her priorities, always took satisfaction in seeing this Unity Circle become the city's "only real open forum" where women could ask the "dangerous questions" and have the benefit of a "frank discussion." [20]

According to both their official historians and members' casual testimonials, when the women's church groups took their ministers' recommendations to heart, they became exciting schools for a new kind of sisterhood in the church. Released from the stultifying small talk and endless sewing and baking, and pressed to set higher goals, club members claimed to have gained better concepts of themselves as individuals and consequently established more satisfying relationships with each other. "There was none of the petty jealousy, gossip and rivalry that mar too many women's organizations," said one of Safford's clubwomen in later years. Her pastor's vision and inspiration had "dominated," she said, and gave her sisters "the highest ideal of womanhood." [21] Proud of their transformation, the women's clubs wanted it put in the record. In 1892, Bartlett's group changed its name from the Ladies' to the Women's Society; Ida Hultin's Ladies' Aid in Des Moines became the Women's Section of the Unity Club; and other groups guided by feminist clergy were quick to follow suit.

In their efforts with these alliances, as in other facets of their ministries, the pastors made greatest headway in changing the image of women's place in the church not by attempting to disengage it from deep-laid domestic allegiances but by yoking the home ideology to their feminist vision. The book reviews, study guides, and syllabi that the pastors prepared show a strong reform interest that yet celebrated the timeless values of family and home and women's roles there as well as in broader spheres. Discussions of literature praised parental responsibility and devotion, while more practical studies gave a new importance to the domestic sphere by examining its component parts scientifically. [22] In Des Moines, the women's society looked at the concept of home so thoroughly—examining everything from architectural styles, materials, cost, and furnishings to what was cooked in the kitchen and read in the study—that it took a full year to get through it, and even then they were not satisfied. [23] They voted to take up additional studies of physical fitness, childrearing, family relationships, clothing, and education. If there were still any doubts about the club's respect for domesticity, several meetings on "How the Club Helps the Home" must have dispelled them. [24]

Some programs built greater pride in the members' unique female art forms, which the male culture trivialized and ignored. To incite a more aggressive spirit along these lines in Des Moines, Marie Jenney spoke to her

Unity Club repeatedly about women's efforts in other cities to save their endangered home industries and gain respect for their undervalued talents before they were lost entirely to machine labor.[25] Mary Collson's prodding along the same lines led the women in Ida Grove to lodge public protests against the men treating their fancy work as "pretty but petty diversion." Together, the pastor and clubwomen sought to reassure the men in the church that they could learn to value the arts that came out of the female domain without jeopardizing their masculinity. The consensus was that "if men would only analyze that group of sensations and feelings which we designate by the word Home, its satisfaction to the tastes and senses and its repose to the soul, they would give a more prominent place to the so-called 'trifles.'"[26]

To some extent, too, the sisterhood's Unity Circles were also following the national women's club trend toward expanding the concepts of self-improvement and domesticity to include not only the study of culture but also an active engagement with social and civic concerns. The liberal ministers' rationale for this fieldwork, known as municipal housekeeping, was that females, schooled through socialization to safeguard and beautify private life, should use their influence to civilize the public arena as well. While cautioning clubwomen not to neglect their families for public service, the pastors warned them not to be self-centered either and urged them to learn how "to make of their cities great community homes for all the people."[27] Like other social feminists, they believed that the private as much as the public domain would benefit from women's presence in both since, in going outside her home to do "the studying, the investigating, the detail work, for which men have not time," a woman became better fit "to rightly govern the kingdom of her own household."[28]

As members of a noncreedal church in which, in the West especially, theology had long had to share the pulpit with science, economics, and politics, liberal churchwomen had never quite had their trinitarian sisters' problem of squaring an interest in practical social relief with ladylike church benevolence and religious education. While orthodox ladies in the 1860s and 1870s came together weekly in "mite societies" to relieve the world's ills through Bible reading and handing out tracts to the poor, religious liberals like Caroline Dall, Antoinette Brown Blackwell, and Celia Burleigh tried to teach the meaning of the Gospels by promoting the work of secular agencies and such independent organizations as the National Conference of Charities. Dall, who helped organize the American Social Science Association and was one of the first females ever to preach from a Unitarian pulpit, urged that the female minister be wary of the strictly academic and bureaucratic approach to ministry, which was "nowhere so narrow as in its human sympathies." The clergywoman should rearrange her brother's priorities, not get caught up in the "pulpit graces," but seek to uplift her "religious household" by leading a "Committee of Comfort" that reached out to the parish's poor, friendless, and emotionally broken.[29]

This practical Christianity had always been fundamental to what Safford's cohort was trying to teach. In the 1880s, they had tried to promote it by having the Humboldt ladies investigate modern theories about public health, social organization, crime, and poverty and suggesting that they use the proceeds from their ice cream socials and Christmas bazaars to help a society for needy children and a home for abandoned women.[30] But the catastrophic economic collapse of 1893 forced them to reconsider what they were teaching and how they were teaching it. The problems of class conflicts, unemployment, financial ruin, family displacement, and hunger, which previously had been largely abstract subjects discussed in Unity Club, assumed a concrete reality in the sisterhood's societies that demanded something more than fine-spun debate. Eleanor Gordon later recalled how distant they had been from their subject when she and Safford arrived in Sioux City during the halcyon days of prosperity. At that time, the church could afford whatever it wanted: the very best music, a new sanctuary, electric lights, and two paid ministers. It had been all too easy to let social conscience grow flabby in such circumstances and feel satisfied in their liberality simply by reading Herbert Spencer and John Stuart Mill. It was only after the banks failed that the ministers fully committed themselves to making the liberal church "something more than just an institution to oppose orthodoxy" and encourage the study of good books.[31]

The social gospel's ascendancy in the 1890s reshaped both the ministers' preaching and their agenda for religious education through club work. The sisterhood's women's groups now sought self-improvement and personal satisfaction by making their clubs into something like part-time schools of social work where they trained in the methods of practical scholarship used by Jane Addams of Hull House. The settlement leader became the churchwomen's favorite exemplar, her standing with them being greatly enhanced by her friendship with Jenkin Lloyd Jones, who praised her progressive experiments as the best of "academic work brought down to date."[32] As a scholar and activist who yet managed to practice a ladylike hospitality that bridged the public and private sectors, Addams offered the sisterhood's circles the perfect domestic model for the pragmatic curriculum they were looking for. Thanks to their pastors' collaborative efforts to put together attractive lecture tours, even the smaller Unity Circles in northwest Iowa had the thrill of having "the sage of Hull House" come tell them in person how women could carry the values of family and home to the broader community. After her visit to Ida Grove, the Unity Circle reported a great enthusiasm for "working toward Miss Addams' ideals" of putting the meaning of hospitality into a public context. There, as in nearby Washta and Cherokee, the reformer's visits inspired the women to start up relief societies and humane shelters for destitute families, while Humboldt's Unity Circle helped furnish a room in a halfway house for ex-convicts.[33]

The Unity groups still had their papers on German theology, Browning, and Emerson, but, by the turn of the century, they were chiefly involved with the sociological issues that Jane Addams raised. Three years after launching their studies of the home, the ladies in Des Moines were still exploring it, now looking at "how the ideal of the city" could be understood as "a well ordered household." Researching every conceivable facet of their city's government, the women reported their findings in an exhaustive array of papers that ranged from the water supply and fire protection to transportation, parks and playgrounds, monuments, hospitals, taxes, and public ownership.[34] This awesome feat was matched in Caroline Bartlett Crane's church in Kalamazoo, where the minister and her sisters mapped out their own city's infrastructure and government networks, the sewer lines, educational systems, health services, and the rest.

The sisterhood's clubwomen had become conscientious if amateurish scientists who examined "The Domestic Problem" through modern lenses that enlarged the subject and sharpened the focus significantly. Their image of motherhood took on the ampler proportions of "City Mothers," and "making a happy home" was perceived to mean instituting "The Social Ideal."[35] Moreover, in broadening what domesticity meant in the larger community, the pastors' approach to religious education put a striking new face on the church as a schoolhouse as well as a home.

Chapter Eight

THE CHURCH HOME

Wisdom has built her house, she has set up her seven pillars.
—Proverbs 9:1

I

Though the first to point out that a house by itself was never enough to make a good home, the clergywomen were just as convinced as the rest of their society that a family's residence had a profound bearing on its religious development. As the guardians of congregations, they therefore took great pains to see that their buildings expressed the ennobling principles that were embraced by the popular ideal of home.[1] Housing the people was always a pressing concern for clergy whose calls came not from the established and well-accommodated societies but from the fledgling or floundering groups most in need of nurture and permanent shelter. This need was so great that, between 1880 and 1913, the Western sisterhood put up and paid for well over a score of new houses of worship, an impressive record for liberal expansion by any standard.[2]

In small towns like Humboldt and Perry, where money was always hard to come by, the sisters' societies built simple Gothic chapels of wood and brick that were indistinguishable from the other Protestant churches except for the absence of crosses on top of their steeples. Citified and bolder congregations showed a preference for styles that put yet a greater distance between them and Christian orthodoxy. A flat-roofed, neoclassical building fashioned after a pagan temple housed the worshipers in Des Moines, and the Iowa City people designed a church that looked like an English manor house and gave no architectural hint of its institutional character. The Kalamazoo and Sioux City groups also designed church homes that bore a resemblance to large private residences, though theirs had the curved arches, stubby towers, and conical roofs of the Romanesque mode that the architect Henry Hobson Richardson had made respectable. The last building to the sisterhood's credit, the church built for Gordon's Floridians, was a humble "plantation cottage" in the Gulf Coast tradition, with a raised foundation, tall clear windows, a wide, sheltered porch, and plain functional columns. Collectively, these structures represented the range of available architectural idioms at the time, but, despite the diversity of their languages, all of them were intended to make the same, insistent statement that the liberal church should above all else be homelike.

Just what this informing principle meant to the clergywomen must again be approached in the context of the nineteenth century's home mystique, which was still gaining force. The Protestant clergy, both liberal and orthodox, were leaders in sanctifying the home, and none were more dedicated to spreading the ideology than the sisterhood's earliest mentors. Jenkin Lloyd Jones's close friend and colleague William Channing Gannett had collaborated with Jones's nephew, Frank Lloyd Wright, in producing a handsomely illustrated volume called *The House Beautiful,* a tribute to the "domestication of the Infinite" in "a building of God." Taking philosophical measure of the home's outer frame while filling it with the kinds of furniture, good books, flowers, and guests that best embodied its lofty character, Gannett had advanced the conceit that a beautiful home reproduced nature's simplest harmonies and ultimately reflected, in the togetherness of its family life, the unity of God's all-inclusive creation.[3]

Jones's pulpit anatomies of the home, based on the same assumptions, were even more extensive than his friend's. Approaching the subject from every possible angle, Jones lectured and preached on "Home-Making, Wooing and Wedding" and "The Higher Politics of the Home." In a six-part series on "House Building," he took his congregation on an exhaustive, emblematic tour through each of the rooms of the ideal residence, from the kitchen and dining area to the parlor, nursery, and study, always speaking more, as he said, of "an inward sentiment that an outward structure." Jones's model sitting room, for example, replacing the dark, stuffy "social refrigerator" of far too many Victorian homes, was to be a sunny and well-ventilated place that fostered warm feelings of human kinship. The wallpaper should be kept simple and the carpet unobtrusive, and none of the furnishings need be expensive so long as there were good pictures and books to keep the family in touch with each other and tug on their sense of the past. Every image should tell a story, Jones said, and everything should "have a memory."[4]

While there is no record of Jones's protégées having attempted anything quite as ambitious from their pulpits, they did render their own elaborate exegeses of the physical features and moral dynamic that made handsome houses good homes. The most extensive and best known of these would not appear until 1925, when Caroline Bartlett Crane published a book called *Everyman's House*. It was based on the plan for a model residence that had won her first place in a national contest sponsored by the Better Homes in America movement. Cast in a conversational tone that suggested the family fireside, the book combined nuts-and-bolts information about construction costs and materials, detailed architectural remedies to common household problems, and gentle homiletics about the needs and responsibilities of the members of a happily sheltered family.[5]

This author's flair for drawing the moral implications of well-structured houses had already been apparent thirty years earlier when, as Miss Bartlett, she wrote and choreographed dedications for her parishioners' private homes and had the scenarios printed up in tidy orders of worship. In a typical service, the pastor commended the owners of a new summer retreat on the shore of Lake Michigan for having used this space and design to convey the reverence for nature and social hospitality through which religious liberals expressed their love of God. The building, she noted approvingly, was as beautiful as it was comfortable, having been fashioned in harmony with the setting as well as the residents' needs. But more than an ideal studio, her interpretation went on, this was a home, "in spirit and in truth," a place of "hospitable intent." One could see it in the broad sweep of the piazza, where chairs stood ready for guests at all hours, and in the depths of the fireplace, whose swinging crane and pot recalled the days "when visits were visits and not ceremonies." The thought of home and hospitality was again visible in the little tower that was lit at night," not as a warning of dangerous rocks ahead, but as a symbol of fellowship" with friends or strangers on shore or out on the water.[6]

Another of Bartlett's dedications, this one for a winter home, shows even more clearly how deftly she used her settings to teach family values that still were preserved within separate spheres that segregated the sexes' roles and space. Held just before Christmas 1895, this service began with the pastor calling the hosts and well-wishers to the foyer, having them turn to their programs, and asking the mother to start with an invocation, a prayer that divine love encircle her family and friends. The father continued by speaking of their desire to make every room "holy by high thoughts," and to this the guests added, "So may it be with us . . . in every home." After several stanzas of Payne's "Home Sweet Home," the movable pageant began slowly winding its way through the house to witness acts of consecration designed for the different rooms. In the parlor, the mother, lighting the hearth, prayed for love's light and warmth in the home, and the father, lighting the evening lamp, pledged to seek truth and wisdom. Another fire was lit in the library to the memory of the man's mother, and then the focus shifted to the little crèche by the Christmas tree, which became the backdrop for re-dedicating the children of all the families present. The group came last to the dining room, where the table was spread for a holiday feast, and the daughter, lighting the candles, invited the guests to sit down and eat.[7]

None of Bartlett's colleagues ever surpassed her when it came to spectacle, but all put obvious effort into producing "house christenings" that would do justice to the domestic ideal. By pooling their talents, Safford, Jenney, and Padgham produced a finely wrought home dedication as a gift for one of their conference's prominent lay leaders. Except for Gannett's poem "A Fireside," which the sister pastors used almost routinely for weddings and house christenings, the readings were all written specially for the occasion, although with such standard motifs that they seemed to be comfortably worn. Safford's opening prayer and the words she wrote for the hymn, Jenney's brief remarks on "The Ideal Home," Padgham's dedication prayer, and the congratulatory letter that Gordon had sent to be read in her absence provided all the furnishings needed to make a house a safe haven, "a school of virtue," and a place of worship.[8]

With its melding of sacred and secular symbols, the praise of the home as a holy space encouraged a good deal of collateral talk about the church being a home. As a poignant figure, this concept gained great popularity among the clergy in general, but, for the women whose orientation to ministry was overtly domestic, it was always much more than just rhetoric. For one thing, their total involvement in a practical, seven-day ministry blurred the divisions between its public and its private areas so that the church and the home sometimes seemed to be not merely similar but one and the same. Certainly, when the parishioners needed their pastor, no place was really off limits, and they were as free to seek her out in the parsonage as in the church study. Similarly, in a line of work that dealt, as service professions do, largely with life's unruly and unscheduled developments, the women's living quarters often ended up doubling as offices and conference rooms, particularly but not only when the church was short on space. It was therefore natural that a woman like Gordon would ask her colleague Jones, when he was preparing to christen his new All Souls Church in Chicago, if the service would include "the domestic part of the building," that is, the second-floor that had been set aside for a parsonage. "I do not see *why not,*" she had volunteered, reminding him that, if ministers' residences were not also houses of worship and "dedicated to the same purposes as the church home, they should be."[9]

So closely akin were the sacred and secular houses of worship in these pastors' minds that, except for their settings, the dedications were almost identical. The hymn that was written by Safford and used by some of her colleagues most frequently for their church christenings wrapped the church in the same domestic phrasing suggestive of intimate family life and the comfort of nourishing, harmonized human relationships. The church was "a home of love that yearns to bless," the hymn declared. An androgynous rather than patriarchal household, it was the dwelling place of children drawn together by common ties to a great Transcendentalist "Over-Soul" who was their "father, mother [and] nearest friend."[10] But, more significant, the sisters moved boldly beyond the metaphor to make their churches functional centers for congregational family life.

With a literalness their brothers never attempted, women had years before shown themselves ready to put into concrete expression the popular domestic ideology that presented the home as a religious sanctuary. The Beecher sisters designed their small church that was also "a school-house and a comfortable family dwelling" at mid-century, when no other architects were connecting the home and religion in more than abstract turns of phrase.[11] A few decades later, a clerical sisterhood viewed their sacred space from a woman's perspective, as the Beechers had done. Understanding that homes, whether private or public, were family centers run largely by females—civilization's appointed architects of home and hearth—they strove to create buildings that were not merely places where people assembled for formal worship but also hospitable dwellings, schools for the young, and workshops for women's essential labors, companionship, and recreation. In short, they saw that the kinship between the church and the home implied more than a one-way transfer of values from the first to the second. Through a reciprocal exchange—one that went beyond talk— the church could appropriate the private home's secular evidence of blessed domesticity just as the home displayed the church's sacred iconography of devotion.

II

The sisterhood's views on church architecture were part of an old and continuing debate between the liberals' traditionalists, who wanted more art in their temples, and the liberals' progressives, who wanted more hospitality. In the 1880s, the Midwestern radicals had begun to challenge the hegemony of the Gothic by housing their congregations in more down-to-earth structures that enunciated the democratic religion and universal community on which the free church was based. Gannett had sought to embody these ideas in the functional quarters he helped design for his congregation in Hinsdale, Illinois, and Jones had created his own, bolder version of the proper church home by combining the practical features of an office building, apartment house, music hall, and gymnasium.[12]

In making simplicity and utility the guiding principles of their church homes, Jones and Gannett had their chance to demonstrate what they had long been preaching. Jones, whose Chicago society started out in a shabby room with nothing more than a few kitchen chairs and a table, had always told his people that the ideal church was a humble abode, not "a Gothic sham" but "a secular hall, a workshop [and] oratory of the Soul all in one." It was a place, he had said, where its members could come together for culture and mutual comfort and the study of God's laws through selfless, community service. The cathedral style, Jones insisted, was "very costly, yet useless on weekdays," and its pretentious display would "frighten away the mechanic and the seamstress." Worse still, "it promoted the sense of individual insignificance that served authoritarianism and medieval super-stition." The meeting place that Jones's society built in 1887 with an eye to avoiding these drawbacks of Gothic style turned out, said some, looking most like a strange cross between a Roman cathedral and a Turkish mosque.[13] By the 1890s, a number of Jones's Midwestern colleagues had joined in promoting the simple and functional church. Davenport's Arthur Judy, for one, met his group in a brick Georgian structure whose horizontal lines and unpretentious facade gave fitting expression to their practical faith and community outreach.

Unitarian and other liberal traditionalists, who deplored what they saw as a spreading aesthetic impoverishment among American Protestants gen-erally, grumbled about their churches becoming too plain and secular. Rev. F. M. Bennett of Lawrence, Kansas, represented their view when the Iowa Association of Unitarian and other Liberal Churches met in 1903. As a former pastor of the Keokuk, Iowa, congregation, Bennett had had the heady experience of preaching in one of the most imposing Gothic churches in the area, a graceful structure with lofty spires and a profusion of stained glass that he felt inspired great religious sentiment. In revolting against creeds, he said, liberal churches were throwing away the corn with the husks, discarding a symbolism that emerged from a sense of divinity's hidden life and transcended any single theology. Appalled that such an appeal to the people's religious sense was being abandoned, Bennett insisted that there could be "more religion" in a beautiful temple than there could "in a club room" and entered a vigorous plea for the return to more cathedrals. [14]

Other ministers at the conference and the women particularly disagreed. Like Jones and Gannett, they maintained that true love and hospitality would "find a way in whatever house" and that the basics of good homemaking rather than outward appearances should be the determining factors in designing a house of worship. [15] "Handsome is that handsome does" was the way Bartlett summed up her guiding principle when she set out to plan the new People's Church in Kalamazoo. [16] Safford and Gordon had felt the same way when they decided to "cradle" their infant Sioux City society in a skating rink, which the people had purchased and ably converted into a versatile meeting place. The members had put in partitions for a kitchen and a cloakroom and still had plenty of space for their auditorium and social hall. They had a grand piano and rows of yellow pine chairs for the services, and for their suppers and other festivities, they moved the chairs to the side and set up light tables along the length of the hall to make room for dancing and entertainment. While this religious anomaly drew mixed reactions from the community, it attracted a great many leading citizens who were dissatisfied with the churches they had. [17]

Religiously liberal women had both theological and feminist reasons for shunning the traditional Gothic design. As a minister's wife pointed out, what a congregation believed and how it behaved were "unconsciously molded" by a sanctuary's physical properties, and unorthodox congregations therefore put their religion in jeopardy when they worshiped in churches constructed along explicitly christological lines. To avoid losing ground in this way, she argued, the liberals should make a clear visual break with trinitarianism by striving for simple design, avoiding excessive embellishment and distracting patterns in glass, brick, and stone. The distaff's advocacy of a less aristocratic idiom was also a way of promoting a devotional language that better expressed the egalitarian ideal on which their liberal movement was founded. The stately Gothic cathedrals in which the East's most conservative liberal men preached had become for the women visible statements of patriarchal resistance to their equal access to leadership roles in the church. This architectural style was so much a part of Eliza Wilkes's fears about the Eastern conservatives trying to shackle the West's liberal missionaries that it furnished the backdrop for nightmares in which she saw Sioux Falls as "a Cathedral town" where the clergywomen had to answer to an officious male bishop.[18] To make a clear declaration of independence from any such "papist" control, Wilkes tried unsuccessfully in the late 1880s to interest the Sioux Falls society in building their church along freer lines, as her friend Jones had done in Chicago.[19]

In Sioux City, Safford and Gordon, who shared Wilkes's aversion to the Roman style and its patriarchal associations, made sure that the church their society built to replace the converted skating rink would not easily be confused with the Catholic cathedral that stood just across the street, and, after it was completed, they often reminded their members what was signified by the structural differences between their church and its neighbor. Their own church home, they explained in the parish bulletin, had been "planned more for convenience, comfort and use than for ecclesiastical effect."[20] Indeed, it was finally these intentions of "workability" and communal well-being, more than the architecture as such, that gave the sisterhood's churches their special character. Even when it turned out, as it did with the Gothic church in Sioux Falls, that the building's visible statement had to be cast in an orthodox idiom, the desired meaning remained secure in the eye of the beholders. The pastors let the world know what their vision was, not only by what they preached, but by how they furnished and used their interior space to express the domestic ideal.

Like all industrious homemakers charged with the smooth operation of busy households, the pastors would not lay a cornerstone before they had given "much anxious thought" to how the buildings could best be designed to meet the entire family's needs. Caroline Bartlett asked her church's building committee to start out by putting themselves in all the various family roles, imagining in succession the positions of preacher, chorister, usher, guest, teacher, toddler, sexton, and cook, and then scrutinizing the blueprints from the assumed perspective of each. As the church in Kalamazoo ended up hosting more than thirty meetings a week before the building was two years old, the minister was glad that she had had her planning board make the rooms adaptable to a wide range of different activities. "We asked the minutest questions concerning conveniences— from where will the kindergartener keep her supplies, to where will the janitor keep his brooms," she wrote afterward. "We had drawn everything exactly as we wanted it, for the sake of use, before we took our plan to an architect, to tell him that it was fixed as fate, and he was to put the best-looking outside to it that he could."[21]

That the physical plant had been designed from a woman's perspective was equally evident in the Sioux City church, where Safford and Gordon had also had the final word in the planning. In Sioux City, as in Kalamazoo, the layout and decor had been governed by the pastors' overriding concern that their members and the public at large be made to feel welcome and part of the family inside. The people had finally settled on a Romanesque building of wood and red quartzite and had it placed right at the street's edge so that, as it were, it could reach out to the community without a large frontage putting a distance between them. Other touches of this sort were detailed immodestly in the parish directory, which explained that the building's broad flight of stone steps extended an ample greeting and led directly into a main entrance hall, which was appointed as comfortably as the front parlor of any hospitable residence. "With its fire-place and other furnishings," the handbook pointed out, this "admirable arrangement" had "done much to foster the social life of the church and make its members feel truly at home." The main auditorium also provided a welcoming atmosphere with its warm tones and friendly arrangement of nearly four hundred upholstered chairs, all unreserved. A "large lecture room, with kitchen, toilet rooms, and two parlors adjoining," had also encouraged congregational unity, having been the scene of many a parish supper at which more than two hundred people had sat down and said grace together. Far from being "a man's castle," here was a place designed to accommodate a balanced, democratized household managed by women.[22]

Iowa City's church home, built during 1907 and 1908 under Gordon's close supervision while she was the Iowa Unitarian Association's field director, also reflected the sisters' concern that the church embody "the idea of comfort" and, according to local reporters, achieved an unusually "cozy and homelike" ambiance.[23] It was well known that Safford and Gordon had gone to "gigantic efforts" to purchase the land after failing to get the AUA to buy the property from the Universalists. The story was often repeated of how the pastors embarked on an all-out campaign, traveling constantly, skimping on meals, carrying their bags to save on porters, and dipping into their small salaries to cover the other expenses.[24] Having invested this much in the property, they were hardly prepared to let just any sort of building be put up on it.

Anticipating the next step, the women had helped to place Rev. Robert Loring, a man with a special interest and congenial tastes in church architecture, in the Iowa City pastorate. Loring had had a nice little cottage church built for his previous congregation in Derby, Connecticut, and there was perfect agreement between him and the Iowa Unitarian Association women that the Iowa church should use the same domestic idiom. There should not be a steeple, and homely touches—dark open beams against white walls, fireplaces upstairs and down, and leaded window panes with amber glass—should take the place of ecclesiastical ornament. They also agreed that the church, which required a seating capacity of some three hundred, should be built as economically as possible without appearing in any way "mean or small" or "stingy," as this would work to hurt the liberal cause.[25] Gordon did not let Loring forget that, even when there was a man in the pulpit, the church was a place where women worked, too. There would have to be space for a "good sized kitchen" and ample areas for socializing, guild rooms, parlors, and fireplaces, all arranged in the interest of family togetherness and comfort.[26]

For pastors whose feminist standard and Protestant ethic both called for material self-sufficiency, the financing of new churches had to be planned as carefully as the physical construction. Whatever else they rejected, Unitarian preachers had always held fast to the Calvinist virtues of thrift and resourcefulness. Long before women had ever appeared in the pulpits, these clergy enjoined congregations to be like the poor but frugal wife who laid out her husband's small earnings so well that her family was able to live comfortably without ever having to borrow.[27] As the customary financial managers of their homes, nineteenth-century women were well aware, without being preached to about it, that being in debt was harmful to family life, and, in church affairs, they advocated saving first before spending. According to one liberal minister's wife who had watched the trends in church financing closely, womenfolk well understood that families did not have "the same sense of home" in houses in which they had small equity as in those that were paid for.[28]

The women who managed church households in the Western Conference agreed entirely. The record establishes that they were much less inclined than their brothers to borrow "easy money" on the long term or to try to balance their budgets on faith alone. Convinced that the happiest congregations were those that could take pride in ownership, they made it their policy to have their people rely on their own hard work and sacrifice and build within their means instead of going outside for financial assistance. Even by the late 1890s, when it became almost routine for growing societies to take advantage of the AUA's low-interest loans, the Iowa sisterhood, loathe to take help from officials who showed no respect for their ministry, shied away from this funding strategy as a lesser evil at best.

For Safford, the idea of using the AUA's money was so offensive that on more than one occasion she drew on her personal savings to keep her church independent and free of the obligations that went along with patronage. "We are asking no outside help but are building the church *ourselves*," she reminded the AUA's secretary Grendall Reynolds in 1889 when the Sioux City church was nearing completion and plans for its christening were under way. What she and her people most needed, she told him with barely concealed irony, was the genuine respect "of eastern friends, who are not asked to help us in any pecuniary way."[29] Ten years later, in negotiating with Boston for local autonomy in financing state development, Safford was able to cite her record of eighteen years in the field, during which she had more than established credentials to manage her churches' money. "My own church is the mother of four self-supporting churches," she told the AUA's secretary Samuel Eliot in 1898, and, in the past ten years alone, the conference she and her sisters directed had "raised more money and established more churches" than any other.[30]

If the people's will to sacrifice for the cause was not tested as fully when a wealthy parishioner, confident in his pastor's wise management, virtually paid for a new church himself—as happened when Bartlett was pastor in Kalamazoo and Buck was in Kenosha—even such good fortune served the ministers as an object lesson on the value of simple industry and frugality.[31]

Extreme thrift had been absolutely essential when Gordon's society started to build its new church in Orlando in 1912. Without any large contributions up front, there had not been much choice except to override Safford's objections and start with an AUA loan, and the prospect of this indebtedness made Gordon all the more adamant about the need for frugality and sacrifice. Some resistance to the minister's call for economy came from a few members who had been part of the Sioux City church when unlimited funds had built them a dream house and who now had a hard time adjusting to present realities. Yet Gordon was firm. She instructed her building committee to find out exactly how much they could raise and then be content with whatever the pledges would build. For her own part, after trying to preach with the litter and noise of their temporary quarters in the local Opera House, she would be enormously grateful just to have a small place that was quiet and clean.[32]

The group agreed on a simple frame building costing $1,800. The only "extra" was a fireplace put into the plans at the last moment at the pastor's insistence—"to give a touch of poetry to the otherwise rather plain room," she explained.[33] With its front porch and chimney taking the place of a formal arched entrance and steeple, the diminutive sanctuary was evidently quite an anomaly, for it came to be known in the town as "the little church that looks like a house."[34] But it was a home that was practically paid for the day it was christened, and Eleanor Gordon, grateful and proud to have it, found nothing wanting. "I shall never forget how fine in every way the chapel was on that March morning," she later recalled of its dedication. To her great delight, it had been just cool enough to warrant a fire in the hearth, and the room quickly filled to capacity with a total of eighty-five celebrants. White jasmine, elderberry, and pink roses decorated the hall, and the plain glass windows allowed a clear view of an orange grove in full bloom. "No stately service in a Cathedral ever meant more," Gordon wrote, than the simple service had meant to her people in this most humble home.[35]

III

All the principles of the well-built church home—the down-to-earth workability, the democratic provision of comfort, and the spirit of magnanimity fostered by self-sufficiency—culminated in the idea that a church's responsibility was not confined to its immediate family but included the whole of society. Though women were not unique in seeking to prod their churches toward greater outreach, with their traditional interest in hospitality and benevolence it was natural for them to think more than men about their churches' relationships with their neighbors on the outside. Liberal churchwomen noted that simply because their churches were untaxed properties, not to mention outward expressions of a democratic theology, there was an obligation to see that the buildings enhanced their neighborhoods, not only in terms of aesthetic effect, but through their ethical influence, too. Even more important than how a church looked was how well it took care of its more distant relatives.[36]

Inspired by Jones's thriving institutional church movement in Chicago, the sisterhood sought to give even their smallest organizations the character of friendly "workshops" that offered their services to the broader community. In Cherokee, Iowa, Collson made her church a clearinghouse for relief work; in Des Moines, Safford and Gordon conceived the new church as a "personal and civic" home that would prove a source of good for all the city.[37] Only in Iowa City, where Gordon attempted to prod a society whose religious consciousness was still entrenched in an academic tradition, did the pastor find it "impossible" to involve the church more in community outreach.

When it became clear that her efforts were futile, Gordon began to look about for a field that would be more responsive. Jones suggested the possibility of her going to Minneapolis. The city had no need at all for a Unitarian church "of the Boston type"—since all its wealthier and "stylish" liberals were now finding that sort of thing in established yet doctrinally relaxed denominations—but it could benefit from a "People's Institute" in which she might well find a future, Jones said. Such a movement might use the Unitarians' present facilities "in a down-town seven-day-in-the-week fashion for all the blessed amenities and humanities, making it not a settlement but a center, with high preaching on Sunday, large studying and noble usefulness all around."[38] Gordon liked the idea enormously, and, although the job failed to materialize, the concept became a reference that helped her chart her future course. When she moved to Des Moines a decade later, she chose to make her "parsonage" the Roadside Settlement House and there fused her ministry with the "large studying and noble usefulness" that Jones had suggested.[39]

None of these architectural histories offered a clearer example of the way the church's role evolved from public to private nurturing under a woman's leadership than that of the People's Church in Kalamazoo. Anyone who compared the original building with the one that replaced it in 1894 could see at a glance just how far this society had moved away from the "high church" ideal of the old Boston parishes. The liberals who had organized in the city some thirty years earlier had wanted as far as possible to make their house of worship a replica of the cathedrals back East and had used their resources to build a bare-bones Gothic adaptation of wood, with stained glass windows, modified spires, carpets, upholstered seats, and a pipe organ. Adopting the covenant of the College Church in Cambridge, Massachusetts, they had not only held weekly communion, using a beautiful set of silver service, but had baptisms every other month. In short, Bartlett said, the old Unitarian building had tried to be a "theological church" and was therefore conceived as "a house of God." Its successor, on the other hand—as its new name announced—was built in the modern style of the "sociological institution" and was meant to be a house for all God's people.[40]

Looking more like a large, later Victorian residence than a religious meeting place, People's Church had taken its cue from Jones's public-spirited All Souls, which was opening a "fellowship house" on Chicago's disadvantaged South Side. From the start, Bartlett's plan was to have her own organization do much the same thing by making its new facility "plain and simple and moving it towards the poorer population" of Kalamazoo, which at the time had some twenty-five thousand residents. It seemed to the pastor that no one was taking responsibility for the town's spiraling social problems because the community was at an awkward stage of development, too big for people to keep an eye on everyone else as they did in the country, but too recently small to have started providing for people's welfare through agencies. Kalamazoo already had scores of juvenile delinquents, but no children's court or jail; it had enough transients to bring in all sorts of communicable diseases, but no way to help drifters get jobs and homes, and no safeguard for the public's health. An institutional church built to care for all the people all week was the obvious place to start addressing these problems.

The building that Bartlett's committee had planned had a large auditorium with adjoining parlors and galleries that could all be combined "by an ingenious device" to seat over seven hundred. On the lower level were workshops for manual training classes. Next to them were a kitchen and dining room where women of all ages and backgrounds came for free lessons in home economics and helped serve hot lunches at cost to as many as three hundred working girls during a single noon hour. Upstairs, a bevy of rooms and offices had been put in for cultural and service clubs and charitable agencies that had no other housing.[41] After a free public library opened a couple of blocks away and the YMCA started offering physical hygiene and exercise programs, the church abandoned its own plans for such facilities and reallocated the space for a women's gymnasium and a free community kindergarten, as "there could be no question" of their urgent need.[42]

The church's accepted identities as a workshop, a meeting place, and a school were yet always subsumed by the broader idea of the church as a home. Therefore, when the building was finished, the board invited the families of all the workmen—from the architect and the contractor to every carpenter, mason, and stonecutter—to a combination "communion meal" and "housewarming banquet" as a gesture of the church's intent to nourish its broader family.

Many others outside the membership also soon found hospitality at People's Church. The kindergarten, the first of the programs to open, began to sign up little scholars the summer before the building was finished and filled up within a few days. To be sure that the program would reach a wide segment of the community, the minister asked women from different churches to serve with her as co-directors. Together they hired a trained "kindergartener" from the Armour Institute in Chicago, provided her with a corps of teacher cadets and the latest equipment, and arranged for a fleet of "buses" to gather up and return the children who lived at a distance and could not have come otherwise. There was such a demand for the new facility that, even after expanding it, half the applicants had to be turned away. After two years, with the figures at hand, the church had no trouble convincing the Board of Education that there was enough need to make kindergarten an integral part of the city's public school system.[43]

The women's gymnasium, furnished with state-of-the-art apparatus and supervised by a professional physical hygienist trained in the East, was run on the premise that stronger women meant stronger families. Like other progressive reformers who focused on balance and symmetry as the ideal in human experience, Bartlett's group fully expected that women's improved health through exercise would also improve their relationships with the opposite sex and produce better marriages.[44] To this end, the church kept the ladies' gymnasium open all day and most nights. In the mornings and afternoons, women and girls of all ages came for fitness classes, which carried a nominal charge that paid the director's salary; in the evenings, the working girls came from the factories and shops to exercise and dance to live ensembles.

It took just a casual question about People's Church and its popularity to set Bartlett off on an endless description of every inch of space and how it was used by all sorts of people one never expected to see together. She loved to detail how women in bloomers and tunics went through their routines in the gym while others in starched aprons bustled about in the kitchen or sat in the meeting rooms learning the latest in cooking, nutrition, marketing, home nursing, sewing, and psychology. She would tell how immediately after school and in the evenings the basement shop filled with boys who had once roamed the streets but now, by studying metalwork, carpentry, and mechanical drawing, were given the prospect of jobs and a future. At the same time, a steady line of traffic passed through the parlors and rooms upstairs, where the Unity Club, the ladies' alliance, a choral union and Sunday School orchestra, and countless other groups—including for several years an all-black Frederick Douglass Literary Club—made their home in People's Church. The minister liked to conclude her tours by pointing out that "the vital thing" was "the spirit and purpose" informing the building and all its practical work and that, like other churches, hers had its regular worship services to keep this religious consciousness alive.[45]

The institutional concept toward which the ministers moved their houses of worship might well be considered the farthest extension of their domestic church ministry. Taking literally and combining the celebrated ideas of the home as a sacred space and the church as a center of comfort and outgoing hospitality, the sisterhood bridged the private and public realms of religious expression and made their prophetic message accessible to the rank and file. Jenkin Lloyd Jones had good reason for offering them his congratulations for using the social sciences to put the Christian message into a language all people could understand. The theologians had "had their day and made sorry work of it," he summarized, but his sisters were showing them how to feed and shelter the flocks by nurturing families and making the church a real home.[46]

Part Three

INSTITUTIONAL BOUNDARIES

*I am amused to see from my window here how busily man has divided and
staked off his domain. God must smile at his puny fences running hither
and thither everywhere over the land.*
—Henry David Thoreau

Chapter Nine

EAST AND WEST

Place . . . provides the base of reference . . . the point of view. . . .
Every story would be another story . . . if it took up its characters and
plot and happened somewhere else.
—Eudora Welty

I

In 1889, while attending the annual meetings in Boston, Caroline
Bartlett wrote Jenkin Lloyd Jones about how important geography had
become to her liberal identity. Several New England colleagues who
frowned on Jones and the Western Conference in general had been trying
all week to bring her around to their side, but she had stood firm.
"The more I see of the spirit of the East," she assured her friend in
Chicago, "the more I feel that I am of the West—and that I am
glad I am."[1]

What Bartlett's group had in mind when they talked of an Eastern spirit
was partly the pull toward centralization that started right after the Civil
War with the founding of a National Conference of Unitarian Churches. It
also referred to the lingering evidence of ecclesiasticism: the retention of the
rituals of communion and baptism, the use of such terms as "Jesus *Christ*,"
and the jealously guarded hierarchical structures that put women at the
bottom. Many who tried to describe the regional differences dwelt on the
physical cues, the low platforms and simple halls that Westerners used to
replace the high pulpits and fancy cathedrals favored back East.[2] Others,
the women especially, went to the heart of the matter and spoke of the
contrast in attitudes. Marie Jenney, laying it out on a great "metaphorical
map," presented the West as "a wide spread web" held together by threads
of cooperation and sympathy between men and women.[3] By situating

119

themselves in opposition to the Eastern tendencies toward a centralized hierarchy, female subordination, and narrow theology, women like Bartlett came to see just how far to the left of center they stood in the liberal scheme of things.

The frontier's demands, which released the hold of old habits and fostered a climate in which all good workers were valued equally, had given the Western women a measure of opportunity and respect that was quite unknown to their New England sisters. Practically twenty years before a reluctant AUA Board of Directors gave a seat to a female, the Western Conference had given all women an equal voice as delegates. While at first, according to early reports, the women had simply "preferred to listen," they soon rid themselves of their inhibitions and took the lead in conference development, turning it into a highly effective umbrella for scattered churches and state groups.[4] Their contributions were innovative and practical. To solve the problem of keeping their traveling missionaries supplied with tracts and books, they devised an ingenious system of using back rooms in their homes as pantries for storing the literature and making it available all along the frontier routes. Frequently, they took on most of the job of distribution as well and could be seen going from farm to farm with their peddler's carts of sermons and flyers. After the war, as demand for liberal religion outgrew their immediate reach, the conference's women decided to take to the mails to missionize. When they heard about families in isolated areas who had no church to support them, they started sending them tracts along with personal letters that mixed a warm sympathy and encouragement with bits of homespun theology.[5]

The distaff became even more prominent in denominational efforts out West after 1875, when Jones took the conference helm and infused the movement with unprecedented zeal for missionary work. In his weekly *Unity* Jones celebrated the efforts that women were making in pulpits and parish service, declaring that they were the strength of the Western movement, "quite as much if not more than the men."[6] Jones's respect for women's intelligence and his way of delivering "good stiff stuff when he talked to them," in Jane Addams's words, "brought out the very best"; he "expected them to do good, hard work, and they were proud to respond."[7] In less than two years after Jones's arrival, the distaff's programs had grown so elaborate that they were organized into a separate division with greater representation on the Western Unitarian Conference board.

Alert to the need for a workplace as well, the women raised money to open a conference headquarters in downtown Chicago and then got a woman elected as assistant conference secretary to keep the new operation running smoothly. Though sparsely equipped, the office on Madison Street served admirably as a paper storage, mailroom, and general clearing house. All through the week, it was thronged by women distributing tracts and Sunday School lessons, editing various publications, and writing letters for the Post Office Mission. Chicago-based Celia Woolley, who helped edit Jones's *Unity,* was one of the office regulars. So was Susan Barber Jones, whose leadership in the Western Women's Unitarian Conference, one visitor said, seemed to have turned its base of operation into "practically a bilateral headquarters for the Women's Rights Movement."[8] A striking contrast to the AUA's Boston offices, the Chicago "sky parlor," where women's work and leadership were most in evidence, left little question about the distaff's importance and place in the Western movement.

Western liberals had also been willing to back women who had an interest in preaching and pastoring. When the Iowa conference discovered a talent like Safford's they not only gave her credentials but made her their chief executive. Given this opportunity, Safford had turned the state organization into the largest and most energetic in the West and anchored her pulpit sisterhood in the process. The women's auxiliary of the Western Unitarian Conference had committed itself to supporting the female ministry when it first organized as the Western Women's Unitarian Conference in 1881. Their members' success as Post Office pastors and lay missionaries— or untitled ministers—legitimized the ambition some had to have their work recognized for what it was. As part of their program of helping those women who had this desire and talent, they gave small stipends to Ida Hultin to take a few college courses and to Mila Tupper and Amelia Murdock to support them in part-time pastorates.[9] While the Western conference's leaders were known for their love of debate and had some significant differences when it came to reform and religion, about women's place in the church and the ministry there was little dispute in the 1880s and the 1890s. Indeed, when the century came to a close, there was scarcely a liberal pulpit in Iowa and the contiguous states that had not at some time had a woman conducting its services, and any liberal brother who so much as hedged on the issue was taking the risk of putting his reputation and contract in jeopardy.

By contrast, the Eastern liberals had always been cool to ambitious women. Historically, they had provided the leadership in the crusades for women's rights, but only a small minority of the Unitarian fold shared these sympathies. The mainstream had disapproved of women in its administration and ministry on the grounds that females lacked business sense and would crowd out the capable men if they could.[10] No woman served on the AUA's Board of Directors until 1870, and females were still routinely excluded from real positions of influence when the Western sisters began to appear in the East in the 1880s expecting that they would be treated as equal colleagues.

Accustomed to being regarded professionally and judged on merit, not gender, the Iowa group had not been well prepared for the second-class treatment they got from the Eastern provincials they found at the AUA. The Beacon Street executives, who had never known institutionalized religion as anything but "a man's world," had a hard time taking the women's leadership seriously. Grindall Reynolds, AUA secretary from 1881 through 1894, was the greatest offender during the years when the women began to come into their own. While Reynolds was able to get along well with his male associates, who liked his "sound common sense," "judicial temper," and "efficient business capacity," Safford's group found him to be officious and condescending.[11] Though Reynolds's part of the correspondence that passed between them is lost, it is clear from the women's responses that, whatever he actually felt or wrote, he failed to communicate the sort of respect and cooperation they considered their due. As far as the women could tell, their record of building thriving societies and running the regional conference affairs more efficiently than anyone else was doing did not impress Reynolds, who allegedly treated them as a bad joke. As a consequence, though they were eager for cordial relations with Boston, the women preferred to cut short the amenities, which seemed only to encourage the cavalier attitude, and confront the men directly about their bias against women's work.

Why was it, asked Safford of Reynolds in 1887, that, when women ministers wrote him for tracts, they were never sent more than a handful? "We have distributed a great many here, as we have a large congregation, but in order to secure them I have to order through Mr. Clute and have them sent to a *man*." The ladies in Davenport's Post Office Mission were having the very same trouble. How did Mr. Reynolds account for it?[12] The question was never answered, and two years later the women still had to forage for pamphlets to meet the demand of congregations that in Safford's church ran from three to four hundred on typical Sunday mornings.[13] Reynolds also had an infuriating way of ignoring requests for appearances at Western conferences and church dedications or reneging after agreeing to come.[14] Even the weathered Eliza Wilkes, whose long years of service had taught her much patience, was often provoked by the AUA's insensitivity and neglect of the Western work. After being stood up a number of times, an angry Wilkes let Reynolds know what she thought. People had taken a good deal of trouble to come from her outlying missions to meet him, and he had callously let them down. "Don't forget," she told this executive who had never worked far from the cities, "it's sometimes very lonesome being a Unitarian missionary."[15]

While the women were willing enough to show their loyalty to the national body by displaying a photograph of its Beacon Street offices at their conferences, they would not yet support the administration materially, explaining to Reynolds that first they would have to be treated with the same respect and cordiality that they always received from the Western conference. Surely, said Safford, such treatment was mandated not only by common decency but by the most fundamental principles of their religious faith.[16] Only if the AUA could assure her that they were prepared to make fitness for ministry rather than sex the basis for recognition of clergy would she ask her churches to send contributions to Boston.[17]

Beyond the personal insult it levied, what bothered the sisterhood most about the Eastern bureaucracy's disregard for their leadership was that, for all their superior ways, these men did not understand Western methods and needed the guidance of those they listened to least. Writing to Boston from the Dakotas, Wilkes tried for years to explain the futility of attempting "to plant 'eastern Unitarian churches' on western soil" or of "simply hiding the leaven and waiting for it to do its work." More damage than good had been done when the AUA sent out its young seminarians with little equipment beyond their fresh stacks of untried sermons, she complained. Many young men who came to her field were still finding their way into liberal religion and tried to preach a theology that was much too conservative for the people, whose thinking was more evolved than the ministers'. "A course at Harvard," Wilkes had to remind the settlement office, was "not [a] sufficient antidote for a lifetime in orthodoxy."[18] Others who came to help had "really good sermons" but little else to their credit. "He has a timid hesitating delivery," Wilkes said of one who was "not at all suited to pioneer work." The man's spirit was good, she told Jenkin Lloyd Jones, and it pained her to see him disappointed again and again, but his failures worked just as much, if not more, of a hardship on her and the movement. "Better [to] make theological schools of our old parishes than our new," was the moral.[19]

But then not even the best of preaching was enough to ensure success. In the West especially, the urgent need was for all-around, androgynous workers who were not just good pulpit providers but also caring, attentive pastors throughout the week. Both lay and ordained mission efforts had shown that the greatest returns came where this nurturing was the strongest. The Post Office Mission, whose outreach had been the real heart of Western development, had come into being, its founders explained, through the understanding of their religion as a "homely faith." As homemakers, they had responded to the practical struggles that families had when they broke off from orthodoxy, when they had to send children to schools where their liberal ideas were condemned, and when they had to bury their dead without a supportive religious community while "the hard word" of scornful neighbors "bruised the heart."[20] As the *Unity* men often pointed out, the same down-to-earth versatility was essential for any successful ministry in the Western field, and no one had shown this more clearly than the women with flourishing pastorates.[21]

Such workers were hard to find, however, when Safford's associates tried to find leadership for their infant societies. "What is the matter with our younger ministers?" Gordon asked of the AUA after reading a stack of letters from Harvard and Meadville men who wanted positions. "They do not look for a place where they may wrestle with superstition, ignorance, materialism, godlessness, but where there is a church built, where the work had been done, where everyone is saved, where all they have to do is write an essay once a week, and perhaps lead a Browning Club. —If only they might have some of the Browning spirit," Gordon despaired. "Does the Divinity School lay a blighting hand on them?" she wondered.[22]

The issue of women's exclusion from Harvard became in itself another capsule for the ideological distance between the East and the West. It strengthened the sisters' affection for Meadville in Pennsylvania, which homespun Westerners proudly embraced as their family's special school. With "no traditions to hamper it, no powerful Establishment to frown upon it," and "no desire to play fast and loose with ecclesiasticism," to borrow Murdock's description, Meadville was giving the women a chance to retire the stereotypes. It allowed them to show that they could be just as eager as men "to solve the insolvable problems of ethics and philosophy and quite as tenacious over disputed interpretations of Scripture"—in short, that the question of ministry was one of fitness, not gender.[23] To the Western mind, Harvard's refusal to follow Meadville's example epitomized the male myopia in the East. In attacking "the shame of Harvard," the women dwelt on the irony of its graduates' poor showing in the West and their own successes, using the contrast as further evidence that a person's sex had very little to do with fitness for ministry.

II

While the Western field was hospitable by comparison with the East, it offered enough opposition to keep women ministers on the defensive. All the feminist clergy had stories to tell about challenges to their authority by the trinitarians and, worse, about their own people's willingness to yield the point to the mainstream culture. Eleanor Gordon recalled how her young engaged women would come to her awkwardly and explain that some other pastor would have to conduct the wedding because their orthodox husbands-to-be did not want a woman to marry them.[24] Elizabeth Padgham, too, recalled how her very own sister, a lifelong Unitarian, used to plead with her not to "embarrass" the family by using her title "Reverend" when they went on vacations together.[25]

Despite the abundant opportunities to debate their fitness for ministry, the Western sisters were not at first willing to make an issue of it. During the 1880s, while getting their toehold in the profession, they said but little about the matter in public and, taking a brother's advice, left the question of their ability for the record of their performance to answer. While the pedants were combing the Garden of Eden for evidence against them, women need only show that they were doing a noble ministry, and the old arguments would disappear before the accomplished fact.[26] For this non-confrontational strategy, the sisters found precedent in the biblical record of Phoebe, whom Paul had appointed to be the deaconess of his church at Cencraea. Marion Murdock preached an entire sermon on this story to show the merits of using actions instead of words to break down deeply set opposition. What was it, she asked, that Phoebe had done to overcome Paul's antifeminist bias and win his heartfelt endorsement? "Knowing the prejudices of her time, she doubtless acted in advance of custom rather than in defiance of it," was Murdock's answer. Aware that the man at the head of her church was "very sensitive in this direction," Phoebe had the wisdom to know "that if she quietly made herself useful, custom would stand back, and Paul would come forward to recognize her."[27] The modern-day Phoebes of the 1880s followed the same approach.

By the 1890s, however, with the growing resistance already beginning to block any further advance, the women began to mount a more vocal offensive, though still deploring the fact that their critics insisted on making gender a factor. They insisted impatiently that they had entered the ministry not just to make a feminist point but, as Gordon explained, for the work itself and that "this work was human work," not man's or woman's. Granted, their disregard of traditional gender-based role assignments had been a conscious, personal imperative, but it had never been an issue professionally until it was forced on them by the opposition.[28]

Compelled to accept the terms in which the debate had been set, the women argued their case on a number of fronts, frequently starting off with the issue of the Bible's inerrancy and a rejection of scriptural teachings considered "unreasonable and unfair." As ministers who still regarded the Bible as a rich cultural storehouse, these women could never accept the solution proposed by Elizabeth Cady Stanton in the 1880s, an alternative *Woman's Bible* that sacrificed poetry to polemics. Yet they fully agreed with Stanton that woman's continuing subjugation to man had resulted from the unreflective acceptance of scriptural myth as prescriptive historical fact. "We can find no reason for holding that the Bible can settle all the social and religious questions of the 19th century," said Ida Hultin. Whether or not Paul meant to circumscribe woman's spheres for all times and places, they would go their own way and correct Paul where he was misguided.[29] Murdock, who took special pleasure in putting the patriarch in his place, explained that Paul had merely reflected the popular thought of his time when he said, "with all his customary rhetoric, but with less than his customary logic, 'Man is the glory of God, but woman is the glory of the man.'" Her group felt that Paul's teachings on woman's place were obsolete in the modern world, and their practice was simply to skip the passages where these pronouncements appeared.[30]

The women ministers also sought to dissolve the obstructive notions about separate natures and spheres by holding them up to plain fact. "While the 'truly feminine,' the 'ever womanly' theory of the vine and oak may be all very well in poetry," Gordon noted, "when she was needed, 'the 'ever womanly' roll[ed] up her sleeves' and tackled what some people still persisted in calling "man's work."[31] Hultin also scoffed at the popular notion that females lacked in physical stamina what they were said to have in the way of spiritual strength and told about how she had driven her horse as much as forty miles a day while filling three or four pulpits a week in Michigan. "When our brother minister objects to woman's admission to the ministry on the ground of physical inability, I wonder if he stops to consider how much of his work his wife does," Hultin said, and where "he would find himself were there only men in his congregation." Even Safford, never strong physically, was satisfied that, "in the face of deep-seated prejudice and opposition," the woman minister had "shown beyond question that she was not only able to preach, but also able to do far more—endure the strain of long city pastorates and build up strong, growing churches." [32]

Equally pernicious, the clergywomen said, was all the talk about women's having especially keen intuitive powers that compensated for their alleged intellectual weakness. While anatomy obviously determined different biological functions, there was to their way of thinking no essential difference between men and women in the realms of morality, intellect, or feeling. Tragically, Gordon noted, such "mistaken psychology" had filled society with "hard-hearted men and hysterical women." [33]

In the area of church leadership, this cult of True Womanhood worked its mischief by impeding the development of well-rounded, ministerial personalities. Good ministers, whatever their sex, needed tenderness and intuition as well as good judgment and intellectual rigor. It was as foolish to imagine that a man could reach the hearts of his congregation with a coldly intellectual sermon as to assume that a woman could guide her people responsibly by relying on her intuitive nature. By the same token, Bartlett reminded her colleagues and younger aspiring sisters, intuitions alone did not "afford a reliable exegesis of Scripture," nor did they supply the "sound information" needed to address "the living questions" of the day. As Bartlett saw it, any woman who relied solely on her native, untrained powers, on her "motherwit or an emotional temperament," would be both presumptuous and silly and bound to preach the pews empty. [34]

In short, in their public debate the sisterhood sought to describe a place for themselves in a balanced and unified institution that stressed the sexes' similarities, not their differences. As positivists who thought of reform in terms of healing societies that were fractured by wars between men and women, they talked about "feminine nature" only to point out that ailing communities like the church needed the so-called womanly traits of sympathy and generosity to correct the imbalance that had made "man's world" materialistic and brutal. Social institutions, like humanity itself, were meant to have both male and female components, the "father and the mother, the sister and the brother elements," as their "ministers, helpers, and saviors."[35] As the process of evolution continued to lift human understanding, they said, and people in all regions, East and West, and all religions discerned that the nature of deity was androgynous, they would accept the broader range of its expression as well, and woman's place in the ministry would be secure.

Chapter Ten

THE ECONOMICS OF POWER

Is it not lawful for me to do what I will with my own?
—Matthew 20:12

It did not take long for the pastors to learn that their institutional fight for a place would have to be waged as a fight for financial control. As with other women who were attempting to enter fields that men still controlled and who had no job market or easy access to real property, economic dependency loomed as a terrible threat to their personal and professional welfare. The problem, as put by Elizabeth Cady Stanton in 1869, was that a woman would always attempt to please a man and "adapt to his condition" so long as he was the one who was feeding her.[1] Nowhere was this danger greater, as far as the pastors could see, than in dealing with their denomination's executive officers, whose enormous economic advantage—Jones called it "insidious money power"—had weakened the very "sinews of courage" in the Western conference. Like Jones, the women believed that the "efficient strength" that came from close dealings with "a moneyed corporation such as the A.U.A." was a dangerous temptation to poor congregations and underpaid ministers.[2]

On the most practical level, the sisterhood's effort to hold their own took the form of a struggle to generate and control their own funds without losing stature as clergy or women. From the start, Safford's circle attempted to place their relationship with the East on the basis of strictly reciprocal fellowship, not economic support. At every opportunity, they reminded the Boston office that their societies had always paid their own way and, while seeking the friendship of Eastern friends, did not want their financial patronage.[3] The return on this policy was that it freed them to spend their own money as they thought best. This nearly always meant spending it close to home instead of for "all the drawers and pigeon holes" at AUA

129

headquarters. Sending their money to Boston, they said, was working from too great a distance, and, for all the effect it had on their parish's practical needs, they might just as well be sending it off to London. It made no sense to try to "work Boston" and local societies at the same time. Better "to do our own work, in our own way, with our own tools," Gordon said, speaking for her associates.[4]

To be sure, it was not always possible to achieve ideal self-sufficiency. Mary Leggett failed so miserably in her fund-raising efforts in Beatrice, Nebraska, that, month after month, the church came up short on the small salary it had guaranteed until the mortified pastor was forced to borrow the difference from her parishioners. On top of this awful embarrassment was that of having to air it back East and appeal to the AUA to bail her out. "It is a sore humiliation to me," she told Boston's Reynolds, "that we are not by this time more *Self-Reliant!* Do I expect too much of this People. Or is it my own lack of address that fails to bring out their resources?"[5] While the details of Leggett's unfortunate situation are sketchy at best, raising the money to run a society in land-poor areas such as hers was often too much to expect from even the most dedicated of workers.

Eliza Wilkes, who asked for AUA subsidies as a matter of course, was a case in point. As she informed Boston just after Christmas in 1893, when it looked as if the Sioux Falls church was about to go under, no amount of talent or dedication could raise local funds when the people had nothing but "land and taxes" and could not afford to buy groceries. With the economic collapse, her husband was getting back less than eight cents for each dollar he sent out in legal fees, and Wilkes could personally testify to the problems the people were having.[6]

In fact, in such difficult territory, not even Eastern reinforcement could guarantee that a church would survive. Though the AUA came through with further funding and in nonmaterial ways the hard times helped the liberal cause by quickening local interest in it—Wilkes was frankly "astonished" to see how easily she could draw congregations of 125 and even more—the depression's ravages and Sioux Falls's surfeit of churches prevented recovery there. In 1897, the liberal church was forced to disband and left its beautiful building to the city for use as a free public library.[7] Wilkes continued to make appeals for outside help for her several country churches until they had adequate "inside resources" to operate self-sufficiently. In the meantime, there surely was no lack of dedication, she stressed in her letters to Boston, noting that all her little societies already had shown their resilience. By 1896, a core of laywomen in Adrian, Minnesota, were conducting the weekly services and had raised $400 to build a new chapel. Luverne, Minnesota, had cleared all its debts and was paying a regular minister. Even Rock Rapids, Iowa, which had nearly folded when the price of oats dropped to ten cents a bushel, was "holding on to the cause" and showing promise.[8] Seeing herself as more of a district developer than a settled pastor like Leggett, Wilkes felt that pleading for help from outside was a mark of strong purpose and not of some failing; convinced that the movement could flourish if helped in material ways a while longer, she sought funds from Boston again and again without feeling compromised by it.[9]

In Iowa, on the other hand, where the workers were younger and feistier and bristled at the slightest hint of paternalism, the understanding was that they would make do without Boston's money, no matter how hard this might be. Just once, in 1889, had the Iowa Unitarian Association softened and accepted an AUA offer to match funds raised at the state level the following year, and the arrangement had been sufficiently disagreeable to discourage any more of the kind.[10] Thereafter, the women resolved to manage their finances on their own, under the Iowa association's auspices, and to let Boston know how well they were able to do this. In 1892, a smug Safford bragged to the AUA that her Sioux City church was so strong that it had been able to pay back the $1,000 loan for its building before it was due and that its infant society in Cherokee was expected to do the same. "We are trying to cultivate the right spirit in Iowa," she reminded the Boston officials.[11]

Indeed, Safford's movement in Iowa had already become "the mother of four self-supporting churches," thanks to its "Helping Hand" policy. As described in the Sioux City church's tenth anniversary handbook—which Safford sent on to the AUA with the section carefully bracketed—the policy was to take no outside monies but work to develop its own resources and share these with family churches in the Iowa association. There were "far too many" societies that did rely on the AUA, Safford said, but her sisters' congregations were rarely among them.[12] One of the things that made Iowa City a "cross" for Gordon when she was the pastor there was that the movement was heavily subsidized by the AUA and that, after years of jealously guarded financial independence, she found herself having to look to Boston for part of her salary. "One thing is certain," she had told Jones during the worst of her ordeal, "if I ever finish *honorably* this Iowa City business, nothing will ever tempt me again to undertake a movement . . . that is not self-supporting. This experience has been good for me, but like most things that are good for us, it has been extremely unpleasant."[13]

It was hard enough living on what Western ministers earned without having to suffer the indignities of dependency. Salaries that started at around $1,200 a year and rarely went higher than $1,500 barely covered necessary travel, which was considerable, and basic living expenses. When Hultin was first starting out in Algona, she had such a difficult time paying bills that she soon fell behind in her rent and apparently had to shop on credit.[14] Even after long years in the field, Gordon still had to get by on a salary of $1,350 a year as the pastor in Iowa City. She frequently wondered how she would have managed if she had had a spouse to support. "I fear he would have fared but poorly," she told the AUA dryly, as would her successor if he should decide to get married.[15] Gordon's personal needs were modest, but, like most of her sister workers, she shared a large part of the little she earned with needy relatives, college students, friends too old to support themselves, and worthy organizations like the suffrage and temperance alliances. Then, too, after she had turned forty, she started to think more about her old age and wanted to save something to keep from spending her last days "in some retreat for superannuated old women."[16] It did not "seem quite fair," as she told the better paid bureaucrats in 1900, that the older ministers like herself should have to do the pioneer work at their own expense when it was young men with advantages who should be doing it.[17]

What made the dependence on Boston officialdom so distasteful to the Western women was that the people who subsidized their wages had little respect for their work. Not only were their requests for AUA tracts and other services slighted, but their insights into the Western work were patently ignored. Eliza Wilkes, with twenty years in the field, cringed each time she recalled one executive—evidently disparaging her prior service as a Universalist—saying that he did not even consider her labors legitimate "Unitarian" work.[18] Safford also smarted at the East's attitude that "any sort of ministerial timber would do for the West," which conveyed such an obvious lack of respect for a field that the women had worked hard to cultivate.[19] She and her sisters could hardly accept Boston's dollars as payment for services rendered when the patrons refused to recognize their services for what they were.

From this point of view, any money received from the East seemed no better than charity, and the work it supported, uncompensated in essence, would have to be exploitation. At least at home, where appreciative congregations paid them as much as they could, their salaries, no matter how small, signified a genuine recognition of their work's merit. The local congregations also had a far better record of delivering the paycheck on time than the AUA, which was notorious for its late disbursements. As Gordon complained, "the uncertainty" and "unceasing financial strain" took away "all the inspiration," and it was demeaning to have to go hat in hand for one's salary every month. Iowa City was proof enough that a woman's "dignity" was put in "greater danger" by money matters of this kind than almost anything else.[20]

The tensions arising from these "money matters" became even worse at the turn of the century, when Bostonian Samuel Eliot took over the AUA's leadership. Eliot, a consummate executive, was intent on putting the loosely run movement on a sound business footing by tightening up operations and concentrating authority in the East.[21] With two-thirds of the AUA's 457 churches still in New England and the sixty societies within ten miles of Boston contributing nearly half the association's annual income in 1900, it seemed clear to him that the national headquarters was well positioned on Beacon Street and from there ought to monitor liberal development in the Middle and Far West more closely.[22] The AUA's new chief administrator sought to have such full control that he held the gavel not only when the Board of Directors met but at all meetings of the standing committees, which he appointed himself. He even had his position upgraded from secretary to president to remove any question of his being the chief executive. Insisting that "a corporation managed by ministers" needed "business discipline more than work," Eliot pressed for a pay-as-you-go policy and called for an end to covering deficit spending with endowment monies. He had his board cut off assistance to chronically dependent churches and redirect the funding to more "promising or important" ventures.[23]

From the time that Eliot first gained visibility on the Board of Directors in the mid-1890s and began to emerge as George Batchelor's heir apparent, Safford's group had had misgivings about his authoritarian influence and advocacy of stronger centralization. These women, most of them first-generation liberals, had entered the fold to escape the oppressive concentration of ecclesiastical power. They did not take their freedom of self-governance for granted, as "born Unitarians" might, but were fiercely protective of their congregational polity. Yet while fearing intrusion, they also felt heartened when Eliot, now as the movement's top officer, expressed an interest in Western growth and took steps to support it more actively.

As the long-standing president of the Iowa body and president designate of the Western Unitarian Conference, Safford was asked in the spring of 1898 to sit on the national Board of Directors and to serve on its Western affairs committee. Though she doubted that she would actually be able to attend many meetings, the cost of the travel to Boston being prohibitive, she accepted the appointment, happy to see some possible change from the AUA's tendency in the past to view the denomination "too exclusively through New England eyes."[24] The "cordial, fresh, and manly" tone of Eliot's letter to her in November, in which he clarified the design and function of his new council, also gave her hope that they would be able to work together productively.[25]

As soon as the parties got down to real business, however, the conflict between East and West resumed. The specific problem was triggered when the AUA's directors met in 1900 and as an experimental venture voted Safford's field an appropriation of $100 monthly for a period of fifteen months contingent on the Iowa people raising the same amount for new societies. Though Safford had been wary of the arrangement infringing on local control, she decided that this chance to double her dollars would be worth the risk and agreed to break with her longstanding policy of total self-sufficiency. Back home, she promoted the plan optimistically, assuring her people that it would not overtax them to raise $2,000 and showing them her calculations of how their investment would grow handsomely.[26] If the WUC and the AUA met their respective obligations, said Safford in *Old and New,* there would be an "ascending series of oversight and invigoration, and no conflict of jurisdiction."[27]

This division of turf was more easily put into words than into practice, however. Determined to hold tightly to the reins, Eliot balked at the idea of giving the local body unassigned funds, as the Iowa associated wanted.[28] Discretionary use of the AUA's matching grant seemed only reasonable to the state and district leadership. For one thing, their experience was unmatched, as the record showed. "I've been in this field 18 years and know its needs as well as anyone, East or West," Safford had reminded Eliot when he first took office; under her management, the Iowa organization had "raised more money and established more churches during the past ten years than any other Conference in the A.U.A."[29]

At the same time, Safford's workers were still convinced that the Eastern bureaucracy had no concept at all of their actual circumstances. In the sisters' experience, certainly, Boston seemed always to think more in terms of managers than laborers. As a case in point, a few years before, when Wilkes was anxious to start a movement in California, she found that the AUA had budgeted funds for a superintendent of coastal mission work but had no money to pay for a minister-at-large, who might have developed something for the man to superintend.[30] The women ran into the same mentality in the present administration, which offered to send an assistant pastor to Gordon in Iowa City to free her to build up some satellite groups and then expected that she would pay him herself from her own meager salary.[31] With this kind of blundering, naive approach to Unitarian mission work, many an embryo movement had already been destroyed needlessly, Safford fumed.[32]

Here, too, the women came back repeatedly to the poor judgment the AUA showed when it used its money to finance incompetent workers. Like Wilkes, Gordon had to tell Eliot, as she had told those before him, that it took a superior woman or man to carry the load in the West and that they would greatly appreciate not being sent yet another "nice average boy."[33] The Rock Rapids church, they reminded him, was "nearly wrecked" by a man who had been assigned there by Boston without prior consultation with them. How often would they have to repeat that ministers who could hold churches together "must know something of the needs of the field and also be able speakers" and that money invested in anyone else amounted to money wasted?[34]

The women were hardly surprised that Beacon Street's bureaucrats were out of touch when—despite Mr. Eliot's boast that he was nationalizing the movement and traveling widely throughout the country—the sisterhood had to ask three or four times before he would make an appearance or send someone else to represent him in their diocese. The men were also officious and given to dickering over the smallest appropriations, yet no less inclined to get the details of the women's fieldwork all mixed up. Charles E. St. John, who was Eliot's viceroy while Safford was on the national board, required a detailed accounting of how matching funds would be used in advance, then lost track of the IUA's plans and acted as if he had never received them. His maddening conduct and petty demands were more than Safford could take. "The fact that you can not carry these things in your mind," she told him bluntly, "points to the need of entrusting local officers with the administration of affairs in their own states." If he did not think that she was qualified to decide how such small sums of money were used in her own missionary programs, she would just get the money without the AUA's dubious "help."[35]

The wrangling between the Iowa and national associations brought into focus not only a conflict between different organizational philosophies but equally a collision of strong personalities in which the factor of gender was a major component. Though eager to have good relations with Boston, Safford was not about to yield on the home-rule principle simply because it put her in contention with men, even men at the center of institutional power. When she failed to convince a voting majority of the IUA that they should insist on complete budgetary control in any financial dealings with Boston, she pressed for at least the drafting of an official position paper that challenged the national body to form "a sound basis of federal union," one that was neither Eliot's brand of "medieval absolutism" nor a totally unrestrained "French Republicanism." At the same time, she took the more practical step of starting to build an endowment fund that she hoped would make Iowa independent enough to obviate any further financial entanglements with the East.[36]

The establishment's failure to recognize and retain the talent that women were offering always remained the key issue in this battle for economic control. In one of the best illustrations of this, a case that increased the sisterhood's alienation and distrust of the East, Florence Buck had written to Eliot for his help in organizing a new congregation in some congenial Midwestern city. She had saved some money, she told him, and would be willing to work for little or no compensation at first, but she wanted a field that was large and promising enough to pay dividends later and justify this initial sacrifice. Eliot's recommendation that she try Des Moines or Kansas City was a shocking revelation to Safford's circle. It told them either that he had no idea of what was happening outside New England or else that he knew very well and meant to defeat them.

Western workers all realized that Kansas City was too far south and conservative ever to welcome a female pastor, and, even as Buck wrote, Des Moines was preparing to call Mary Safford from Sioux City to fill that vacancy. More damning still was Eliot's suggestion of a third possibility, and "the most promising" of the three, a position in Minneapolis as an assistant pastor. As she and Murdock had always been full and equal pastors together, the idea of any subordinate post was unthinkable, and Buck declined it politely, explaining that she and her partner would just keep her money and use it instead for travel and study in England. This enrichment of her "own resources and equipment," she told Eliot, would in the end be of greater benefit to the cause of liberal religion.[37] While there had sometimes been reason enough to make material sacrifices, there was never an adequate justification for sacrificing one's self. Buck, like her sisters, had learned the meaning of "money power" and what to do with it.

Chapter Eleven

RELIGIOUS DIVISIONS

Ours is a precarious language, as every writer knows, in which the merest shadow line often separates affirmation from negation, sense from nonsense, and one sex from another.
—James Thurber

I

Maneuvering for a place on this rocky institutional soil was made all the harder by gulfs that were opened when Unitarians tried to describe the ground of belief that united them. In the one camp, the more traditional "liberal evangelicals," who rejected only the negative features of orthodoxy, insisted on a theistic faith that was clothed in the warm and comforting language and forms of Christianity. Their opposition, the "liberal radicals"—sometimes called "Ethical Basis liberals"—argued that ethics provided an adequate base for religious affiliation and resisted the sort of explicit affirmations of Christian belief that had been demanded of Murdock's classmates when she was a student at Meadville. Historians who have described the collision between the radical and "evangelical" forces have shown how it challenged the liberal church to become more responsive to changing times and new sociological trends.[1] What has yet to be told is what this dispute meant to the sister ministers who through it all had to struggle to clarify and defend where they stood in their faith and profession.

The rifts arising from differences in religious emphases were not as closely attached to geography as were opinions about women's place in the church. The conflict had actually started to build not between East and West but within the Western conference itself in the 1870s. The Western Unitarian Conference had been doctrinally conservative since its organization in 1852, and its missionary development, a conference priority, had

137

presumed an acceptance of Jesus' divinity and its miraculous evidence. It was only after the war, with the entrance of Jones and Gannett, that radical religion began its ascendency and the factions began to form. The *Unity* men allied themselves with the Free Religion movement that had been started in the mid-1860s by a small circle of disaffected Unitarian ministers who wanted to shift their religious faith from supernaturalism to science and from sectarianism to universal fellowship.[2] They pressed for a freer Unitarianism that required no statement of theistic belief but only a shared commitment to moral improvement and service to society, as summarized by their motto, "Freedom, Fellowship, and Character in Religion." This principle of association was not enough for the opposition, who certainly had little quarrel with the rejection of dogmatic creeds, with humanistic outreach, or with ethical emphasis but were deeply disturbed by what the motto omitted. They said that "without any mention of God or Christ, the Unitarian body, a faith that had always been "broadly Christian," would lose its religious identity.

Actually, despite its departure from orthodox Christianity, the rational faith of the *Unity* men and the women they mentored still had a strong intuitional element that might best be characterized as a lyrical fusion of social psychology and religious sentiment. Their more traditional brothers, however, regarded the radicals' faith as nothing much more than ethics. Accordingly, when one of their camp, Jabez Sunderland, followed Jones into the secretariat of the Western conference in 1884, he set about putting the movement back on "a solid religious foundation," by which he meant taking a "stand for belief in God and worship in the spirit of Christ."[3]

The controversy, the women's initiation to institutional hardball, came to a crisis in the spring of 1886, when Sunderland delivered a brief on "The Issue in the West" before the Western conference convention in Cincinnati. Word of the showdown had reached the sisters' parishes months before, and, when the delegates finally left for the meetings, Gordon admitted later, it was with the awful feeling that whatever happened would save or destroy her life's calling. Though Sunderland had distributed printed copies of his statement ahead of time, on the day of the conference the issues themselves got lost. As Gordon recalled, it was hard to believe as the hours wore on and the bad feelings simmered, that anyone knew "just what he or she was voting for."[4] The worst of it was that afterwards everyone felt that their side had lost.

As Gordon's group saw it, the question was one of how much autonomy was allowed by the congregational polity governing Unitarian churches. It amounted to whether this form of government gave each society the right to define the words *Christian, God,* and *religion* for itself and express in its own way what held them together or whether there was a "copy-right on the word *Unitarian.*" When it came right down to it, most Unitarians could have been said to have shared much the same theology; most practiced a theistic worship of the One-in-All as well as embracing a Christian reverence for the historical Jesus as a great religious prophet. But Gordon's more radical faction considered it not just presumptuous but dangerous for an omnibus organization to set forth the views of its members in any but the broadest terms and therefore ended up voting with the majority to base their union on common commitment to "Truth, Righteousness, and Love."[5]

Having failed to swing the delegation in their direction, the angry minority broke off from the conference the following month and formed a rival Western Unitarian Association with the hope that its collaboration with the AUA would return the West to what they perceived as liberal religion's mainstream. This put the dispute on a national level and opened up a schism between East and West that was felt immediately and for years afterward at the congregational level where the sister pastors were trying to shape a sense of religious identity. Thus, ironically, though the women had technically won the debate, they came out as losers. After the Cincinnati convention, Gordon told Jones anxiously that all she could hear was "the death knell of Unitarianism in the West." An aunt of hers who attended his church in Chicago was so incensed by Jones's "godless" position that she had vowed not to pledge to his building fund any more, and it seemed the same story everywhere. When she arrived back in Sioux City, Gordon told Jones, she found the congregation in turmoil and "poor Miss Safford," who had stayed home, "nearly frantic" with all the rumors. The people knew "just enough of the subject to entirely misunderstand it" and suspected the delegates of having somehow betrayed their best interests.[6]

The disquiet, it turned out, was only beginning. As soon as the Western dissenters had formed their own regional body, the AUA openly joined the debate over whether, as Sunderland's pamphlet had put it, the Unitarian body was ready to give up its Christian and theistic character. While *Unity* and its rival, the *Unitarian,* tangled in public view, a barrage of circulars sent out to the Western parishes by the "liberal evangelicals" agitated the people even more. They continued to come to the parsonage "to be straightened out," Gordon wrote Jones in October. "Over and over, I tell my little story of the conference, how it all happened. Over and over Miss Safford explains." It was "dreary to spend one's time so," she said, when there was so much work to do, but there was "a grand principle at stake," and, frankly, she was glad to be living while there was "something worth contending for."[7]

Like most of their feminist generation who tended toward what was called Free Religion, whether or not they themselves accepted the name, the radical Unitarian clergywomen saw themselves not as rejecting Christian principles but only as staking out the broadest possible compass for their liberation. Since the Free Religion approach "put the Church on the level of all other institutions, the Bible on the level of all other books, and Christ on the level of all other men"—as Francis Abbot, the movement's most vocal advocate, expressed it—it released women from the sweep of oppressive hierarchies that impeded their social, political, and spiritual aspirations.[8] Committed to the widest interpretation of Free Religion, the Unitarian women ministers were aghast at the movement within their own fold toward restoring the patriarchal structures that had shackled their sex for centuries.

As outspoken critics of this "backward trend," the women were soon drawing fire from some of the opposition's most prominent men. "The meanest thing," in their opinion, had come from Meadville's usually gracious president Abiel Livermore, who charged that the Western conference had been "ruined" by "a company of women" whose vote had been "controlled" by Gannett in Cincinnati.[9] None of this helped restore the laity's trust in the radical clergy's position. Confused and disillusioned by the institutional politics, the people refused to respond when the ministers tried to raise funds to help pay the salary of the Western conference secretary J. R. Effinger. The best the pastors could do was be faithful to the cause themselves, promising to dip deeper into their own pocketbooks and to go without their new winter dresses if necessary.[10] They also made sure that their organization stood firmly behind "the larger thought" when the Iowa body took up the relative merits of the Western conference and its rival the Western Unitarian Association. "Miss Safford did nobly as President," Murdock reported to Jones afterward, while Bartlett, Hultin, and Wilkes had lobbied on the floor. When the question was called, "five earnest women ministers were ready to rise in defense of the faith, through 'Truth, Righteousness, and Love.' A little strategy by someone changed the subject and saved a division by vote."[11]

At the AUA's annual meeting in Saratoga in September 1894, a younger group of liberals who had not taken part in the earlier squabbles was able to steer the National conference to a reconciliation that compromised neither denominational wing. A majority accepted as its common statement of purpose a commitment to "the religion of Jesus, holding, in accordance with his teaching, that practical religion is summed up in love to God and love to man." Then the body invited to fellowship all those who shared in a "general sympathy" with their spirit and practical aims, whatever the differences in their beliefs.[12] With this, according to press reports, all the old wrangling finally disappeared "in the one great holy spirit of God's peace."

As far as the women could see when they returned to their work in the West, however, little was changed by the Saratoga compromise.[13] If anything, in its aftermath the battles over religious boundaries grew even more heated and destructive to liberal religious unity. The sisters now had to contend with an angry reactionary remnant of "liberal evangelicals" that resisted the radical trend toward a more humanistic, inclusive religion.

This element was particularly virulent in the Iowa City parish when Gordon went there to revive its moribund church in 1896. Liberal religion had been in this academic community for forty years, having been planted by Universalists and cultivated by Unitarians; at one time, with Oscar Clute in the pulpit, it had been one of the best-attended churches in the town.[14] The movement had later declined, however, and after a string of men sent in by Boston had failed to turn things around, Safford's group got their chance to see what one of their own could do. Gordon had just resigned from her post in Sioux City when she returned to the town where she had once dreamed of earning a college degree. Now twenty years later, she found the community larger, with ten thousand residents, twelve hundred of whom were students. The church, too, had changed from the popular place she remembered from her student days—when Clute had had to preach twice on Sundays to meet the standing-room-only demand—to an organization that was "as dead as possible."[15] Even so, Gordon initially saw some ground for hope. The students, she told Jones when she first arrived, were "eager, earnest, narrow, untrained, asking everything, not knowing what they want[ed] and yet wanting something." With the right leadership, she hoped, a strong, "rationally religious movement" might well be initiated.[16]

Out of sympathy more than conviction, Jones wrote back commending Gordon for having the courage to take on this "tough place" and saying that she would be equal to the challenge, for it was no time to convey his real doubts about her chance of succeeding.[17] Privately, however, Jones wondered how his sister was going to draw a following of any size by preaching her humanistic theology where Unitarians acted like evangelicals. Gordon had come with these doubts herself, and they were quickly confirmed. After a year in Iowa City, she was certain that the effort was hopeless and was just about ready "to let everything go to smash." [18] Her work had been made "a cross" by these so-called liberals who were "afraid of losing caste, position, and chance of advancement" and so "trained under the orthodox banner." Only when she forced the issue had the straddlers, the "most contemptible of all contemptible human beings," chosen one side or the other, and now their empty pews left no question of where their priorities lay.

Gordon's immediate predecessor had been so demoralized by this "cowardice" that he had finally stood in his pulpit and actually questioned the worth of his faith, but the present pastor was not about to have her spirit broken this way. She would leave the parish as soon as possible, and when she went, she assured her brother, she would go "pledged as never before, to work for progressive, unsectarian, universal religion." "I am not going to beat my life out or work *myself to death,* but 'work *myself to life*' in doing it." [19] Obliged to remain in the parish until the church had purchased its property, Gordon spent several more years in what she called "solitary confinement" among academics who took no risks and refused to embrace the kind of values and spirit that she considered the heart of liberal religion. [20] Composing new sermons each week and making her parish calls gave her plenty to do, but she felt herself growing a "coat of mail" and withdrawing to books and her correspondence to find any sort of sympathy or sustaining companionship. At the earliest possible moment, she turned in her letter of resignation, leaving the liberal impostors to her successor. [21]

II

Even as they were arriving at a clearer position within the fold by joining the Ethical Basis block against the "liberal evangelicals," the women were drawn reluctantly into a second, more wrenching conflict that put them at odds with their own beloved ally Jenkin Lloyd Jones. Jones had moved farther than ever away from denominational identity after the Saratoga settlement of 1894, insisting that its reference to "the religion of Jesus" constricted the meaning of Unitarianism in a way that precluded an ideal religious fellowship. Though he kept his All Souls church in the Western Unitarian Conference, he shifted his loyalties from the denominational groups to the American Congress of Liberal Religion, an embryo organization of Jews, Unitarians, Universalists, and others committed to fostering progressive, nonsectarian societies. Aware that a great many Unitarian friends shared his feelings about Saratoga, Jones appealed to them as the congress's newly elected secretary for their financial help and affiliation, and, failing to appreciate how hard it had become to sell his methods of pulpit iconoclasm outside Chicago, he was deeply hurt by his colleagues' tepid response. It therefore happened that, while the Eastern establishment castigated the women for having moved too far from orthodoxy, their old standard bearer complained that they had not gone nearly far enough. The record of how Jones's sisters in ministry claimed their right to "innocent passage" and tried to steer a course through free waters without violating the claims of either a valued friendship or their religious integrity further illuminates their difficulty in staking out a place within the church's institutional boundaries.

Theologically, the Western sisterhood could not have felt more at one with their brother; they hoped for a broad and inclusive religion as fervently as he. But with Western Unitarianism right then in the throes of a complex identity crisis, they had impassable reservations about moving toward this ideal in the way Jones would have them, by merging with loosely defined, nonsectarian groups. Their part in the reconstruction effort that followed the national reconciliation convinced them that any affiliations would be ill advised until the Western conference was back on its feet and its own character had clarified. Unitarians East and West, they said, were simply too worn out with haggling over territorial markers and names to consider another complication at present. For the moment, said Celia Woolley, the Western conference should think about paying its debts and rest on its oars until it could get its bearings. Then it could chart its future course with respect to the Liberal Congress.[22]

Although their position seemed simple enough to the women, they found it impossible to explain it satisfactorily to Jones, who took it as a personal betrayal. He had never felt part of the national movement and looked for no sympathy there, so it had not surprised him that W. W. Fenn, the AUA's man in the Western conference, had called his Liberal Congress "all tom rot" and swayed some of the Eastern transplants to this point of view. But he had thought that his longtime comrades in the Iowa conference would welcome his congress and marshal their people to it. Instead, the Iowa leadership had submitted a resolution urging the Western conference to protect its local associations' autonomy, and this apparent "distrust and coldness" coming from friends, Jones told Gordon, had taken away his joy and courage.[23] Anxious to "keep things right" between them, Gordon rushed to explain her state's actions, again stressing that Unitarians outside the major cities were less secure and justifiably afraid of letting a new group absorb them church by church before they were sure that it would be a change for the better. Their difference was simply one of method, not of principle, she insisted. In her lexicon, as in his, *religion* had always been an inclusive word, and, as he knew, this had kept her from casting her vote for the statement at Saratoga. However, when it came to methods for bringing about this inclusive religion, they simply did not agree, and he, of all people, ought to accept this. After all, Gordon reminded him, "*You* have taught us younger ministers in the West to be true to ourselves no matter what the result."[24]

Jones agreed that method had much to do with the break that had opened between them, but he put his own interpretation on the breech. The Iowa group particularly, he told Safford in 1896, had long "been disposed to elevate the 'expedient' and 'available' into an ideal" and to make what seemed "'practical' into a religion." He had always believed, to the contrary, that the methods of work were secondary, that the ideal was always "impracticable," but that it was also the more important, and that it was their business to stand for it. It was presumptuous to suggest that "Freedom, Fellowship and Character in Religion" could be confined to the Unitarian name and endeavors.[25] The women's answer to this was that Jones was simply ignoring the psychological truths: people's thinking changed faster than their emotions, and, for a good while yet, most liberals as isolated as theirs would "need a definite name to cling to" as a brace for standing together as a unified group.[26] Gordon's cohort was especially sensitive to this need since the rampant religious prejudice in smaller parishes usually meant the exclusion of liberal churchwomen from the clubs and associations that formed the primary webbing for female community. Fearful of any action that might weaken their only citadel in this environment, Western Unitarian women, though theologically broader than their sisters in the East, were narrower when it came to institutional organizations and names.

The intensity of these territorial feelings had been decisive in 1889, when a national movement was launched to form an Alliance of Unitarian and Other Liberal Christian Women and the Western Women's Unitarian Conference had to decide whether they should disband and become part of the larger body. The intent of the name proposed for the group seemed harmless to those who had drafted it: Jews would be welcomed as unitarian, and others whose early training was orthodox could come in under the second clause if they were liberal enough. "Help realize what we are working for," the women of the East urged those in the West. "We do it that we *all may be one.*" They need not repeat the mistakes of the men, who were "more theological" and thus "sore with bruises" and "slower" in working together. "*We* shall forget theology in our living faith and burning love."[27] The Western women, however, found the conception and name more "complex and perplexing" since, in their experience, self-described "Christian women" were rarely inclusive or hospitable to the broader religious thought.[28] Including the word *Christian* seemed to dilute and muddy what Unitarians stood for, and it remained an obstacle to the West despite the reasoned and welcoming arguments from the sisters in the East. The need for a secure, unambiguous, liberal identity was more compelling, and it was a number of years before the Western Women's Unitarian Conference could bring itself to merge with the National Alliance.

The same inhibitions took hold when the question of joining the Liberal Congress came to the floor of the Western Unitarian Conference in the wake of Saratoga. While the women were grateful to Jones for leading the fight for the broader spirit that had supported their work, they were loathe to abandon the banner under which he had led them in battle, fearing that, if they did, their forces would dissipate. Marion Murdock, fully convinced that it would be "a mistake and indeed a calamity," reminded her brother that he himself had taught them to read the name *Unitarian* as synonymous with "the largest liberty of thought and the widest of fellowship." This is what they taught their own people now, encouraging them to wear the name proudly to set them apart from the narrowness of evangelical orthodoxy.[29]

The tensions increased in 1897, when, with the Iowa block's full support, the Western conference replaced the weekly *Unity,* which Jones had put out for twenty years as the conference's official organ, with *Old and New,* the monthly paper that the Iowa group had been publishing since 1891 to provide closer coverage of its local and district news. The feeling was that Jones's paper had clearly become the Liberal Congress's voice, as signaled by its change of name to the *New Unity* two years before, and that this had left the Unitarians' interests without proper representation. Gordon had tried to explain this decision dispassionately in *Old and New*'s columns, but, after she read Jones's anger between the lines of his own notice in the *New Unity,* she again hastened to write him directly to make her position clear. While *Old and New* had continued to urge its readers' support of the congress, she said, the *New Unity* had nonetheless lost a great many of its subscribers because of what came across as its open contempt for their denominational ties. There was no longer any use, she told him, in trying to sell his publication to people who took what he said as an insult.[30] Jones's suggestion that stronger leadership could correct such false impressions was too much for Gordon, who also knew how to deliver a lecture: "I, too, believe that ministers may *lead,* but it is not wise to attempt to drive, at least not in Iowa."[31]

Until its publication ceased in 1908, *Old and New* continued to be a sore spot for Jones and a source of contention for all the parties concerned. His occasional swipes at the paper cut its editors deeply, and Gordon confronted him angrily, trying to shame him for speaking so well of the Catholics and Boers but barely acknowledging old Unitarian friends who had worked with him for so many years. As a rule, however, the women's rebukes were gentle; for as Gordon told Jones, even though they might have "no time to be 'sweet'" they would always be grateful to those who had thought they were "worth doing something for."[32] Determined to keep their friendship with Jones from being destroyed by politics, the women worked hard to convince him that they were still standing on common ground. No narrow sectarian banners had ever flown over their pulpits, they pointed out, and the fact that they still named their new churches "People's" or "All Souls" or "Unity" was evidence of their shared ideal of inclusive religious fellowship. Their ties to the Unitarian work, Mary Collson told Jones in 1899, were much less denominational claims than personal bonds to people they loved.[33] This love, which extended to Jones as well, would not let them choose between cherished relationships and their religious ideals but insisted that old friends must work together where there was still common commitment. Jones, too, felt that it was essential to work out their differences "into daylight and . . . harmony again" and kept his pledge to speak honestly and accept others' plain talk to him. If it had meant that they must "hurt each other a little" in order to keep alive "the movement of the Zeit Geist" working through them, the pain had been worth it.[34]

Chapter Twelve

WOMAN'S PLACE IN A
"MANLIER MINISTRY"

STRONG men are not afraid to work with women ministers.
—Rev. Mary A. Safford

I

In the twenty years following Mary Safford's ordination in 1880, she and her sisters had put together an organization that even Sam Eliot had to concede was a model for getting things done. Whereas many of the most prominent churches in Eastern parishes were barely solvent and, in his judgment, "lazy, indifferent and helpless" in managing their affairs, Safford's outfit, as she let him know frequently, had founded no fewer than fifteen churches and rescued others, and these had been "living" churches, not "mere paper organizations" that might with less effort have simply been started, to be listed in the AUA *Year Book,* and then left to die a lingering death.[1] Most of their churches, moreover, had been housed in handsome new buildings that were not just paid for but paid for promptly with money that had been raised locally.[2] On the denominational level, the women had taken efficient command of the West's strongest conference, tended its monthly publication, and held just about every office. From such a list of credits, one might have expected their place in the movement to have been secure and expanding at the end of the century; yet at precisely this time, their position, damaged by recent erosion, collapsed. Their members dropped off precipitously and, by the outbreak of World War I, there was little evidence of the West ever having been woman's terrain.[3]

The sisterhood's decline came at a time when the focus of Unitarian expansion was shifting to university centers and urban showcases. The rural and small town Midwest had ceased to be a growth area for liberal religion. The children of the first liberal settlers on the frontier were now dropping out of the rational church of their parents and being absorbed by the dominant evangelical culture. By the later 1890s, with the penetration of the social gospel in mainline Protestantism, many of this accommodating second generation were satisfied that they could hear "liberal" preaching without going to Unitarian churches.[4] Nor was there any shortage of other Protestant pews to choose from, as Mary Collson had learned in Ida Grove, a town with fewer than two thousand residents, where in 1897 her church had competed with seven others. The overchurching, moreover, took its heaviest tolls in these small communities, where female clergy had found most of their pastorates. Thus, Safford's network watched six of the twelve congregations that had been holding their own in 1899 dwindle away until their buildings were all standing vacant a dozen years later.[5]

While these currents hurt almost all liberal clergy, the Western women complained that the situation was made "doubly hard" for them by a resurgence of opposition from the higher administrative levels. Previously held at bay in the West while the feminist Jones and his *Unity* group were a force to be reckoned with, the feeling against female ministers had re-emerged with new virulence when W. C. Backus was handpicked by Eliot to represent the AUA's interests in the Western conference.[6] With Backus opposed to putting women into the dwindling number of vacancies, the sisters' prospects were bleak.

The high command's aversion to having females appear in their pulpits was part of America's larger reaction against its cultural "emasculation" during the nineteenth century.[7] Convinced that the nation's ills had resulted from a loss of the toughness and vigor that gave the young country its greatness, Americans had been campaigning since the late 1880s for more "masculinity" in all facets of their society. Sports had become more combative and violent. Educators looked for ways to control the preponderance of females among grade-school teachers. Novelists fed the public's taste for animal instinct and brute force. With Theodore Roosevelt—boxer, cowboy, Rough Rider, and policeman of world and domestic affairs—America's ideal of tough masculinity eventually assumed presidential proportions.

Nowhere was the desire to regain a lost virility felt more keenly than among the clergy, and particularly Unitarian clergy, whose loss of status as the established New England church at the start of the century had made them the most susceptible to the impact of feminization. With no firm creed to brace their evangel, the liberal preachers had always been easy targets for critics who disparaged their faith as a spineless imposter of real religion, an effeminate surrogate that had nothing more substantial to offer in place of rejected doctrines than a flimsy literary piety. Once deprived of their former political clout and forced to court an overwhelmingly female constituency, liberal preachers felt exiled from the virile world of male power and leadership. As the church's womanly ambiance began to attract a gentler, more delicate breed of minister, often men bereft of executive skills, who found it a haven from public pressures, the more robust, fearing for their masculinity, fled from the field.

Ralph Waldo Emerson had decided by the 1830s that the Unitarian pulpit had become too "effete" and personally debilitating for him to be "a man quite and whole."[8] The trend continued, and, by the new century, more men—an average of fifteen a year—were leaving the Unitarian ministry than were entering it. As one young pastor acknowledged in 1907, the peception of the minister as a weakling and "sort of ladies' man with soft hands and a polite manner" had not disappeared since Emerson's time and still made it "hard for a thoroughly masculine man to identify himself with the ministerial class."[9] Enrollment at Harvard Divinity School had dropped to scandalously low levels, and it was only the dozen or so defectors arriving each year from other denominations that were keeping the Unitarian pulpit supply from bankruptcy.[10] Settled ministers who shared the same anxieties as their younger brothers abandoned the profession they had trained for or eased out of parish ministry and into writing, teaching, and lecturing.

As a consequence, by the end of the century AUA placement officers faced a critical shortage of men whom they thought fit enough to lead their societies.[11] Samuel Eliot's correspondence during his first year as secretary read like a catalog of every sort of ministerial disability. One candidate who was judged to be "as good a man as the churches [could] afford" was known for his "missionary spirit and unselfish zeal" but also for "some capacity to say and do indiscreet things."[12] Another was "excellent in dealing with a small company of boys, 6 at the outside," but, being "mild and gentle," had "not sufficient force to control a large company" and got "rattled" easily.[13] The clergy were also plagued by poor health, and word came to Eliot daily of workers laid up or hospitalized for nervous exhaustion and various physical problems.[14] It is hardly surprising that leaders whose remedy for an ailing ministry was to give it a "manlier" image were eager to move women out just as quickly as possible.

Historically, the AUA's top brass had been men accustomed to public power and influence. They had been Civil War officers, mayors, senators, governors, and cabinet members. Their experiences in political office and military service had geared them to think of their work for the church as an opportunity to display the sort of tough masculinity that they felt the clerical brotherhood desperately needed. American Unitarian Association president Carroll D. Wright, who preferred to be called by his title of Colonel, talked about his responsibilities as head of the Unitarian body and the job's demands for great valor and sacrifice in the line of duty as if he were leading a military campaign. The Colonel's own colleagues smiled at his absolute seriousness when he spoke of his work as "a battle" and pledged himself ready to "fall on the field" if it came to that.[15] Yet they themselves courted a manly ideal that paraded about in uniform. Soon after Eliot came in as secretary, he put up a portrait of J. B. F. Marshall, the AUA's first treasurer, who had been a Civil War general, and presumably under its inspiration started dispatching letters that sounded like military alerts.[16] A message he sent to his Western commander concerning the dearth of strong personnel warned that their airship was sinking and would lose its cargo unless the ballast was thrown overboard and some of their own "flesh and blood" were sacrificed.[17]

Samuel Eliot came to this high office at the age of thirty-five exquisitely prepared to lead the campaign for a manlier ministry. A New England Brahmin, his script for success had been written by his family's brilliant history of male accomplishment. His paternal grandfather, for whom he was named, had been a congressman, mayor of Boston, and one of the AUA's founding fathers. His maternal grandfather had been the minister of King's Chapel in Boston, the oldest Unitarian church in the world. Young Eliot's father, the innovative and vigorous president of Harvard College, further enriched his son's distinguished legacy, and, after the boy's mother died when he was six, the masculine model became the absolute standard in his private and public endeavors. His own success in public life and happy marriage to a woman who, taking little interest in outside reforms, devoted herself to the care of their home and seven children, merely reinforced his belief in keeping the sexes' spheres discrete. Unable to see any reason for tampering with the existing social structures, he voted against women's suffrage when it was put to a vote in Massachusetts and just as confidently opposed women having a voice in the pulpits.[18]

Unaccustomed to treating the opposite sex as colleagues and business associates, Eliot's office was never quite sure how to handle the Iowa bunch, and Safford's prickly performance as the Western conference's representative to the Board of Directors had only increased the tensions. Anything but the pliant go-between Eliot had expected when he gallantly welcomed her to his executive council, Safford had turned out to be her "own man," not his. She persisted in asking for "clear and considerate" explanations whenever she felt—as she usually did—that Eliot's men deliberately put things ambiguously to gain the upper hand.[19] Headquarters hardly knew how to respond when, in order to keep their positions from wobbling, she took it on herself to write out a policy as she understood it and asked that one of the officers sign and return it to her for her files. Nor had they ever imagined that Safford would not sit quietly by when she thought they were taking advantage of her absences to work around her or undermine her influence. She protested hotly when, after having to miss a meeting in Boston, she learned that one of Eliot's viceroys had taken the opportunity to accuse her of not sending in her reports when in fact she had done so faithfully and he had had them to prove it all the time. She confronted them angrily again when she heard that one of the officers had blatantly disregarded the record to say that she no longer had the undivided support of the Western conference.[20]

Safford had also shown that she could be just as quick as they to jockey for position if her authority were challenged. When Eliot tried to designate her as the Iowa Unitarian Association secretary in order that she might report to him regularly on the Iowa work, she declined the appointment because, as she told him, it discounted the force of home rule and presumed an authority that he himself did not have. In fact, she was Iowa's secretary already, having been "properly" chosen by the power of the local churches. If Eliot wanted her as liaison, he would have to reword his request, which was to say that, if it came to it, she, not he, would be giving the orders.[21] Just as boldly, she gained the advantage by chiding the men for being defensive, for taking her simple questions as complaints and personal attacks—though ironically they saw this tendency as a defect confined to females—and for failing to keep things on a professional level as she was doing.[22] On the other hand, when they went on the offensive, the woman was just as quick to disarm them politely by counseling more generosity and a change in approach so that they would no longer treat those they worked with, and for, as if they were training in boot camp.[23]

Needless to say, once Safford's term on the AUA expired, Eliot had an easier time ignoring the women already in pulpits and moving to keep those without anchorage from making further encroachments. While he handed down no ultimata as such, none were needed to let the ranks know where he stood on the question of women's ministry. The intention was clear, for example, when Eliot's secretary wrote Buck to suggest that she offer herself as a candidate for the pastorate in Manistee, Michigan, where, she happened to know, the situation was so precarious that the people had already voted to close down the church.[24] With word of such dirty tricks spreading rapidly through the women ministers' network, Caroline Bartlett Crane, when asked to comment about the prejudice, answered, "We all feel it. We all know it; men as well as women"; and the AUA leadership ought at least to "be frank enough to say it."[25] Safford went farther. If officials "would minimize this prejudice, if they would make it a rule to recommend good women ministers as heartily as they recommend good men," the clergywoman "would cease to be an anomaly," and the denomination would be all the stronger and more vigorous because of it.[26]

Eliot's methods of operation and staffing practices made it clear that, in his estimation, women were poor professional risks, being creatures designed for private life and supportive roles and therefore naturally prone to abandon careers for marriage and domesticity. In such a climate, a woman like Margaret Olmstead, who did find that being a wife, mother, and minister all at once was too much for her to handle, was all the more reluctant to ask for the leave that she felt would be best for everyone. While Olmstead had wanted to drop out of ministry for a time when her son was born, she had held on for another eleven years so as not to injure her sisters by seeming to prove their detractors right about their lack of commitment. Not even when her boy had been hospitalized for several weeks and she had had to leave her pulpit to the care of her minister husband had she been able to bring herself to bow out.[27]

Only in 1908, when the return on her preaching to near empty pews in dwindling Iowa parishes could no longer justify the time away from her family, did she write her letter of resignation, and even then shuddered at the reaction that she knew it would get from the regional settlement officer. "I did not say to him that I considered myself a failure, you may be sure," she told her sister Gordon, "but between you and me," she went on apologetically, "I wish I had not felt it necessary to ask him to secure my successor, for . . . I know his attitude in general toward the woman minister, and when she drops out of the ranks, for any reason, or even temporarily, I imagine him thinking, along with some others, 'I told you so.'"[28] Gordon, for her part, could well imagine Eliot saying the same thing about those "foolish" and stubborn females like herself who meant to stay put in their pulpits no matter how difficult it became.[29]

II

Hopelessly out of step with the prevailing politics of the day, the women despaired at the triumph of the muscular standard by which social ills and solutions were being defined. When Gordon heard a lecturer in Iowa City tell an audience of college students that people who were too refined and well schooled rarely amounted to much in "the world's battles," she had wanted to stand up and shout him right off the platform. Instead, she later wrote Jones to say what she had been aching to scream: "I suppose that was what was the matter *with Jesus,* and *Buddha* and *Channing,* Dorothea Dix and Florence Nightingale, &c, and all the other *failures* (?) in history!" She vowed that, with a balanced perspective so desperately needed, she and her sisters would not be sitting by silently while civilization fell.[30] *Old and New* kept up a steady attack against the advancing virility culture, with masculinity written large and female elements "not worth considering."[31] They especially took aim at writers like George Albert Coe, whose "muscular Christianity" sought to restore the people's respect for religion by changing its colorations from "feminine saintliness" and "gentleness" to "the rugged virtues of the athletic field." They spoke darkly of their fears for the future when a society raised its youth on this barbarized kind of religion, thinking mistakenly that it could strengthen its churches by purging them of female influence.[32]

The exclusion of women was not the whole of the church's offense in crusading for manliness. The reassertion of its male prerogatives also called for more of the "womanliness" that depreciated the female's abilities and pressed her into subordinate roles. At the turn of the century, church periodicals like the *Unitarian,* whose masthead promised its readers "A Virile Optimism in Religion," were urging women to cultivate their special quality of "unobtrusiveness" that went along with "intuition" and "purity."[33] Their "Home" and "Family" pages reminded their female readers that, though they could never be "preachers" and "heroes," as homemakers they could evangelize to souls within their short reach and fill a lifetime with small and kindly acts.[34] Just how short this reach was in the minds of the men who were running the AUA was evident from Eliot's idea of asking his leading laywomen, prominent ministers' wives and alliance officers, to wait on tables at luncheons arranged "for the men" at the annual meetings.[35]

Another of Eliot's schemes for putting church women to work in their proper place again brought the sister ministers to their feet in bitter protest. The idea, as he presented it in his 1906 presidential address and in letters sent out to potential contributors afterward, was said to be a response to the many young women who had the potential for service careers with the church but needed to be instructed in how "to do it wisely and successfully." To provide this training, he wanted to see the Unitarians open a school for parish assistants, where programs like those the Methodists had for their deaconesses would teach liberal women to be superintendents and teachers of Sunday Schools, visitors in the homes of the sick and elderly, and general program coordinators. Such a school, he said, would provide "an appropriate field of service" for many who presently found no chance to do the kind of work that interested them.[36]

Despite a published announcement worded so as to include both the sexes, there was little question about the targeted market, and the ordained sisterhood in the West pounced on the implications. Since the minister's job had always been propped up by women who worked without title or pay as parish assistants and who trained under each other far more effectively than the men ever imagined, Eliot's plan to open a school for them was at best gratuitous. The worst of it, Safford observed in letters she wrote to the *Christian Register,* was that the urgency now was for ministers, not for more assistants, yet the AUA's leader, who pledged to develop the free church's untapped resources, was bent on keeping the women from serving where they were most needed.[37] Indeed, historically, it was when women finally realized that they had already been making the church run and doing the work of the minister all along that they found the courage to ask to be ordained.[38] Such women as Mary H. Graves, the first to have done so and gotten credentials from the Unitarians, found it ludicrous to be told after years of proving themselves that their sex was not only unfit for ministry but incapable even of parish work without the special instruction provided by men.

As expected, the protests were largely ignored, and the plans for training assistants went forward. In 1907, bearing the name of Joseph Tuckerman, who founded the Benevolent Fraternity of Unitarian Churches in Boston before the Civil War, and memorializing as well the "noble band of women" who perpetuated this tradition of aid to the needy, the new institution opened its doors near AUA headquarters with three students enrolled.[39] Eager to have the curriculum in step with the modern-day church, whose interest in social services had replaced the concern with abstract theology, Eliot, presiding over the Tuckerman board as expected, set out to develop a close partnership between his school and the nearby School of Social Work that was run by Simmons College and Harvard. In their first year,

Tuckerman students were to spend three-fifths of their time at Simmons and devote the rest of their program to courses in "parish and Sunday School administration, mission work, the art of teaching, hygiene and the elements of nursing."[40] At the same time, however, the school's underlying philosophy gave the program a highly conservative cast that reflected Eliot's total failure to comprehend the ambitious "new woman." The students were told that Tuckerman graduates never forgot their "domestic mission," did not try to enter "conspicuous agencies for doing good in the world," or get caught up in such foolishness as "the folly of the Woman's Movement." They were being trained not to exercise their minds in the "abstract study of social problems" but to use their hearts and hands to improve life's "personal side." The tools that they would be using in their work were "not eloquence in preaching" or "great schemes for reforming the world" or persuasion in "public speaking or writing." Their sufficient equipment would be their affection, friendship, sympathy, and kindness.[41]

As Safford's group had expected, the Tuckerman School had few takers and still fewer graduates; after fifteen commencements, there were only some forty alumnae all together. As they had tried to explain to Eliot at the very beginning, any woman who was looking for a service career outside her home in the twentieth century was precisely the sort who would want to develop her analytic skills and talents in reaching the public. She was the most keenly interested in broadening, not narrowing, her opportunities and would be the most inclined to join such "follies" as the crusade for universal suffrage. Most of the small number who did start out in the Tuckerman program were lured away into social work once they had started attending the classes at Simmons College.[42]

Those who did not leave before graduation frequently came to regret it after discovering that there was not nearly the call for parish assistants that there was for social workers and that, once a job had been found, the terms were likely to be disappointing. Apart from the mothers with Sunday School children who liked the idea of a trained superintendent, church members rarely could understand why they should pay to have someone do the same things that they had been doing as labors of love. Societies willing to pay an assistant generally did not intend to pay much, although they might want her to be at the church all day long and several evenings a week. One Tuckerman alumna from the class of 1916, who went on to work for the Montreal and Omaha congregations, complained to her former dean that the men who ran the churches did not seem to know how to go about treating a woman as a professional. They seemed to have "no idea" of what she was trying to do in the church, she said, and therefore expected her to be a clerk and a maid instead of an educator and a program director. As a further consequence, though they were willing to pay the minister $5,000 a year, the leaders in Omaha balked at budgeting more than $500 for her, though she was spending more time at the church than he. Disappointed by the realities of what the church offered them as a vocation, the younger women, and some of the older ones, left for the secular ministries of social work and reform, there joining their ordained counterparts whose own careers in the parishes had been cut short by the church's attempt to institutionalize their sex's subordination.[43]

To this exiled sisterhood, it was obvious that the church had become no stronger, but only weaker, by keeping its women in inferior roles, excluding them from the pulpits and boards and other positions of real leadership. "Heartsick over the outlook," as Gordon described their feelings in 1909, the women despaired that "never before in the history of the liberal church" had there been "so great a need of religious inspiration" and never a time when the Unitarians' movement "had so little to offer."[44] As Marie Jenney Howe pointed out, the vigorous women who had been "unloved" and uninspired by the church for so long were beginning to find a more meaningful gospel elsewhere and taking their energies with them. As a result, the church was now more effete than ever, and the menfolk who once came in healthy numbers to hear the women preach wanted no part of it and just stayed home.[45] Failing to see that the only true test of a "manly religion" was woman's equality in it, the church had effectively alienated its most devoted and talented women, who had no choice but to turn to the secular sphere for a place to do ministry.

Part Four

PROPHETIC MINISTRIES

I think that "all SERVICE ranks the same with God," but naturally I regard my own vocation—the ministry—most highly since the TRUE minister is teacher, preacher, student, pastor and "all around" worker for "MORE ABUNDANT" life."
—Rev. Mary A. Safford

Chapter Thirteen

PREACHING REFORM

*I believe from this pulpit and from these pews will go forth an influence
that will make for honor in politics, truth-telling in business, justice in
the home, and high ideals of human obligation and responsibility
everywhere.*
—Rev. Eleanor E. Gordon

Religious liberals a hundred years ago were not nearly as keen
about having their pastors preach social reform as many today might suppose. Largely well-educated and privileged individualists who went to
church to worship in freedom from pulpit pressures of any kind, they were
just as averse to having political or social gospel imposed on them as they
were to being fed the old Calvinist theology. Few liberal clergy were willing
only to mirror their people's opinions, but most did take the moderate
course that steered clear of controversy and kept their congregations content
and intact.[1] Remaining in neutral waters was less of an option for women
who chose the ministry as their life's work, however. Not only was their
very presence in pulpits a statement offensive to many, but their calling
most likely had been inspired by those who had in the past been uncompro-
mising and risked the people's wrath to preach a faith of social responsibility. They looked back to William Ellery Channing, who in the first half of
the century had pressed increasingly for an engaged Christianity, "preeminently a social religion . . . disposing its disciples to joint services."
While his call for public action inspired the efforts of followers like Horace
Mann, Joseph Tuckerman, Dorothea Dix, and Samuel and Julia Ward
Howe, he lost the support of his solidly middle-class worshipers as he
became more radical, drawing closer to the working classes, the poor, and
the blacks and coming out on the side of abolition.[2]

The radical preacher and abolitionist Theodore Parker, who held the seat of honor in the Iowa sisters' pantheon, not only agreed that belief alone was inadequate—"a sacrament of works," he said, was the essence of meaningful worship—but called for a "church militant" that would sound the alarm wherever it found "a public sin in the land." Ministers who were sincerely intent on fostering religion, said Parker, had no choice except "to meddle with the state, business, the perishing classes, literature, science, morals, manners, everything that affects the welfare of mankind," and from there lead their congregations into reform.[3] Safford's cohort identified also with the early Universalist preachers, whose ethical rather than theological precepts distinguished their sermons. Here, the clergywomen considered themselves the legacy of Hosea Ballou, who recast the concept of universal salvation in terms of the early Christians' ideal of universal community and thus provided the impetus for later social crusaders. Among their more recent inspirators, the Universalist clergywomen Olympia Brown and Phebe Hanaford had helped convince these younger sisters that the reform evangel, like women, must be given their place in the pulpit.

The quieter colleagues were prone to justify their reticence, or "neutrality," by explaining that they were primarily shepherds whose roles were pastoral, not prophetic, and that they, too, had a solid tradition to draw on. Henry W. Bellows, who waffled on slavery back in the 1850s, had built his defense on the argument that prophets, obedient to some divine madness, were meant to address bodies politic and speak out on public issues whereas pastors were called to tend flocks and follow the sensible rule of "sober discretion." It was only when the pastor's and the prophet's duties coalesced, Bellows said, that he could step into the prophet's place, "and then only haltingly and in second-rate style—as a *minor* prophet indeed."[4] For the women who entered the ministry twenty years later on Parker's authority that the preacher's function was both "to instruct and serve," such distinctions were specious.[5] Ever since the war, more and more women, defying the notion that females attained their "highest glory, not on the platform . . . but in the center of the home," had been mounting stages to urge the reform of public institutions.[6] Once they gained access to pulpits, they used them to preach the regeneration of social systems as well as of people, thus answering those who argued that pastors should tend to their flocks and not try to run the world. Joined at the podium by mentors and friends like Mary Livermore, Julia Ward Howe, and Anna Howard Shaw, they were proud, they said, to belong to such "an eloquent . . . household of faith."[7]

Caroline Bartlett Crane once explained what her group understood as the essence of prophecy after a newspaper commented on her charm and diplomacy in the pulpit. While she was happy to have the personal compliment, she replied, she would have to decline being called *diplomatic,* if this implied dodging the issue to avoid disagreement. Crane's sermons, which not only took unequivocal stands but took them on all the most highly charged issues of her day—like legalized prostitution and prison reform—more than justified her disclaimer. While she was aware that her office required her to be a shepherd who kept the flock whole as well as a prophet and teacher, she was convinced that "the simple, fearless saying of what one means" served the versatile minister's "every purpose."[8]

As pulpit discourse, the sisterhood's sermons displayed the unmistakable contours of the Unitarian preaching that had evolved since the early years of the nineteenth century, when Joseph K. Buckminster introduced the higher biblical criticism. The new homiletics relieved liberal ministers of the need to expound a rigid body of doctrine supported by Scripture, and this gave Buckminster's progeny a new flexibility and potential for turning their preaching into a lively art. Though the pastors might still take their texts from the Bible, and Safford's group usually did, they were not bound to do so and, rather than render close exegeses, tended to range over all the vast record of human culture, past and present. Their themes and "proof passages," topical illustrations, and language were just as likely to come from current events and history as from the Bible or to draw on ancient and modern philosophy, world religions, science, and art.

To "demystify" the pulpit and bring it closer to the pews, the women frequently sermonized about the sermon itself, its proper character and purposes in a rational faith. Repudiating the pietists' method of feeding the people "fancy and sentiment" and letting them have religion "by proxy," the women maintained that a sermon did far greater good as a teaching instrument that stirred deep thought, not just feeling. The pulpit paper, they said, should put the congregation "on the footing of students before a lecturer" who dispensed information and points of view but deliberately left to the class the work of absorbing and finding the applications. As the sisterhood saw it, successful sermons were those that made everyone "priests" and had them accept the responsibility of forming and defending their faith.[9]

Not surprisingly, those who heard the women preach and sought to explain their effectiveness often remarked how much they sounded like teachers. John Howland Lathrop, who was eighteen when he first heard

Murdock deliver a sermon and found there the inspiration for his own life's work in the ministry, was struck by the way she dealt with her theme as "a teacher of philosophy might have handled it." "The sweep of her thought, its poetic expression, and the suggestion of mystery in the voice" all combined to stimulate "exactly the sort of searching thinking" that the young Lathrop craved, and this came to serve as the critical measure for his own efforts later.[10] Sometimes, as in her exegesis of the Ninetieth Psalm, Murdock guided her students toward a broader religious vision by helping them enlarge their imagery for divine revelation.[11] At other times, she gave them historical surveys that culminated in a crescendo of moral and ethical truths. "The Growth of the Hebrew People," for instance, treated the congregation to a colorful excursion through early cultures and language development that ended up with a plea for the open mind that would neither blindly worship the past nor abandon it.[12]

Gordon, whose "schoolmarm" persona followed her just about everywhere, loved to coax congregants back to the schoolrooms in which they had first learned to read and work through mathematical problems. "How plainly we see the picture," she beckoned in one sermon, conjuring up the blackboard, the vertical line drawn in chalk, and the factors arranged on each side of it, all calling to mind the challenge and pleasure in proving one's calculation. Likening these early lessons in balance and ratio to the lessons of life, Gordon deftly developed the metaphor through every stage of her argument, until the problem, stated as simply as possible, read, "Given life, to find its meaning." If people applied themselves to choosing what really mattered most and were willing to redo the careless and faulty work they had done in the past, Gordon said, then "little by little the factors in the problem would find their proper place."[13]

It was a source of great pride to the preachers that theirs was a rational pulpit grounded in the best of modern scientific thought. Indeed, they bragged that liberal religion was "the science of the sciences" and that their churches stood "resolutely by naturalism, pure and simple, eschewing miracle and revelation as the basis of faith," while finding God's grace in the optimistic assumptions of reform Darwinism.[14] As positivists who believed that their efforts to comprehend divine law put them on the same track as the students of social, political, and biological systems, they preached that humanity's progress was ongoing and inevitable, that science assured them, to use Gordon's words, of a universe that was "alive, fluid, flexible," and animated by a "germ of expanding life" containing "all sorts of divine possibilities."[15]

In reading Scripture and human experience through the lenses of reason and science and connecting moral and spiritual growth to the natural cycles of life, these modern-day prophets were able to render out of the abstract issues of regeneration newly positive and accessible messages. When Rowena Morse, for example, presented the liberal interpretation of sin and punishment, she used the behavioristic concepts of cause and effect and social conditions instead of the terms of corruption and judgment inherited from the Garden of Eden.[16] If all things were really evolving and people were not fallen angels but rising souls, then their corporate structure was also designed to reach higher levels, said Eleanor Gordon when preaching about it. It followed, she went on, that everyone who was a part of this changing universe was a reformer, collaborating with God in the daily process of natural progress.[17]

Not that the women accepted as allies all systems that claimed to be science. Though keenly interested in the new psychology, they shied away from dubious schools like phrenology and mind cure, which had found a wide sympathetic response among the liberal clergy only until the appearance of germ theory struck a blow to their credibility.[18] In the 1890s, the Unitarian clergy were especially harsh in their censorship of Mary Baker Eddy's fast-growing Christian Science movement, which they were persuaded was quackery that exploited the public's awe of anything that was presented as "scientific." Even among the most tolerant parties like *Unity*'s editorial staff, who took great pains to deal fairly with all religious traditions and sects and who acknowledged the immense importance of mind over matter in healing, there was grave concern and even anger about Mrs. Eddy's denial of sin, disease, and death and the consequent disregard of medical advances and common sense in matters of hygiene and public health.[19] Less charitable critics, writing in *Old and New,* charged angrily that the curists' unfounded, irrational claims just muddied the waters, making it harder for qualified and objective researchers to get the real facts that could actually help people.[20] There was, moreover, among Christian Scientists no philanthropic concern. This was noted by Caroline Bartlett Crane, who best summarized the reform pulpit's quarrel with the Eddyites when she wrote that responsible scientists, teachers, statesmen, and preachers all were trying to help people see things as they were and thus to relate most constructively to their present surroundings. Those who thwarted this effort by failing to do anything concrete about sickness, crime, and poverty, because they refused to acknowledge their reality, could hardly be called either "scientific" or "Christian."[21]

More than incidentally, the Iowa group was especially harsh in its censorship of Christian Science after a sister's defection to it. Her experience had underscored its dangers to women lured into its pulpits and pews by false promises of a feminist sympathy and the personal power to make the world perfect. They could well appreciate women's hunger for Mrs. Eddy's androgynous concept of deity and the opportunities to serve as Readers and well-paid metaphysicians. But, unlike the uninitiated observers who assumed from these benefits that the church was informed by a genuine feminism, the Unitarian preachers, who had always been somewhat skeptical, acquired a very different picture of the organization when Mary Collson became entrapped by it in 1902.

Small town pastoring in the late 1890s had been a letdown for Collson, and, in the course of looking for a more rewarding context for ministry, she had become involved in Chicago's burgeoning mind cure movement. Though the Unitarian sisterhood did all it could to snatch her back, she slipped away and remained a captive to Eddyism for thirty years. The stories that got back to them about their protégée's tormented struggles to free herself gave them a shocking picture of institutional fear and repression. Far from strengthening women, singly or as a community, Eddy's chain of command and doctrines akin to witchcraft seem to have reinforced women's dependency on male authority while isolating them from one another. As local congregational leaders and Christian Science practitioners, whose standing required denial of all unpleasantness and human loyalties, Collson and her sister Eddyites, she reported afterward, had never talked to each other about their problems honestly or formed the close friendships that grow out of such exchanges. Instead, she had found her colleagues to be a conservative and selfish lot, "more competitive than cooperative" in their relationships, uninterested in any social service, and oblivious to the working-class problem and need for reforms like the child labor laws.[22] This lack of solidarity and social consciousness, a cruel and tragic disappointment for the ministers' well-meaning prodigy, was a warning to them to choose their routes to reform with the greatest care.

Along with pseudosciences like Eddyism, the liberal sisters rejected the social Darwinian theory that people's progress was limited by their heredity, as this seemed just as oppressive as Calvin's doctrine of predestination.[23] The far more appealing view, and the one that formed the basis for their reform sermons, was the social scientists' idea that education and culture had more to do with one's destiny than genetic inheritance. By the mid-1890s, the pulpit sisterhood was also preaching reform within the new frame of historical economics that challenged the classical paradigms that they had learned years before from their reading of John Stuart Mill and Herbert Spencer. Back in the Humboldt days when Eleanor Gordon was just discovering Spencer, excitedly giving reviews of his *Data of Ethics* at the Unity Club, the force of laissez-faire doctrine had been entirely academic. There had been no test of its merits in rural and small town parishes that knew nothing of the kind of poverty, labor problems, and neighborhood squalor that blighted big cities, and rather than any perceived utility, it had been its sheer beauty that won the preachers' allegiance to Spencer's construction of moral progress. In the realm of pure theory, it made good sense that competition was healthy and desirable and that the working class should accept its lot without complaint since the unequal distribution of wealth was but a natural consequence of the unequal distribution of talent. Thus, the ministers took Spencer's word that, if allowed to function without interference, the law of natural selection would harmonize all society by reconciling people's selfish and altruistic motives.[24]

Yet, after the women saw more of what was happening in the urban centers, where poverty and social disintegration were reaching alarming proportions, they started rethinking the classical economics. By the late 1880s, they were listening more intently to the small group of clergy—Jenkin Lloyd Jones, Josiah Strong, and Washington Gladden among them—who were already anticipating the social gospelers of the next decade in calling for a realignment of business ethics and Christian principles. The critiques of Karl Marx and Henry George also raised serious questions for them about the efficacy of entrusting society's desperate conditions to natural law when there seemed to be no correspondence between laissez faire in theory and in practice.[25] The sisters' conversion from theory to empirical prophecy was completed by the devastating depression of 1893, which brought home to them, as no textbook could, the full impact of economic dislocation, unemployment, and financial ruin. In Sioux City, where many prosperous Unitarians lost their fortunes, the church could no longer afford two paid pastors, and Gordon felt obliged to resign to avert a financial disaster. Similar losses among the major contributors to Wilkes's work meant that she had to do most of her mission work without pay at her family's expense. The plight of the working classes also became more visible in the communities, and preachers in even the smallest of parishes were being told by the people to "throw theology to the dogs" and focus their energies on "the burning necessities of the present."[26]

The social gospel that called for the Kingdom of God to be built on earth through reforming the social and economic fabric had found a place in a number of Protestant pulpits at the end of the century, but nowhere was it more at home than among the radical Unitarians, who had for years been preaching a fundamentally ethical faith that stressed salvation in the present life through a cultivation of character. In the East, Harvard's Francis Greenwood Peabody published *Jesus Christ and the Social Question,* one of the movement's foremost works, after almost two decades of having his seminarians ponder how Christian ideals, reinterpreted in the context of modern socioeconomic relations, could cure society's ills.[27] In the West, the radical Unitarians like Jones, Gannett, and Mann had also prepared younger pastors to preach applied Christianity.

Like social gospelers elsewhere, the sister clergy who worked in the Midwest did not all agree on how to attack the problems systematically. The younger generation of Collson, Jenney, and Morse was persuaded that peaceful conversion to a socialistic commonwealth was the only solution. Safford, Gordon, and Murdock believed that capitalism was no more corruptible than any other human system and, if salvaged, would be the best way to realize the nation's ideals. These differences were barely discernible in what they preached from the pulpit, however. For there they said very little about economic constructions one way or the other. Instead, they spoke with one voice for the restoration of the Christian virtues to rescue a fallen humanity and produce a healthy society.

When during the fall of 1900 Marie Jenney took up the issues of "Reform, Leadership, and Christian Socialism" in a series of pulpit papers, she set about doing exactly what she had promised the year before when she introduced herself by letter to the author of *Women and Economics.* She was going to do her part to hasten a just society, she had told Charlotte Perkins Stetson, by preaching a stiff dose of individualism to the women and a spirit of Christianity to the men. While her pulpit analyses put the problem in economic terms and utilized the language and tools of political science and sociology, they always came back to the point that, since corporate structures were only as good as the individuals in them, the people would have to reclaim and defend the personal traits that Jesus exemplified.[28] Rowena Morse, another Christian Socialist, also shied away from prescribing specific systemic remedies. Instead, she attempted to prod the businessmen in the pews toward reform with the point of Paul's words to the Romans, "None of us liveth to himself." "The unscrupulous haste to get rich at other people's expense," said the preacher, was the cause of their society's moral impoverishment.[29]

While Caroline Bartlett Crane was less comfortable with the socialistic solution, she, too, attacked the imbalances of the capitalistic mentality. In an 1896 sermon provoked by the prizefighter John L. Sullivan's popularity and the wild reception he got when he came to Kalamazoo, she lectured her audience sternly about the natural law of competition, how it had been grossly misunderstood and confused with a selfish combativeness, and how that brute mentality was fast destroying the social order. There were Sullivans outside the boxing ring, the preacher told her listeners, looking especially hard at the businessmen in the pews. They thought that, to be respected, they had to show that they were "the fittest," the champions; for their understanding of what success and personal power meant had never developed beyond the crude terms of controlling or conquering other people. Really successful and strong men and women, Crane said, were able to gain self-respect just by doing their jobs as well as they could, and they did not need "to turn every relationship into a combat to prove their worth." [30]

The preaching of Safford and Gordon, though firmly secured to the Protestant ethic and spirit of enterprise, also stressed personal service and self-sacrifice as keys to saving society. Safford, as proud of her entrepreneurial skills as any successful capitalist, yet emphasized mutual caring and doing one's part for the common good. Since divine love expressed itself through the happy community, Safford sermonized, slouchers did violence to a higher law when they failed to contribute their share and made others' lives more difficult. [31] Eleanor Gordon's proof passages, taken from novels like Wharton's *The House of Mirth* and Ecclesiastes, dramatized the disastrous effects of selfish and profligate living. [32]

While they would continue to preach Christian virtues to uplift individual character, as the century drew to a close, these clergy became much less certain that theirs was the way to solve all society's problems. Throughout the 1890s, the expression of Christian conscience through the social settlement movement had been suggesting a more expansive prophetic ministry that directed the pulpit to an unaccustomed community involvement. Murdock and Buck were already exploring alternative ministries in 1893 when they preached to the people in Cleveland on the Salvation Army and neighborhood houses. About the same time, in Kalamazoo, Bartlett was moving her church toward institutional outreach, Collson was writing her college thesis on labor unrest and unions, and Jenney her seminary thesis on the social settlement movement. For most, there was little question by the new century but that real reform ministry must go beyond the abstractions of character building to a demonstrated commitment to social programs through direct involvement. "The sheer prophet who was content to talk about things," warned Jenney, might captivate the people and even restore their faith in progress, but only "the prophet in action" was going to spur the people to change. [33]

Rowena Morse, who only started to preach on a regular basis in 1906, also challenged the view that preachers should talk just about hell and heaven and not get involved with picket lines or government policy. Both the Old and New Testament writers, she said, had provided a much broader guide for prophetic ministry when they taught that God wanted the faithful to show their devotion not by fasting and ritual but by seeking justice, relieving the oppressed, and befriending the helpless. These prophets had taught that collective needs must be put before individual interests; certainly, Jesus' purpose was not merely "to cure a few sick Jews" or "to make a tub of wine eke out the cheer of a wedding" but to relieve the world's miseries by achieving a universal good. In the present day, Morse told her people, the "priests" with their sacred forms were still guarding the old order jealously, but the visionaries were placing religion in the service of humanity. The lines had been drawn, and now they must stand with those who were willing to look beyond their own salvation to that of the broader community. [34]

It took Mary Safford much longer to yield on this point. Almost until her retirement in 1910, she insisted that it was unfair of more radical social gospelers to accuse moderates like herself of taking the path of least resistance if they chose to teach individual kindness instead of the redistribution of wealth. When these critics dismissed her sermons as just preaching platitudes, not charting practical paths, she reminded them that her methods were those of the great moralists of the past. Surely, she said, there was a place in the modern pulpit for ministers who still believed in the value of teaching the Ten Commandments. [35]

Gordon was also slow to accept the activist gospel, for it seemed to her to excite more enthusiasm than intellectual rigor and well-informed planning among its proponents. Her uneasiness about it vented itself in at least one full sermon that dwelt on the dangers of giving oneself to service without taking time for the quiet study that people also needed for moral growth. Gordon acknowledged the world's need for Marthas, the people who labored "early and late to improve the tenement houses, to clean the streets, to do away with the smoke," and to see that there was pure food and water. But this was not all that was needed, she said, citing Jesus' words to

Martha. Mary had sat at his feet while he taught his disciples, had chosen "the good part," and this thoughtful time should never be sacrificed for the demands of the world. Proper housekeeping, ethical business practices, and fair pay for an honest day's work would all have to be assured before the kingdom of heaven arrived, but these alone were not the kingdom, as some of the gospelers seemed to think.[36] The same distrust of the social gospel's high spiritedness caused Gordon to criticize Charles M. Sheldon's charming best-seller *In His Steps, or What Would Jesus Do?* as a facile recommendation of poorly researched and shortsighted social reforms. Unshakable in her attachment to the rational ideal, she could hardly believe that, if Jesus returned to save the modern world, he would plunge into any such "bungling" ventures as Sheldon depicted. He would surely be thoroughly scholarly and deliberate in seeking reforms.[37]

Yet for all these reservations, Gordon and Safford also acquired strong doubts that the minister could fulfill her prophetic responsibilities from a disengaged pulpit. These doubts were fed not only by their internal ambivalence but by their church members' growing indifference to what they were trying to preach. Once more radical pulpits than theirs had dispensed with the niceties of teaching virtue and started attacking the evils of the capitalistic system head on, it was hard not to see their own as but trying to nudge people gently out of a deepset complacency, and even then having to answer to protests that they were pushing too hard. Disheartened by the doubtful results of their effort to preach Christian character, and drawn to the possibilities of doing more good from broader platforms, the sisterhood gradually ventured beyond their conventional pastorates to the suffrage crusade, settlement work, municipal housekeeping, and kindred fields where they tested the possible reach of their vocation.

In extending the definitions of ministry to include these reforms, the women were braced by knowing that there had been liberal clergy before them who had left liberal pulpits to forge a yet freer ministry. Some like Collson spoke of themselves as following Emerson's lead, but for the most part the model was Parker, not the Concord sage.[38] For Emerson had been born, as he said, with a seeing eye, not a helping hand, called to social witness but not to active social engagement. Parker, on the other hand, envisioned a ministry of reform that gave the women their clearest mandate for outreach in the new century.

The growing appeal of reform and corresponding decline of detached prophecy was a general trend that resulted in pulpits everywhere losing their visionaries to fields of service in the secular sphere. The Ethical Basis radicals in the West and the East's mainline liberals took different views of this exodus from the parish ministry. Jenkin Lloyd Jones, more averse every year to any form of sectarianism, and barely within the denominational borders anyway, took it as an inevitable and healthy if disruptive development that so many Unitarian clergy had come to "feel the irritation of the 'vest,'" even though they stood in the freest of pulpits. As far as he was concerned, this depletion of the ministry was, if nothing else, forcing the church to see that there were other roads to reform.[39]

Understandably, this was no consolation for the officials in Boston. The AUA's Eliot viewed the flight from the field as a sign of "progressive decay" that was threatening to put his denomination out of business. Faced with the declines in lay membership and the clergy's plummeting salaries at a time when the cost of living was rising, Eliot watched his "fittest men" leave for other careers with the feeling that he was fighting a losing battle.[40] "The widespread desire to get more of this world's goods" was without doubt a major deterrent to choosing the ministry, acknowledged one young Unitarian pastor, whose own career choice had proved that there were yet some exceptions.[41] But these few who still were concerned more about saving souls than about making money formed a new breed who wanted to practice their ministry in closer connection with social work.

As radical gospeler John Haynes Holmes warned his colleagues, the new generation could see all too well that the Protestant church was out of date and "like some old man in his second childhood . . . utterly oblivious to the facts of the present."[42] Not even the free church, another young pastor conceded, had altogether outgrown the polarized thinking that made religion and science enemies, pitting a God of reason and nature against a God of revelation and Scripture. This as much as anything had discredited the church and the ministry among his generation's "thoughtful young men," he said.[43] Without being asked, the clergywomen were quick to add that the so-called free church had lost its credibility with its thoughtful women as well. Given the opposition that they had met at the institutional levels and the disappointing returns on their efforts to change human nature at the grass roots, the pulpit sisterhood had cause enough to move to new fields of service that bid them warmer welcome and promised better results, and it was among their ranks that the emigration to secular ministry was most dramatic, if least lamented by the church's establishment.

Chapter Fourteen

BLESSED NEIGHBORLINESS

Woman's function, like charity, begins at home; then, like charity, goes elsewhere.
—Rev. Theodore Parker

I

It was inevitable that the Western conference's clergywomen, displaced and restive, look to the social settlements as the most promising sites for rebuilding their ministries. At the start of the new century, the Protestant leadership was touting the community house as a paradigm for giving the work of the church a more practical shape. "The saint must become a social reformer," Rev. Henry S. Nash of the Cambridge Divinity School told American colleagues; he must "seek his ennobling vision of the being and beauty of God . . . in the slums, not in the religious leisure of the monastery." [1] In the same year, 1900, Jenkin Lloyd Jones, having long before made this evangel his signature, was underscoring the message by having Jane Addams deliver the principal lectures at his Tower Hill summer school. At once religious and secular, institutional and domestic and embracing through its broad methods the principles of both science and sympathy, the settlement concept promised the sister clergy a more supportive vocational structure than they had found in the church.

As their sermonizing has shown, the pulpit sisterhood, like other social gospelers, had followed the settlement house idea from the time it began taking hold in America in the late 1880s. The travel logs Bartlett and Murdock kept when they went abroad in the 1890s show them eagerly "poking in" at Women's University Settlement and Toynbee Hall in London and other places that stimulated the same sort of ventures back home. It was a powerful inspiration to them, Bartlett wrote in her journal, to witness "so many heroic efforts" on the part of people who chose to live "right among the poor, drawing them about them into study circles, teaching them 'religion from the near end' by daily *kindnesses*." [2]

While Bartlett funneled this inspiration into an institutional church that embodied the settlement principles, others, whose pastorates were less secure or whose visions of ministry were not as clear, began to enter the neighborhood work more directly. From the rigors of rural parish life in Humboldt, Amelia Murdock had gone to Chicago, enrolled in a kindergarten college, and spent a two-year practicum in the city slums. This test of endurance, ironically, was in itself so exhausting that, when Jane Addams offered Amelia the enviable opportunity to use her credentials working with her as the head of the new kindergarten at Hull House, she was too worn out to accept and went back to country teaching. [3] This was just at the time, too, when Mila Tupper stepped down from her pulpit in Grand Rapids, Michigan, married her Unitarian colleague, Rezin A. Maynard, and spent an unorthodox honeymoon working with him in the slums as Hull House staff.

The pulpit sisters would not have been drawn to the settlements if they had understood them to be secular substitutes for their sacred calling. What they wanted and found in the movement was a real if unlabeled religious animus that secured their sense of a pastoral continuity. Even where, as at Hull House and the better-known settlements generally, the leadership's principal goals were political and the staff cultivated a nonsectarian image, the neighborhood centers were vitalized by a religious fervor that was undeniable even to those who were most averse to churchly associations. [4] Settlement pioneer Mary Kingsbury Simkhovitch noticed throughout the years that, whatever their other motives, and "no matter how variously constituted," the settlement family aspired "through its common life . . . toward a common faith" and in this way contributed "to the religious experience of the world." This was so, said Simkhovitch, whether its residents saw it or not, and regardless of "how non-religious or irreligious" they claimed to be. [5]

The clergywomen who came to the social settlements fully agreed. They believed that "all *Ideals*," as *Old and New* put it, grew out of a basic religious spirit, if by *religious* one meant possessing a fundamental reverence for life. [6] Yet, while it was easy enough to speak of the bond between philanthropy and religion, existing tensions between the settlements and the traditional church-sponsored charities frequently made it hard to forge a good working relationship between the two. The settlement workers' cultivation of a scientific ground for reform, with an emphasis on the social and economic causes of poverty, had often set them in heated opposition to the charities, which saw the problems in terms of individual needs and moral character. The settlement theory that rich and poor were dependent on each other further increased the distance between its practitioners and the religious philanthropists, whose work with the needy remained paternalistic.[7] The clergywomen who came to the settlements seeking to rest religious belief on the firmest empirical base, yet eager to maintain those churchly connections that also provided a place for the spiritual life in reform, sometimes got caught between the claims of the two philanthropic camps.

Mary Leggett became one such casualty when, after fifteen years of trying to prop up weak rural churches, she decided to change her direction and went to Chicago to live in the slums. Her plan was to learn all she could about settlements and then become a head resident somewhere. After short stints at Hull House, the Eli Bates project, and the Chicago Commons in 1901, Leggett was offered what seemed from a distance to be the ideal position for her. This was the post of head resident at the Friendly Aid Society—later the Warren Goddard House—which was run by the All Souls Unitarian Church in New York City. Leggett's letters to friends at this time show that she was self-consciously trying to reconstruct, not abandon, her ministry and was therefore intent on doing the kind of neighborhood work whose deepest purpose touched "every side of human nature—including the religious instincts."[8] A Unitarian settlement had seemed to Leggett the perfect place to achieve this until she actually got there and saw how complicated and stressful the life of a church-run neighborhood center could be.

In fact, what Leggett learned when she arrived was that the project's staff and the All Souls directors had been at odds for some time and that her job had become available when the residents walked out en masse. According to Mary Simkhovitch, who had been the head resident just before Leggett, the church-appointed board apparently thought of the Friendly Aid House "as a mode of altruism for the church members, rather than an attempt at social understanding and a cooperative effort for social betterment." Thinking little about the actual character of the neighborhood, and guided instead by their own beliefs and customs, Simkhovitch later recalled, they seemed unaware of the glaring incongruity of holding Unitarian services on Sunday evenings in an almost entirely Catholic community or of giving geranium plants as gifts to children who had no shoes. "The idea of a settlement run as a charity was so uncongenial" that, after several stormy encounters, the group of ten residents or so had made their break—with one of the janitors bringing up the rear—and started the Greenwich House, where they could frame their own policies without the frustrations of church interference.[9] One can but speculate as to how well Mary Leggett fared during this time of transition. The record that has been recovered shows only that, after a year of trying to reassemble a staff and keep up the programs, she had a chance to return to the parish ministry in New Hampshire—and took it.[10]

In Mila Tupper Maynard's experience of settlement work, the conflicting territorial claims of organized religion and sociology led ultimately to the dissolution of her denominational ties and a permanent departure from parish ministry. Stimulated to greater social involvement by their summer at Hull House, the Maynards moved to the West, missionized on the coast for a while, and then settled down in Denver, where they joined the radical Broadway Temple of Christian Socialist Myron Reed. The AUA, fearing a blunting of its identity, viewed the couple's involvement with this social action group as a defection and dropped them from the roster of Unitarian clergy "with cause."[11]

It was certainly possible for religion and the social sciences to work together in harmony when the conditions were right, as they were at Roadside House in Des Moines when Eleanor Gordon became part of the resident staff in 1906. Serving a largely Protestant and assimilated clientele in a smaller Midwestern city, the Roadside project experienced none of the philosophical conflict that fractured the Friendly Aid program on New York's East Side. Though their field of service was secular, the religiously liberal, though not exclusively Unitarian, Roadside workers could run their program quite openly as a form of religious outreach. This was possible, said its head resident Flora Dunlap, who had interned at Hull House, because the native-born people could still be reached through church influences that were either repulsive or ineffective in immigrant neighborhoods. In cities the size of Des Moines, the influence of the church was still great enough for centers like Roadside to rely on the missions and Sunday Schools to help accomplish what those like Hull House attempted to do by themselves in the church's stead.[12] Roadside's self-described Christian but "absolutely non-sectarian" spirit was so close to Gordon's engrained approach to pastoring that the change from a church to a settlement base of operations seemed minimal. Because, she told her friends, the situation allowed her to keep "working on a broad basis of religious culture" even while testing new waters, she enjoyed it thoroughly.[13]

The settlement movement's domestic phrasing was yet another source of its appeal for these women, for it echoed the principles that had earlier made their churches homelike. A cooperative residence whose outward structure implied that its workers were family, the neighborhood house operated within a matrix of comfortable homely constructions. It was based on the theory of kinship between society's more and less fortunate and aimed at strengthening home life and the female's position within it. Jane Addams presented the settlement as an environment in which a woman enlarged her "maternal instinct" and "family conscience" by supplementing them with "a social and an industrial conscience" and widening "her family affections to embrace the children of the community." [14] While not all the ministers liked the "maternal instinct" and "moral energy" arguments, they agreed that, as Addams envisioned, women were needed to be the "Mothers of Civilization," and they were drawn easily to the settlement purpose of widening family affections. An enthused reporter for *Old and New* summarized its appeal in a word: "Home! Yes, that is the key-word to the social settlement movement," she wrote. "Its residents seek to express the highest ideals embodied by the idea of home." [15]

The settlement idea in action seemed an exciting application of the pastoral model that had been recommended to women some fifty years earlier by Caroline Dall, one of the first Unitarian women to preach. Already alarmed that the age's industrial forces were making most social relations, including pastoral care, less intimate, Dall had envisioned a new, nonsectarian ministry based on the "tender, reverent caretaking" of troubled people. Rather than trying to be bureaucrats, which always narrowed the human sympathies, these pastors would try to be a "Committee of Comfort" that reached out to the unfortunate, the poor, the friendless, and the emotionally broken. [16] Drawn to this model of ministry, Dall's successors noted approvingly in the 1890s that, however imposing the physical plant, the settlement house was following Dall's basic blueprint for Christian service. It was managed no more like a big business than a palatial estate. It might have a good many rooms, but all were used to express "this blessed neighborliness of service." [17]

Nor were the pastors who went to the settlements disappointed in this expectation. Roadside Settlement, Hull House, the Friendly Aid Society, and the others all tried to be surrogate households that served to shore up the family life of the poor. "Like the well-managed home," Flora Dunlap explained of Roadside, the settlement tried to foster a "self-sustaining, self-respecting standard of citizenship" and the skills needed for "hospitality in the word's fullest sense." Taking over the daytime domestic duties of wage-earning mothers, the volunteers staffed well-equipped nurseries where they encouraged their charges to be neat and orderly. There were classes for older children and adults in sewing, cooking, carpentry, reading, and music. In the evenings, there were parents' clubs and sociables that brought together the young and old, all intended to strengthen the family and the home.[18]

II

The most complete picture of what it could mean for a Midwestern clergywoman to move from parish ministry to the secular calling of settlement work emerges from the experience of Mary Collson, who made this transition in June 1900. *Unity's* senior editor, who had known the woman since she was a young girl in Humboldt and watched her dutifully follow her mentors into the Iowa parishes, welcomed her to Chicago with a few paragraphs. Not long before, when spending a day with her in Ida Grove, he had been much impressed by her ministry's emphasis on the "neighborhood needs and village culture."[19] Now, not surprisingly, he told his readers, she had come to the city "to study the new application of the old law of love" at Hull House. Although she was leaving her church work behind, they should not suppose that she was leaving the ministry, for "the old work and the new" were "one in the hands of the devoted."[20]

Actually, Collson had not been entirely comfortable in her parishes, where the people were far more conservative and typical of small town liberals than the enclave of Humboldt radicals who had formed her views and audacious ambitions. Like Jenney, Padgham, and Morse, the "second generation" in Safford's ecclesia, she had answered the call to her first church believing that socialism, the settlements, and the ideals of Unitarians all sprang from "the same reservoir of religious impulse and attitude," to use Padgham's phrase, and therefore were all appropriate subjects for the liberal pulpit.[21] Her parishioners, however, had no more taste for papers on Marxist philosophy than they had for sermons that scrutinized fine points of theology. Nor did they altogether approve of women who stepped outside their private sphere to do the "masculine work" of the ministry. The trauma of being told that what she wanted to preach was not relevant and, even worse, that she ought not to be in the pulpit at all because she was a female led to a nervous breakdown that forced her to reassess her position. Facing the truth that she had practically no sectarian loyalties and no desire to be identified as the "Reverend" Collson, she admitted to herself, as she did to Jones, that her obligation to friends was all that was keeping her in the pulpit.[22]

An unusually empathic woman who always had taken on nurturant roles, Collson returned to her pastoral office with a mind to discarding its priestly trappings and putting her energy principally into organizing small relief outlets for needy families in the rural areas. By taking this new direction, she finally met Jane Addams personally and found through the settlement leader's image of secular priestess the role she was groping for. From there it was just a short step to Hull House and a new precinct for ministry. Addams had asked the young pastor to come when one of the settlement's mainstays, Alzina Stevens, died suddenly and someone had to be found to replace her as liaison with the city's new Juvenile Court. Seeing a rare opportunity to bring her work "up to date" and resolve her vocational ambivalence, Collson had left immediately for her new home in one of Chicago's worst slums, where she envisioned Miss Addams working "a miracle of people" that was making the world a better and happier place.[23]

Though her background of poverty set her apart from the social settlement's leaders, in other respects Collson's profile was that of the typical Hull House resident. Most of her new associates were young and unmarried Protestant women of English or Scotch-Irish ancestry, highly educated, and brought up in a tradition of public service, precisely the sort that she had presumed would understand and support her most readily. As she soon learned, however, her job made her life so consistently different from that of the settlement's "regular household" that there was not nearly the ground for identification and sympathy she had expected. Whether they were the administrative staff or professional people and students who spent their off hours at Hull House transforming slum life—by putting on plays, mounting art exhibitions, and serving their poor neighbors tea—the others all seemed to have some regular respite, some daily reprieve from the neighborhood's harsh conditions. By contrast, Collson's position as a full-time caseworker brought her face to face all day with ghetto realities far removed from the well-meaning busyness back at the settlement.

According to the *Hull-House Bulletin,* Collson's job as the neighborhood's Juvenile Court officer was to look after children who, through their delinquency or dependency, had become the state's wards and needed help with school or family problems.[24] While this had not seemed to the program's creators too much to promise the public, with no state funding, just private subsidies, and but a skeletal staff the demands of the assignment were overwhelming. It was not at all unusual for the youngsters themselves to rush in to report family crises, and Collson could always expect to find the spindle on her desk filled with messages telling of drunken parents and beatings when she returned in the evenings.[25] By the time Mary Collson came into the program, its architects realized that, as things were, only a woman with superhuman qualities could survive as a caseworker. She would need not only "the strength of a Samson and the delicacy of an Ariel" but also wings to rise above her own "depressing financial worries." Paid piece-meal through private contributions, Collson was somehow supposed to live on $60 a month, which one of the program's own patrons described as "a pitiful remuneration." Out of this she was expected to pay for her room and board at the settlement.[26]

Although the official word that was sent to the state, along with a bid for funding, was that the staff was seeing "gratifying progress" with a rate of success close to 85 percent, another story was being recounted in the caseworker's ledger.[27] There the notations told of daily rounds that brought Collson into "dark, stuffy" tenement flats with "bare, dirty rooms" and "garbage heaped up" in corners and rancid mattresses piled on the floors. One typical house "seemed filled with quarrelsome people," and another had been left "deserted and filthy" by an alcoholic mother who "was in hiding" from the law. Collson encountered one family's children alone just before Thanksgiving trying to put their "dinner" together with nothing except "black coffee without even sugar, and bread without butter."[28]

The work of helping her boys find jobs and hold onto them was no less discouraging. For, while she knew that a family's next meal often came from the few coins a small child brought home, in placing the youngsters and trying to keep them at work she could not but feel party to what was at best their crass exploitation. At worst, and this proved the more likely, she knew that she was sending them into situations that were apt to cause some physical or psychological injury, and then she was wracked with guilt when the damage was done. Mandel's case was not unusual. In bed with a raging fever when Collson checked up on him, he explained that he had been carrying crates for the bottling company where he worked when one of the bottles exploded and cut him severely. Infection had set in, but he had stayed on the job for another week until the pain had gotten the best of him. Stanley, another of Collson's "good boys," who had gotten a job in an iron factory, came to report to the Hull House officer with his hands "blistered three times across" and his voice hoarse from breathing in air "filled with filings." Then, again, there was Fred, whom the caseworker sent out of town to a farm that had asked for "a boy" and then sent him back immediately because he was too small to do what they needed. "They want [him] to do a man's work for $5.00 a month," Collson fumed in her notebook. "Fred is greatly disappointed. What chance do these poor boys have!" The answer came shortly when Fred was arrested and sent to the dreaded John Worthy reform school.[29]

The similar frustrations in trying to get the youngsters some education further eroded Collson's belief that her work could repair at least part of the frayed social fabric. State laws already required that children of certain ages attend public school and be provided with free books if they were in need, yet Collson was told that the district school had neither space nor texts for the students who were already enrolled, much less for others.[30] This irony became all the crueler when it came to light that the local politicians had been taking bribes on contracts for school book adoptions and defrauding the city of millions of dollars, more than enough to build another school for the Nineteenth Ward. When Collson learned of the scandal, she could only weep bitterly for her boys who had been arrested for nothing more than playing truant from schools that had no place to put them.[31]

Having known almost nothing about urban problems before she had started at Hull House, Collson had fancied that social work there would be much the same as it was in the parishes, where the ethic of neighborliness and cultural continuity had made it easier to give people in crisis a basis for hope and religious faith. As a consequence, her initial response to the suffering in Chicago was to offer some sort of spiritual as well as material aid, as she had always done on her parish calls. When, for example, she started to visit a frightened young prostitute who was dying of syphilis in the back room of a dirty flat, she routinely announced her arrival by singing the hymn she had used as the invocation when she was still leading Sunday services. The girl said she hated the pious words of the hypocrites who had preached to her all her life about right and wrong, but she loved Collson's song and thought that if she had been taught to pray in this way, her life might have turned out differently. Yet even as Collson was trying to help the girl overcome her fear of death through communion with some divine power, the weight of ugliness all around them was fast undermining her own confidence in religious uplift, and soon her own faith was "growing dim and flickering."[32]

It had also become obvious to Collson that, however advanced the court's theoretical base, her one-on-one efforts at personal rehabilitation had little effect and that, if conditions were to be improved, the political systems and institutions supporting the poor's exploitation would have to be the targets for reform. Involvement in the labor movement was the norm for Hull House residents, and even the measure of aptitude for the work as far as some staff were concerned. Collson's predecessor, Alzina Stevens, had once stated bluntly that people who could not discern that economic injustices were the root cause of all social problems "did not make very valuable settlement workers."[33] Since Collson had inherited, along with Stevens's job with the court, her obligations to a number of labor groups that met at the settlement, she had no trouble finding ways to put her new sympathies into action. Aware that her own kind of leadership skills were no substitute at all for the tough political savvy of women like Stevens, Collson was grateful to have at least her pulpit and platform experience to contribute by speaking to women's organizations on labor's behalf.[34]

Labor activism, in turn, led Collson into the growing socialist movement, as it did most of the middle-class intellectuals who got together at Hull House to air their pro-worker sympathies. Collson joined the Socialist Democratic party, worked hard for the Debs presidential campaign, and was given a seat on Chicago's Socialist Central Committee. She found that after her long and discouraging days at work, the spirited strategy sessions and speeches gave her an outlet for anger and a locus for hope in politics that momentarily eased her sense of futility. Unfortunately, despite its official endorsement of equal rights for women, the party was just as patriarchal in the way it conducted its business as any religious institution. As one of her sisters complained, females were "just as much an afterthought" with the men in the socialist movement as they had been "with the Hebrew god." The brotherhood had "the absurd idea that man is the race" and woman "his appendage."[35] As a consequence, Collson, like other reformers at Hull House, made her political base not at any of the city-wide forums but at the settlement, where she could be independent of male control and set her own priorities.[36] She organized the Hull House Socialist Woman's Club to focus on just those women's issues the brothers preferred to subordinate to "the larger labor question."[37]

Yet here again, though Collson could soon speak the party vernacular fluently, she preferred to translate political principles into personal acts, that is, to try to live her politics in the same way she had lived her religion. Her goal, she would later explain in her memoirs, was to make socialism her way of life by establishing "real equality" in her dealings with all other people. As a confirmation that she was achieving this, it meant a great deal to her when the immigrant women began to borrow her clothes as freely as they did each others', though Collson's own wardrobe consisted of only two outfits at the time: a serge coat suit and her pulpit gown, "a relic" from her pastoral days. Once the neighborhood matrons caught sight of the dress, which Collson now wore when she went out to speak, it was launched as a regular loan garment that circulated throughout the ward.[38] Unfortunately, these personal triumphs were easily lost in the rubble of human defeat that Collson encountered at every turn.

The settlement's veterans tried to warn the new resident not to set unrealistic expectations for herself or confuse public and private methods of influence, but, the more she saw of the squalor, the more determined she was to live as she thought a good socialist should, giving of herself not only as a professional but "as a friend." Thus, she rushed headlong toward the breakdown her colleagues predicted. By the end of nine months, Collson had reached a state of such severe nervous exhaustion that the several country vacations arranged for her were of little benefit. The end of her settlement venture became imminent when she befriended a terminal cancer patient whom the hospitals would not admit. She brought the woman back to her room at Hull House, over the anxious protests of the other residents. The woman soon died, and, not long after that, Collson returned to Iowa.

In many respects, Mary Collson's unhappy experience followed a common pattern of burnout and disillusionment among the settlement's rank and file, who were blocked on all fronts by insurmountable obstacles and soon gone from the scene, unsung and largely forgotten. In Collson's case, as in many, the odds against her survival were raised by the strong empathic tendencies that had brought her into the work, an open nature that had overloaded within a year even in small town pastoring and was bound to be short-circuited by the high volume of urban suffering. Collson's associates also believed, and she came to agree with them later, that she had been handicapped by being raised among people who treated her as "exceptional," constantly feeding her appetite for praise and turning her into "a glutton for admiration," to borrow her own description. Moreover, having so recently basked in the "artificial" aura that the public attached to ministers, even to those who were women and Unitarian, Collson was unaccustomed to being seen as anything but her "superior self." She was easily wounded not only by real criticism but, as Addams once pointed out, simply by failing to get the reinforcement and praise she expected.[39] Given this constant need for personal validation from others and from the work itself, she was devastated by being unable to solve the neighborhood's problems.

Collson's settlement effort was also undercut by the fact that, in moving from church work to Hull House and trying to substitute politics for liberal religious reform, she had severed herself from a vital support group. Gordon's disappointment and anger at her defection weighed heavily on her, and the rift proved all the more costly because, despite Collson's expectations, she had not found another sisterhood as attentive and caring at the settlement. "At the time of my experience with my poor cancer victim," she later wrote bitterly, "nearly all of the permanent residents were away. Miss Addams herself was gone—probably on some important errand"; "the nurse at Hull House that summer was more romantic than professional, which accounts for my never finding her accessible, and the doctor who happened to be representing her profession among us seemed to me to have no real interest in problems of sickness among the poor."[40] Yet, even when the devoted regulars were at home, there was a formality and reserve as well as a cliquishness that isolated more than one resident who was not in the charmed inner circle.

Mary Collson was not the only one of the clergywomen to be disappointed when they looked to the settlements for a more secure home for their ministry. Mary Leggett had also signed the Hull House roster in 1901, imagining that she would spend a year or so learning the ropes of administration under the watchful eye of her chosen mentor, Miss Addams. Yet she, too, found that the head resident "was necessarily engrossed with the new building enterprise" and had so many other demands on her that she did not have any time to give an apprentice the sort of attention she wanted.[41] The summer that Collson arrived, longtime resident Alice Hamilton, who had herself found that the climate took getting used to, wrote her sister Agnes about it. "We get into the habit which I think all large, clannish households do, of laughing at outsiders," she said, explaining this as "a pose in the house," a studied casualness among the veterans who feared that an obvious enthusiasm might make them seem inexperienced.[42] Whatever the explanations, the Hull House family failed to be a substitute for the close, caring sisterhood that women like Collson had come to depend on.

Eleanor Gordon was able to reap the satisfactions of neighborhood work and spend four enjoyable years at Roadside precisely because, unlike Collson, she was not detached from her female support community. Gordon, in fact, had been introduced to the Roadside project by friends at the church when she was called to fill in during Safford's illness in 1904. As she had not for some years shared a home with Safford, the settlement seemed the ideal "parsonage" from which to practice a modernized ministry. Since Roadside, in contrast to Hull House, had trouble securing a large live-in staff, Gordon's settlement family was made up of volunteers whom she already knew well from her church and club activities throughout the city.

Then, too, though Gordon's transition from a church to a street ministry drew her into the cause of the working class, it never led her as far from familiar ideological paths as Collson was led in Chicago. To be sure, her view from the settlement gave her a new perspective on poverty that made her see things much differently, she said, from the way they were seen by "the good samaritans who lived in comfortable neighborhoods." But, while this fostered greater identification with the disadvantaged, leading the residents "to feel *with* less fortunate people instead of feeling *for* them," it did not make many converts to radical politics.[43] Socialism had few takers at an institution like Roadside, which made no apologies for its Christian identity. Like all settlement workers, Gordon discovered that any attempts to rout social evils could not but involve her in organized group strategies, but, again, she believed with her cohort that their female network could build the required political muscle by pooling the resources of Roadside House, the liberal church, the suffrage groups, and the women's clubs.[44]

Buoyed by the warm community of friends and sister reformers and the "ready response everywhere," Gordon was still enthusiastic about social settlement life after four years of it. The experience had persuaded her that neighborhood work and "the taste of practical politics" were "the really *live thing*" and that they had been of such "immense value" to her that she felt "like recommending it to all ministers."[45] Indeed, Gordon might have stayed on at Roadside indefinitely had she not been such a practical woman and at fifty-seven feeling more than ever the need to save something for her retirement. "If only I did not have to think of money," she wrote her friend Jones wistfully. "If some one would say to me: 'Go ahead, I will see you have bread and clothes and a place to die in,' I could do better work."[46] As no such offer presented itself and the church's needs still seemed paramount to her, the minister left her neighborhood house and went back to tending church homes.[47]

III

Settlement work became a permanent outgrowth of parish ministry for only one of the Western clergywomen who tried to make it the stage for their liberal gospel. This was Celia Parker Woolley, who opened her own settlement in 1905 to accomplish what seemed impossible in the all-white churches she served. Leaving behind a comfortable home and unbelieving neighbors in the Grand Boulevard district of Chicago, the minister and her husband, now both well into their fifties, moved down to the edge of the "black belt" on the city's South Side and settled into the upstairs head resident's flat of the Frederick Douglass Center. There the couple remained for thirteen years, until Celia's death.

A daughter of New England abolitionists, Celia Woolley had carried through life a deep sense of outrage at the inequities suffered by black Americans. During her many years as one of Chicago's most active club-women, she had acquired a reputation for being a skillful champion of racial justice who knew how to win her point by disarming the opposition and applying a friendly but firm persuasion. In the late 1890s, after a number of years agitating behind the scenes, Woolley had led what an ally remembered as "one of the bitterest fights that ever occurred" in the Chicago Woman's Club by introducing a motion that opened the way for the club's integration. She confronted her sisters with their hypocrisy in reciting a motto that claimed, "Nothing that is human is alien to us," and then routinely excluding women who happened to be the "wrong" race or religion. When the dust cleared, the bylaws were changed, and Fannie Barrier Williams became the first black woman ever to cross the club's color line.[48]

This achievement of helping a little to move the club world toward a higher ground of human relationship was one of Woolley's greatest satisfactions, and it saddened her that she could not accomplish as much among Unitarians, whose infighting and fragmentation seemed to be getting worse all the time. After years of involvement with church committees, editorial boards, and conferences, she had reached the conclusion that religious liberals were "stranded in an era of individualism" and so self-absorbed and disconnected that all they could do was "touch fingertips, and with gloves on at that."[49] It was largely this discouragement that persuaded her to loosen her ties to Western conference politics and move into parish ministry. There, she could feel in a daily way that she was really of some use to people who needed her, and she could better promote the ideal of responsible community.[50] Her friend Jones, himself now estranged from the movement, agreed that she could use her talents more fully once she was "free from the courtesy and love bands of denominational carpentry" and, though dubious of her remaining under the Unitarian aegis, agreed to preside at her ordination.[51]

Taking pastorates first with a Unitarian church in nearby Geneva and then with an independent society organized on the Chicago Northside, Woolley had sought to instill in her people an active social conscience that would stimulate their generosity. But when after two years of hearing her preach against competition in social relations and being warned particularly about the destructive nature of gambling, Woolley's people announced that they were going to start holding card parties to bring in her salary, Woolley was forced to conclude that her efforts had been just as futile in the pulpit as in Unitarian politics, and she resigned on the spot.[52]

The founding of the Frederick Douglass Center five years later showed clearly that Woolley had not lost her interest in, or belief in the possibility of, creating a workable setting for an effective prophetic ministry. The idea of having a neighborhood house had appealed to her as a more evolved form of the liberal church homes that had been too insular and complacent to nurture an extended family. Woolley's object in calling her project a "center" was to let people know that it was going to be her ministry's "radiating point," not some foreign missionary outpost but her base of operation and personal family residence, from which she hoped to be of some help to her neighbors.[53] In choosing its name, Woolley also meant to identify her project unmistakably with the black community, which almost all social settlement services shunned in favor of the immigrant and white working-class populations. The Frederick Douglass "experiment," Woolley pledged, would meet the "crying need" for the same kind of outreach in the city's black neighborhoods.[54]

It took some time, however, for the project's approach to become entirely clear, not only to the public but to the organizers themselves. During the planning stage, Woolley spoke of the need to uplift the unschooled "colored people who were coming up from the South" and lowering their community's standard; indeed, when it opened, the three-story, white stone house on Wabash Avenue was prepared to offer most of the usual settlement services for the disadvantaged: a free kindergarten, a reading room and library, classes in cooking, sewing, and manual training for girls and boys, and a bureau of information that functioned largely as an employment agency. A small basement gymnasium for recreation and exercise classes was added a year or so later. Yet, as it turned out, the real clientele was not to be these unwashed "hordes" at all but, in Woolley's own words, "the best people of both races," in short, the element that was uplifted already.[55] As Fannie Williams, Woolley's assistant at the center, defended it, the aim was to help the cause of Afro-Americans not by doing slum work but by providing a meeting ground where, again, "the best whites and blacks" could get acquainted and discuss their differences "on a common ground for common aspirations and common action."[56] Woolley's visitors came to attend teas, recitals, and concerts and to hear the same kinds of talks that had been the standard bill of fare at the Unity Club in the minister's Northside parish. A series on poets and poetry with interpretive readings, a course on George Eliot's fiction by Woolley and another by Jenkin Lloyd Jones on John Ruskin, and even a lecture on vegetarianism were typical of the events that were listed weekly and sent to the local papers.[57]

It was inevitable that Woolley would draw sharp criticism from some members of the black press and labor groups, who sneered at her calendar of interracial teas and forums and sedate "religious ethical" services on Sunday afternoons, charging that they did little for the people who most needed settlement help. Nor is it any wonder that some historians in our own time have found it easy to question the sincerity and depth of Woolley's liberalism, considering how, in order to win support without feeding public fears about racial mixing, she reassured her patrons that she was working to bring the races together only in "non-social" ways.[58] Yet to belittle Woolley's commitment to overcoming racial barriers is to forget that, while she may have hedged on "absolute racial equality" and—as detractors noted—moved just to the edge and not into the heart of the Negro community when she made a new home on the city's South Side, she offered up her private life to the service of what she believed in as few others did. Certainly, to her sister clergy in the Western conference, Woolley's total commitment to her ideal of blessed neighborliness was an inspiration and a sometimes humbling measure of their own convictions. While all of them prided themselves on being ministers of a religious faith that was wedded to human equality, not many of Woolley's sisters were really at ease with more than a limited integration or able to reconcile what they believed in principle with what they felt privately.

This conflict, obviously not one that was frequently aired, is nevertheless clearly documented by the record of Caroline Bartlett Crane's interest in race relations. Crane prided herself on having included the city's blacks in her ministry's outreach. She often reminded the public that, from the time she arrived at People's Church, she had made sure that any occasional Negroes who came to the services were warmly welcomed and given good seats up front. She was proud, too, of having opened her meeting rooms to an all-black cultural club until it was able to find a home in the members' own neighborhood churches. After Celia Woolley opened the Douglass

Center in 1905, Crane, who by then was out of her pulpit and looking for other ways to be useful, attempted to set up a partnership of black and white leaders in Kalamazoo and hosted an interracial luncheon in her home to explore the idea. Knowing the city as well as she did, Crane most surely anticipated the scandal that this get-together created and welcomed the opportunity to proclaim, in a public defense afterward, that she would never "hesitate to meet and break bread with respectable people in the interest of any good cause," including the cause of racial justice.[59]

Yet Crane was never able to go much further than public endorsement of self-help programs for the black community and extending the hospitality of her home to "fine or gifted negroes" like Booker T. Washington, Fannie Barrier Williams, and the "one or two others" who were her guests over the years. The awkward truth was, she confided to a friend in 1927, that she never could quite convince herself that the races were actually equal and therefore could never dislodge a basic fear of racial mixing. She had felt that it was only fair, of course, that the blacks "must have their 'place in the sun'—education and opportunity to develop their racial and individual gifts—" but her "wish to recognize and honor them" had "always been uncomfortably mixed with the feeling" that she "might be helping along the wrong sort of thing if one looked at larger and more fundamental issues."[60] Women who shared Crane's conflict were never able to give both their public and their private lives to the cause of race.

Celia Woolley, for her part, obviously had fewer fears about helping along "the wrong sort of thing." Although she agreed with Crane that blacks had evolved much more slowly than whites, she also believed absolutely that, with sufficient sponsorship, they would make up for lost time. Thanks to the close support of her family and friends, she was able to weather the critics who disparaged her methods as too far to either the right or the left. Safford, Fuchs, Gordon, Crane, and Morse, who dropped in on her now and then, worried about the toll the abuse had taken on her nerves, but they deeply admired the way she had stayed with her project and made it a meeting place for the city's most influential black and white leaders. Good things had been born of it. Through the joint efforts and combined resources of the center's regular visitors, the local chapters of the National Association for the Advancement of Colored People and the Urban League came into being. When her age and the strain of the work made it seem advisable, she was happy to pass her agenda on to their younger executive boards, and by World War I, her center on Wabash Avenue was no longer active enough to be kept on the list of organizations approved for local fund-raising.[61] Just a few weeks before her death in 1918, Woolley turned the first floor of the settlement over to the Urban League to use as its headquarters, and in time the organization occupied the entire building, in effect absorbing and carrying on the Douglass Center's broad ministry.

Though neither the self-perceived Christian endeavor that Gordon found at Roadside nor the church's direct philanthropic extension of Leggett's Friendly Aid House, the Douglass Center had both the domestic contours and the religious foundation that anchored these women who turned to the settlements as a revision of church ministry. Indeed, it was Woolley's religious conviction that coworkers most remembered about her. Jones, who continued to run his own neighborhood center until his death just six months later, noted at her memorial service that she had triumphed in settlement work because "good old-fashioned religion . . . new-fashioned to the need of the hour" had fueled it. George C. Hall, the center's president, also spoke of the woman who started the project and led worship services there as a resident minister, a modern-day Huldah, a "prophetess," who had "dwelt in the temple" where people seeking a better world came and "communed with her." As a homemaking pastor, Woolley believed—and left this belief as her legacy—that "bringing people together" accomplished "more good than a hundred sermons on ethics." In short, the minister did her best teaching by practicing what she had preached.[62]

Chapter Fifteen

MINISTERING TO MUNICIPALITIES

By the blessing of the upright a city is exalted.
—Proverbs 11:11

I

The possibilities for extending the clergywomen's reach did not stop with the social settlements. What had come to be called "public housekeeping" was a boundless field that beckoned to women to make "every place on this rounded earth . . . Home-like," as Frances Willard proclaimed.[1] For women who thought of the ideal church as an intimate congregational residence and the neighborhood house as a home for a yet more inclusive family, it was natural next to view the municipality as a larger home still. Moreover, it seemed to Progressive reformers only fitting that this "large apartment house"—which Gordon sketched metaphorically "with each individual dwelling place as but a single room"—should be cared for by those whom some debatable mix of biology, socialization, and myth had made most responsible for family welfare and social relationships.[2] With the rest of their generation, these pastors maintained that their sex, being less militant than males and more concerned with health and harmony, brought to the public realm a desperately needed perspective and expertise. Their efforts, Marie Jenney said, "showed the defects of masculine housekeeping" and, even more, their brothers' need for "feminine assistance."[3]

Many ordained women who could not get good positions in parish ministry satisfied their sense of mission by carving out other careers for themselves in the social sciences, promoting the rational reform of society through teaching and writing about the solutions suggested by modern scientific research. No doubt the most prominent of these transplanted clergy was Anna Garland Spencer, who had the distinction of being the first woman ever to pastor a church in Rhode Island before going on to help direct the New York School of Philanthropy and become a professor of sociology at several universities. Of the Safford network, however, Caroline Bartlett Crane was the only one to achieve a national reputation by putting her ministerial talents to work as a public housekeeper. Often calling herself "a minister" to neglected municipalities, she developed a new vocation out of inspecting the public health systems and infrastructures of large communities and telling the people how to improve what they had.

Crane sometimes suggested that she had made her way into her second career by inventing it accidentally after leaving the parish ministry, and sometimes that she had gotten there by more or less conscious design after her marriage started her thinking in new directions. In either case, the novel, one-woman profession was a perfect fit for a woman who liked to give orders and play the sleuth as much as Crane did. Bringing as much as $100 a day plus expenses and lots of press coverage, Crane's new line of work, like her church ministry, also satisfied her desire to do useful work, be paid a wage, and stay in the limelight.

When asked what led her to move from the church to civic evangelism, Crane liked to put on her wifely persona and talk about her predicament as a new bride who suddenly found herself with a large home and no idea of how to take care of it. For her own domestic survival as much as her congregation's benefit, she had talked the women at church into starting a School of Household Science complete with expert instructors from Chicago's Armour Institute, and then she enrolled in the program. From there, one thing led to another, she said. While she was soon able to show her maids how to cook and clean in the most advanced ways, her dinner conversations with the city's bacteriologist stimulated an interest in public health. To learn more about the city's water and food supply, its sewage disposal, and other sanitation procedures, she started to go to Chicago a few times a week to take sociology courses in urban support systems and used what she brought back to lead her Unity Club through a comprehensive investigation of Kalamazoo.

After taking a rest from professional life, and failing to get pregnant as she had hoped, the unemployed pastor returned to her sociological studies as a way of reentering public service. Without a pulpit and eager to build a new base for leadership, Crane had soon worked up a model curriculum on city housekeeping for the state's Federation of Women's Clubs. After testing it out on her club friends in Kalamazoo, she suggested that they set up a

Civic Improvement League to tackle the problems that they had uncovered. Initially, the league concentrated on philanthropic programs like free job placement, visiting nurses, and a house-to-house banking service to teach the poor to stay clear of the loan sharks. However, these promptly took a back to seat to public sanitation when, in 1904, Crane got the league women into the street-cleaning business.[4]

With horse-drawn carriages still the principal mode of transport, keeping the streets passable was a major problem, especially for the long-skirted pedestrians. Sweeping crews left piles of dirt standing overnight to be redistributed by traffic and wind, and their rotary brushes damaged the asphalt without achieving much else since pavements were never flushed systematically. It was obvious to the women that this was a worthless gesture toward sanitation, and their attempt to show the city council that there was a better way made the instigator a national celebrity. Having read about the procedure developed by George E. Waring for New York City, where crews in white uniforms used carts to haul off the dirt and hosed down the streets at night, Crane talked her city council into letting her league adopt six blocks of Main Street for three months to see what they could accomplish with Waring's methods in Kalamazoo. Crane herself went out at three in the morning to supervise the flushings downtown, and, as word of this unladylike experiment got around, news photographers started to meet her at daybreak. One morning, she counted no fewer than eight cameras leveled at her at one time. As always, Crane loved the publicity, graciously dropped everything to give interviews, and at the end made certain that all the papers got copies of her report. The good news, Crane said, was that the project had shown that the city could have cleaner streets and have them at a savings of 40 percent for the people who used them. The bad news was that, for reasons never given, the city fathers ignored these findings and continued to have the streets cleaned as they always had.[5]

Crane's word in matters of sanitation came to carry a good deal more weight after she reappeared at the head of a bold campaign against unsafe meat processing. Crane had gotten involved in this battle after her League made an unannounced tour of the local slaughterhouses and found that the roasts and chops that they had been feeding their families were being produced in filthy barns from diseased as well as healthy animals.[6] Outraged, Crane went home and drafted a bill to empower municipalities in the state to regulate the inspection of any meat sold within city limits. Her legislators, when contacted, shied away from endorsing a law of this kind, but Crane was determined to win their support, and she packed a suitcase and went off to Lansing to argue her case in the House and Senate corridors. Through persistence, she also was able to speak in the Senate chamber and there watch the bill's fate unfold. The long, blow-by-blow account Crane gave her father of how the bill barely squeaked through at the end leaves no doubt that, however nerve-racking for her, the fight was immensely fulfilling as well. When she vowed afterward that she would much rather stay home all day and scrub floors than repeat it, nobody really believed her.[7]

As her family and friends expected, as soon as the meat bill caught on as a model in other municipalities, Crane entered yet other battles, some now fought out on a national stage against federal agencies. The most highly publicized contest placed Crane at congressional hearings in Washington, pitted against the Department of Agriculture, whom she charged had so vitiated its own supposed safeguards that the imprimatur "U.S. Inspected and Passed" had come to mean nothing.[8] Within a few years, Crane had covered just about every facet of public housekeeping, from the protection of water supplies to food processing and school sanitation. Widely regarded as one of the country's most capable guardians of the community, she had regained and enlarged the public influence she had had in the ministry by recombining its component roles of homemaker, preacher, and scientist.

II

While Crane liked to say that her need to learn how to take care of a home launched her second career, it was actually by bringing her into a partnership with the medical brotherhood that her marriage did most to professionalize her new vocation. With sulfa drugs and penicillin still weapons of the future and only the application of germ theory with which to fight disease, physicians like Warren Crane were trying to win confidence and respect by doing their best with the science they had and selling the public on the idea of preventive medicine. Obviously, articulate advocates like Mrs. Crane were allies worth courting, as they were at least bound to get a more courteous hearing than doctors who tried to tell people what the politicians and businessmen liked to keep quiet. Once Warren's colleagues around the country became aware of his wife's enterprise, they asked her to give public addresses in their communities and, beginning in 1907 to make her appearances more visible, also to make inspections of how well their cities were doing their work. From then on until war preparedness sidelined the sanitation issue, more than sixty cities in fourteen states had Crane make these surveys.[9]

Primarily out to market a product, Crane's sponsors within the medical league were clearly not asking her for any expert opinions, only for helpful publicity. Indeed, though her husband's close tutoring and her own observation and reading had made her as knowledgeable in her specialized field as any certified health official, even Warren's closest associates tended to think of her as but a zealous amateur. Interested more in her press appeal than in her actual methods, one Louisville man could not understand Crane's balking at being asked to rate his filtration plant's operation when she had never seen anything like it before. Crane's correspondence and final reports show that she nonetheless went ahead with her work in a highly professional way and spared no effort to keep it from being compromised.

Having learned from the parish ministry the importance of knowing the territory, Crane sent out exhaustive questionnaires to her clients ahead of time. She asked them about their forms of government, property values, population, industries, and public services and then requested that she be sent their daily papers for a couple of weeks to get a fuller sense of what was awaiting her.[10] Having also learned as a minister how to promote her own work, she was just as adept at handling her own publicity in her new field. Crane began announcing her visits months before her arrival dates, sending her sponsors elaborate promotional packages with stacks of press releases, photographs, notices, and precise instructions for using these materials. Certain articles should be "mounted and put up in school corridors, book store windows &c," she told her contacts, and others displayed in the public libraries.[11] It was "best to *push* the press notices in the last ten days or so" and not to "tire the people with constant notices stretching over weeks." "Have one or two good but rather brief" blurbs initially, she coached, and then lay off until the final stretch, when there should be "something in the papers every day."[12]

Again with an eye to reaching and winning the widest possible audience, Crane stipulated that she be given the chance to present her findings and recommendations at a mass meeting on her last night in town. As a preacher whose sermons had once filled as many as twelve hundred seats in Kalamazoo, Crane was confident that people elsewhere would be just as eager to hear her. She specified that she be booked in "the largest and best place" available, explaining, "I don't want to half waste my time and efforts on an audience in 'the court House' or a church that seats two or three hundred only." It was equally important to her that her audience represent a cross section of the community and that she have a chance to meet with the working class as well as the affluent. "Whatever you do," she asked of one clubwoman who was arranging a dinner for her, "I beg that you will not make this a fashionable or exclusive affair. . . . Above all else, I want to have the poor people, those who have little influence or power to right conditions for themselves, feel that I am their friend, and am thinking of them at least as much as of any class in the community." The labor unions, she pointed out, were doing "some splendid work in the lines of health and scientific philanthropy," and she hoped that one or two of their leaders would also be invited. [13]

After Crane submitted her written reports, she usually had the pleasure of seeing them published by the sponsoring organization. [14] But her greatest reward, she claimed, was in seeing her surveys bring real improvements to city housekeeping all across America. From Iowa to New York and from Minnesota to Florida, almshouses, schools, and hospitals were replaced or renovated to meet recommended standards as a result of her visits. Cities adopted new methods of road repair, paving, and lighting, and more than twenty communities organized Civic Improvement Leagues to initiate saving collection and home nursing programs like Kalamazoo's. Nashville, Tennessee, formed an Anti-Smoke League. Deluth, Minnesota, removed a cluster of cesspools that had been polluting its water. The people in Saginaw, Michigan, started testing their street wells routinely and replacing broken or rusted pipes. Even Kalamazoo eventually changed its method of cleaning the streets. Most important of all, Crane wrote in her memoirs, beyond the physical progress, a body of legislation was passed at the local and national levels to see that the cities would be safer places to live in the future. [15]

Though Crane often told her promoters that she was really "a home woman" first and foremost and just as frequently billed herself as a "civic engineer" or an attending physician to ailing cities, the title she valued the most, she said, was "minister to municipalities." For, no matter how useful or apt the personae of homemaker and social scientist, neither captured the deeper identity that she had gained through her ordination. [16] In talking with her biographers, Crane made much of the similarities between her career as a sanitationist and the church ministry that led into it. As a pastor, she reminded them, she had been called to countless homes and seen every kind of misfortune firsthand, and, as a preacher, she had spoken before large audiences who came voluntarily to be told what their failures were and how to improve. [17] She was still a pastor and preacher, she told the journalist Helen Bennett. She had merely changed her texts and, instead of recounting what happened to tribes of wanderers thousands of years before, had taken to preaching reform from the book of twentieth-century life.[18]

More than this, Crane's sense of remaining within a cohesive process of ministry was grounded in the belief that liberal religion and science went hand in hand and could help people only when taken together. Her very first Unitarian mentor, Oscar Clute, had emboldened her to befriend the much feared Darwinian dragon and harness her faith to it, and her later studies of social organization under C. R. Henderson—along with her reading of Albion Small and George R. Vincent—reinforced her belief that "sociology must be essentially Christian."[19] In short, Crane believed that her down-to-earth faith was bound to be sociological and that using science to stimulate ethics and urban reforms was the way to teach liberal religion.[20] Continuing to denounce the church for excluding its women, Crane never forgot that she had lost the option of parish ministry and, when it came down to it, had turned to municipal housekeeping by default. But, while she resented not having more choice, the pain was eased by her sense that both callings were part of a single, unified ministry, one that embraced as equal prophets the scientist, teacher, statesman, and preacher, all of whom tried to help people achieve an ideal society.

Chapter Sixteen

CRUSADING FOR SUFFRAGE

*Think of it, three women ordained in two days—Surely WE are coming
to the front—and to-night I am to give a lecture on Equal Suffrage.*
—Rev. Helen G. Putnam to Jenkin Lloyd Jones (1889)

I

Yet another arena to which the clergy's sisterhood carried their
banner was politics. Indeed, as their champion Julia Ward Howe once put
it, crusading for suffrage became "a religious duty" for them and a "part of
their ministry."[1] Fighting for equal political voice and religious independence had gone hand in hand ever since women started demanding their
legacy from the Enlightenment. Margaret Fuller, Elizabeth Cady Stanton,
Louisa Alcott, Susan B. Anthony, Lucy Stone, and Howe—all Unitarians,
Universalists, or kindred free church iconoclasts—were forces behind the
early women's rights agitation because, as they saw it, the ideal of freedom
and dignity in religious faith implicated the ideal of universal political
rights. Like this older generation, the women who sought ordination after
the Civil War developed their feminist notions along with their theological
discontent.

The Murdock sisters, indignant that neither the church nor the state
were displaying the kind of enlightened egalitarianism that their parents
practiced at home, became the precocious defenders of Anna Dickinson
about the time they became the eager disciples of the radical Unitarian
Jones. Similarly, Mary Safford's revolt against women's second-class status
had been incited by listening to her smug orthodox preacher defend it at
church while at home her widowed mother, the shrewdest farm manager for
miles around, complained about having to pay the heaviest taxes in the
district without being given a say about how they were spent.[2] Such experi-

196

ences convinced the clergy's female contingent that their fundamental religious and civil liberties were "bound up together" and must be affirmed as part of the same universalist ideal.[3] Anna Howard Shaw had reached this conclusion and taken to "fighting the devil" through politics after the Methodist church refused to accept her credentials for ordination. She had never withdrawn from the battle, however, or ever conceded defeat, she insisted; she had simply packed up her ammunition and carried it to a different front. The issues had never changed, said Mary Safford, restating Shaw's point. The democratic ideal that gave women their right to preach in the church also gave them the right to vote in public elections.[4]

The Western frontier that provided Safford's group with their opening to the parish ministry also supplied a ready audience for their preachments on women's rights. Iowa had already had a long history of feminist agitation that always aroused great popular interest, if less than full legislative support. Large crowds had come out to hear women's advocate and dress reformer Amelia Jenks Bloomer, who started her first lecture tours in the state after moving from New York to Council Bluffs in 1855. In the late 1860s, feminist Anna Dickinson offset the losses incurred when the lecture halls booked Clara Barton or Ralph Waldo Emerson.[5] Not long afterward, in 1872, the first defeat of the suffrage bill in the Iowa legislature started young Carrie Lane (later Chapman Catt) of Charles City on her way in a career of feminist advocacy that carried her all the way to the presidency of the national suffrage movement.

The ministers added their voices to these as soon as they started to lead congregations. The 1870s found Augusta Chapin and Olympia Brown in Wisconsin and Iowa preaching enlightened religion from Universalist pulpits on Sundays and riding the women's rights circuits during the week.[6] Once the Unitarian sisters also gained access to pulpit ministry, the female clergy came to be seen as a major franchise force on the frontier, and there was hardly a month when the *Woman's Standard,* the Iowa franchise paper, did not report one or another of them out evangelizing for suffrage. In addition to mounting the platforms and lending the cause their clerical aura, the ordained women helped lay leaders reach thoughtful audiences by extending their pulpits to them. Rowena Morse later recalled how she was awakened to the women's crusade when the local Unitarian ministers, Ida Hultin and Marion Murdock, brought advocates like Carrie Chapman Catt to the church to proselytize.[7] Up in South Dakota, it was the veteran Wilkes who drummed up a crowd that rescued a nearly disastrous visit by Susan B. Anthony after she appeared in Sioux Falls quite suddenly one cold November day without letting anyone know in advance that she was coming to speak.[8]

As directors of active church programs, the ministers also had valuable organizational talents to offer the local suffrage interests. Indeed, it was here, where the common desire for equal rights took priority, that the bitter sectarianism that had earlier kept many women apart gave way, allowing the nontrinitarians to enter a mainstream of female community and be accepted as sympathetic leaders. As Elizabeth Padgham wrote later about her experiences in Perry, Iowa, once a Unitarian minister joined the local suffrage work, the orthodox women who had shunned her as a heretic before were likely to change their minds, decide that she "did have religion" after all, and then turn to her for direction.[9] Padgham, Hultin, Jenney, Wilkes, Collson, Murdock, and Tupper were all asked to serve as the presidents of their local suffrage associations. Safford and Gordon went out and started the Political Equality clubs in Sioux City and Des Moines; and Woolley, using the apparatus of the Chicago Woman's Club, helped set up the suffrage league in her city.[10]

Meanwhile, the liberal ministers were working within their own congregations to cultivate the common ground for coalitions with sisters of other faiths. Their commitment to raising the level of feminist consciousness was turning the social clubs from their accustomed study of literature and the arts to suffrage and women's rights and replacing programs on "Home Manners and Conversation" with suffrage teas and papers on how the vote would affect family life. Like the radical Free Religionist clubs that displaced suffrage clubs in the East in the 1870s, the church groups that the Western ministers steered toward suffrage in the 1880s and 1890s became places where women learned to coordinate their political and religious concerns.[11] As the forces behind ecumenically-spirited women's rights groups and the stewards of churches whose heresies made them the easiest places to plot strategy, the clergywomen were soon gaining wider visibility as delegates and speakers at suffrage conventions. Program organizers were eager to have them reinforce the older "assisting ministers," Phebe Hanaford, Ada C. Bowles, and Antoinette Brown Blackwell, who, in offering opening prayers and benedictions and preaching the suffrage sermons, witnessed to their sex's fitness for roles that men sought to keep for themselves.

By 1886, the suffrage tacticians, having moved well beyond the narrower framework of prewar polemics, were ready to fight with the full array of available weaponry. In the first edition of Iowa's main suffrage paper, the

Woman's Standard editor, Mary Jane Coggeshall—a member of Hultin's church who had used her Des Moines Unitarian operatives to build a state suffrage network—promised that her propaganda would draw on "the Home, Hearth, Purity, Culture, Temperance, Education," and woman's right to the franchise.[12] In the interest of reaching all true believers, the paper gave fundamentalists as well as liberal church women regular columns from which to argue the case for suffrage from their respective religious viewpoints. This postwar generation of franchise crusaders still made some use of the "natural right" and "common humanity" issues that had been the stock-in-trade of the earlier suffragists. Postbellum campaigners, and certainly clergy whose churches had their roots in Enlightenment precepts, still stressed that, since women were human beings before they were anything else, they had the same right as their male counterparts to consent to the laws that governed them. It was this essential entitlement, said Rev. Anna Norris, that mandated equal voice for both sexes and must "overshadow all other questions."[13]

At the same time, however, these franchise evangelists tended much more to invoke the arguments of expediency that explained how access to the ballot would help produce the concrete equality that was woman's natural right. Adjusting their pitch and emphasis to gain the most favorable hearing, they described what the vote would do for women and what voting women would do for humanity. Eleanor Gordon's paper "Just Like a Woman" took the first tack. It stressed that, so long as wifehood and motherhood were the circumference and center of female experience, women could have "no civic ideals, no wide outlook on problems of human destiny and human character" outside the home. Only when women were given the chance to take part in the world's affairs, said Gordon, could they overcome the effects of their social confinement. If nothing else, equal suffrage would help to reduce the number of flighty, hysterical women and bring in a higher cut of mothers with actual qualifications for teaching their children the meaning of citizenship and intellectual rigor.[14]

Ideally, of course, the vote would accomplish much more. Its impact would become apparent in the improvement in all domestic relations. As women would no longer occupy a position of servitude, they could finally interact with their husbands and brothers and sons as equals, fulfilling the gospel's prophesy that in God there was "neither bond nor free."[15] Then, too, as Hultin remarked, though the home was supposed to be woman's sphere, the truth was that many married women had "no homes for spheres or anything else" because their husbands were "worthless" and never around when they were needed, and failing to provide for their families, forced their wives into sweatshops or prostitution. If but given the power of the ballot, woman would "lift herself, her child, and her brother to a higher level of civilization."[16]

The suffrage crusaders spoke also of how women, with their experience in domesticity, were the best qualified to solve problems affecting the family outside the home. One of the Iowa Suffrage Association's most widely distributed tracts was Jane Addams's essay about city government being essentially large-scale "housekeeping" that was badly managed because the traditional housekeepers were not consulted.[17] Women needed the ballot, said Safford, who thought of church governance in the same way, because civic housekeeping needed the practical knowledge of the practiced housekeeper as much as it did the businessman's expertise. The influence of enfranchised women would make a healthier home of the larger society by bringing its male and female resources into a balanced relationship.[18]

Once empowered to be public homemakers, women would first of all wipe out the enemy ground, the saloon, and put an end to its breeding of drunkenness, gambling, prostitution, and other moral corruption that weakened the family and home and, by extension, the whole social fabric. The ordained sisters' pronouncements on this particular issue were well rehearsed, as the opposition to liquor had always been one of their pulpit staples. Religious liberals had marched at the head of the temperance crusades from the start. They took great pride in having established the country's first antiliquor societies in New England and in having made abstinence part of their covenants when they colonized on the frontier.[19] Given this strong tradition, which had prompted Safford and Gordon to send off for Unitarian Temperance Society tracts when they first came to Humboldt, it could not have been more ironic that these two were refused membership in the local Women's Christian Temperence Union because they were not trinitarians.[20] It was this tradition that also inspired the eighteen-year-old Carrie Bartlett to make her first public address a reasoned appeal for temperance.[21] Not that the sisterhood's advocacy of temperance derived only, or even primarily, from its history in their denomination. Right in their own immediate circle, the alcoholism of the Wilkes's son Paul was a shared grief that shook them all, and such direct knowledge of drinking's tragic costs were incentive enough to wipe out the liquor trade by getting women the vote.[22]

Although the brewery interests were seen as chief adversaries of suffrage and played a despicable role in defeating the franchise in Iowa, the suffragists tried not to let the campaign be reduced to "a dry and wet job," choosing instead to stress the full spectrum of benefits that would follow if women could vote. The importance of having pure water and food, good schools, sanitation, and "city house cleaning," the same problems women had learned how to tackle on a lesser scale in their households, were presented as compelling arguments for bringing them into the political process. To these they added the need to keep peace in a world where men made war, insisting that far fewer lives would be sacrificed senselessly if the women, who had "the hardest time of every war to bear," were consulted about it beforehand. In short, said Woolley, it was time "to enlarge the offices of the home" and to run society as one would run a healthy and stable family, not as a competition for power, but as a cooperative partnership between men and women who cared for each other.[23]

II

The clergywomen's involvement in the suffrage crusade intensified markedly after the turn of the century, when they started to move from local and regional leadership to the top state positions that carried them onto the national stage. It was no coincidence that this transition took place at the same time the women were losing their anchorage in the liberal ministry. Forced to concede that their fight for a place in the pulpits was getting them nowhere, they turned, much as Shaw had changed her approach, from direct confrontation with the church's power base to the secular political front as an alternative "line of march towards the goal of true democracy." Their goal was "suffrage at large," a free and equal vote in all fields. The open pulpit was only one "form and symbol" of women's franchise. The ballot was another, and no less important.[24]

The sisterhood's sense that their struggles were of a piece, whether fought out for matters of church or state, was reinforced by the fact that on both fronts they found themselves facing the same adversaries. Once again, they were met by familiar voices of the religiously orthodox, who invoked the authority of Genesis and St. Paul to deny woman's right to vote, as they did woman's right to preach. Again, among the antis, they ran up against the same religious liberals who, while ready enough to acknowledge the Bible's fallibility, found in the theory of evolution grounds for barring women from public life: they were too emotional to understand the workings of government, too vulnerable to escape the contamination of political power, and too weak to uphold authority and promote the nation's virility.[25]

Taking the common position that suffrage would "never do any good" even where "woman's influence" was "supposed to be strongest," one religiously liberal anti who wrote to the *Unitarian Advance* said that he was repulsed by the thought of women getting pulled into "ward politics, wire pulling, and bribe-taking," as they were bound to be. Why destroy their refined and superior ways for nothing, he asked angrily. Other readers, observing "its close relation to socialism and feminism," predicted that suffrage would lead to the downfall of the home and society. Their fear, they said, was that too many crude and ignorant people were voting already and that, as there was no way to sift the wheat from the chaff, there would just be that many more to weaken the process if women were also brought in.[26]

The fact that in this political fight, as in their denominational struggle, the battle lines were clearly drawn between the East and the West reinforced the sisterhood's feeling of déjà vu. Jenkin Lloyd Jones, representing the freer spirit in the heartlands and unsurpassed in his feminist zeal and stamina, worked for the cause for so many years that by the time he reached his seventies, he was billing himself as "America's aboriginal suffragist."[27] In the West, it was hard to find a religious liberal, and harder still a minister, who did not support the women's fight for the vote. In the East, on the other hand, there was the same intense opposition to women's involvement in politics as there had been to their intrusion in matters of church administration. Many born and bred Unitarians on the Atlantic seaboard and in New England still harbored their parents' dislike of passionate and aggressive crusading along with any radical break from established social convention. For years, they had nodded approvingly as their ministers preached that the women's movement was folly, and they applauded vigorously when clergy and lay leaders started to say so before wider audiences. These liberal parishioners rushed to congratulate those Unitarian brothers—including Charles Eliot of Harvard College—whose names appeared in the *Boston Herald* on Valentine's Day, 1885, endorsing a full-page advertisement placed by the Anti-Suffrage Association of Massachusetts as one of its first public protests.[28] Since AUA president Samuel Eliot's views were, by his own admission, almost always "identical" with those of his father Charles, it was only to be expected that, in the climate created by his leadership at the turn of the century, the opposition to equal suffrage among self-described "old-fashioned" Unitarians would become stronger and less inhibited than ever.[29]

While it was disappointing enough for the feminist clergy to find themselves pitted against their own denominational kin, it was even more painful to find that their stiffest opposition was coming from liberals whose sex should have made them the most sympathetic. Not that this was a new disappointment for them. More than one of the women ministers looking back on their parish careers remembered with sadness how often the strongest resistance to their position of leadership had come from the women in the pews and not from the men who were sitting beside them. The problem, they all agreed, was usually more complex than it first appeared and certainly had a number of possible causes. The most obvious was that the women who were likeliest to support a female minister and convert others had gradually left the church. Disaffected by the AUA's "masculine" outlook, they had traded in their denominational interests for secular movements in which they received more respect and therefore more satisfaction.[30]

Yet, in their suffrage experience, the ministers found—primarily when they went East—that not even all women who warmly embraced them as pastors were able to cross the line of convention when it came to the matter of woman's vote. For many, the issue was simply more threatening to the concepts they had of themselves and of the hallowed traditions of the family's roles and relationships. Elizabeth Padgham recalled in her memoirs how a delegation of women from her church in Rutherford, New Jersey, had come to her all up in arms when they heard that she planned to march in the first big suffrage parade in New York. They told her that she would disgrace the church and that their husbands agreed, and Padgham began to fear that they would be asking for her resignation. Not about to back down, she replied that the people would someday be proud to know that their minister had been broad and courageous enough to support women's rights, and she went on and marched. Nothing more was ever said of the matter, but it was the sort of experience that made a minister wonder how well she was teaching the principles of her faith and despair that those who should be most unified were yet so deeply divided.[31]

There was no better illustration of this collision of values among liberal churchwomen than the emergence of Kate Gannett Wells as a leader of the antisuffrage forces in Massachusetts. A prominent social philanthropist who came from a distinguished Unitarian family, Wells's opposition to suffrage contrasted ironically with the profranchise stance of her brother, Jenkins Lloyd Jones's close friend William Channing Gannett, and even more with the value she placed on women's education and female coalitions as ways of increasing their influence in society. But from growing up watching her widowed father preside as minister of a large conservative congregation she had absorbed the conventional concepts of female benevolence and womanhood—and all the attendant fears about the perils of woman's involvement in politics. Convinced that the vote would corrupt her sex and destroy their capacity for uplift and moral purification, Wells enlisted in the resistance against the suffrage petition when it was brought before the Massachusetts legislature in 1884 and was instrumental in forming the state's Anti–Woman Suffrage Association. Thanks to Wells and other fiery leaders like her, the Western women were met by a steady opposition of Eastern church sisters until the very end of the fight for the vote. Even after the strength of sentiment outside New England had forced the AUA to pass a prosuffrage resolution in 1911, just months after Wells's death, angry sisters insisted that the statement did not represent the position of most women in the liberal church.[32]

Privately, the clergywomen spoke with contempt of the habits and attitudes that were responsible for their not getting a rush of broad-based support from their sisters. They complained that most women whose family incomes allowed it got caught up in empty externals, thought only of dressing well and looking good, and remained indifferent to issues that mattered. Then, too, from the pastors' perspective, the suffrage campaign showed more clearly than anything else how entrapped females were by the notion that theirs was intended to be "a man's world." This was all too apparent to those who, like Gordon and Crane, worked a good deal as lobbyists and got to know how the legislative community functioned behind the scenes. They found it almost impossible to get congressional wives to cooperate, so great was the fear that the husbands would be "boomed" if they rallied to the cause and their speeches were circulated by rivals. Crane, for one, learned that, "aside from the differences in opinion" on suffrage, a "personal element in the Congressional set" prevented "any *real* work from them." They would help out "on strictly social lines, and on some kinds of philanthropic ones, but not in fundamentals," as they were "too easily sidetracked and tangled up in the meshes of social and political jealousies."[33] They had little idea of what the campaign was really about or how much was at stake for *them*. The ordained women thus learned that the battle lines in the fight for political suffrage were to be determined not by gender but by point of view. The quarrel, said Gordon, in later years, "was simply between men and women who believed in democracy opposed by those men and women who did not."[34]

The clergy, of course, were happiest when their struggle was seen not as combat at all but instead as an effort to heal and harmonize a badly fractured society. They had always hoped to work out their differences in a realm suspended somewhere above mundane politics where discord might be resolved through a higher process of integration. They had tended to think of suffrage itself as being less a political question than a social issue involving the reformation of society. Indeed, as late as 1898, Gordon, like Carrie Catt, was still urging Iowa suffragists to follow "the teaching of evolution" and practice "patience and still more patience" as progress slowly unfolded.[35] However, the preachers themselves grew weary of waiting for concrete results, and by the time they had moved to the front lines a few years later, their stance was a much more aggressive one that showed a new willingness to recognize and exploit real political sources of power.

Certainly, in 1907, when Gordon took on the presidency of the Equal Suffrage Association in Iowa, franchise workers had justification for being impatient and angry. While many had thought that the state, with its liberalized marriage and property laws, would be one of the first to grant women full voting rights, the legislation, proposed for the first time in 1871, was not passed until 1921, after the Nineteenth Amendment preempted it. As Catt remarked when it was finally over, the long campaign in her native state was most "remarkable for what it failed to achieve."[36] This failure was due to the machinations of the liquor trade and big business and a consequent loss of focus on the part of the prosuffrage forces.

Seeing this, Gordon set out to turn the campaign around by insisting that it concentrate on the single issue of the vote and abandon all other crusades, which only played into the hands of the antis. In language that tested a new political militancy, she chided the troops for not understanding that they were involved in a struggle for power and were not just debating about ideals. As long as women did not have the vote and the liquor traffic did, morality was going to lose to big business. However narrow and unkind it sounded, said Gordon, the women would have to stop seeing themselves as all-round philanthropists and start thinking like politicians. Their time-honored tactics of speaking to civic groups, leaving tracts in public libraries, setting up clever displays in store windows, and giving out fans at the fairs was obviously not enough. The "forts of resistance," said Gordon, had not fallen and never would when bombarded "with rose leaves." Iowa women would have to become more aggressive.[37]

Gordon's chance to test her troops' readiness for a bolder approach came in the fall of 1908 when the Iowa Equal Suffrage Association held its yearly convention in Boone. Inspired by the suffragettes' recent demonstrations in England and the silent procession in New York City the winter before, Gordon had hit on the notion of staging a full-fledged parade with music and banners, the first of its kind in the country as far as anyone knew. There was not much enthusiasm for the idea among the delegates, who were accustomed to working for suffrage by handing out pamphlets and putting up posters and felt that a parade and mass meeting would be much too militant. Such public demonstrations conjured up images of their English counterparts, whose unladylike confrontations with the police had led to arrests and brutal imprisonment. Gordon and her committee, however, went ahead with their plans to assemble at the Universalist church and march to the center of town.

The committee had got National American Woman Suffrage Association president Anna Shaw and two English suffragettes who were studying at Bryn Mawr to come for the event, and they all rode up front in an open top automobile just behind the tiny Boone band. Then followed the delegates, no more than thirty of them altogether, who marched in twos and spread themselves out to maximize the effect. Braving strong winds that were blowing up great clouds of dust, they waved flags and wrestled their banners so people could make out their messages. Timed to arrive at the downtown hub right at noon, when the offices, schools, and stores were emptying for the lunch hour, the strange procession brought all traffic to a standstill. The car was whirled into the center of the throng, and Shaw and the suffragettes mounted the front seat and spoke for about fifteen minutes. The crowd cheered and joined the delegates in chanting campaign slogans. Then the exhilarated marchers got back in formation and "with dignity," Gordon wrote later, retraced their steps to the church, sat down for a luncheon, and celebrated their greatest triumph ever.[38]

The Boone parade, applauded locally and written up by the press nation-wide, emboldened the Iowa women to start fighting more aggressively. Several weeks later, when the opposition in Des Moines tried to keep women from using their limited franchise in city elections by putting the ballot boxes in hard-to-reach places, Gordon's forces made news again by dismantling obstacle courses and taking the prize. In one precinct, where the box was in a woodshed behind a huge pile of coal, the women came back with shovels, tucked up their skirts, and cleared out a path to get through; and when they discovered a whisky bottle lying in the shed by the box, confirming suspicions that liquor interests were back of the dirty tricks, they had a good time going out in the alley and smashing it.[39]

The experience that did most to convert Gordon to the hardball tech-niques of this "practical politics" was the ugly defeat of the suffrage amend-ment in 1909, when state senators killed the bill in "the meanest way possible," by striking out the enabling clause that was needed to give it its force. Outraged at the insulting and flippant way that their interests had been thrown aside, hundreds of women assembled the following day at the Baptist church in Des Moines for what was known thereafter as "the Indignation Meeting." Quick to channel the angry mood and make it "politically effective," Gordon declared that Iowa women would spare themselves further humiliation by changing their tactics radically. No longer would they waste their energy circulating petitions. Henceforth they would fight their campaigns in the offices of legislative incumbents and hopefuls and work to defeat those not willing to make public statements pledging support of the franchise. "Direct influence" would be the keyword in the future, Gordon promised.[40]

Determined to beat the antis at their own game, the members of the Des Moines Political Equality Club committed themselves to adopting "obstruction methods" of their own and began openly to defend the actions of their militant sisters abroad. "As in England, so in Iowa!" was the new rally cry. The *Woman's Standard* carried the message that the women of the Midwest would have to stop the government from doing its work as usual if they wanted the right to live decent, healthful, and fully productive lives. Nothing could be more important, and, if it could not be had without "a fight or fuss, then fight and fuss must come." Thirty years, the span of a lifetime, was long enough to establish that "rosewater politics" were not enough. Like the New York Equality League that Harriet Stanton Blatch had recently founded, Gordon's organization began to experiment with other "militant" tactics like holding open-air rallies and noontime meetings at factories, using posters and dodgers, and stationing young women as sandwich girls on downtown street corners, all in daring "imitation of the English suffragettes."[41]

Feeling their way unsteadily, Iowa suffragists spent a good deal of time alternately backing off from their new confrontational style and stoutly defending it. While assuring alarmists who charged them of flirting with criminality that they were not really out to "break windows, or knock men down, or storm the legislature," they wanted it known that they were still ready to take "aggressive action" and "become insurgent if need be to secure what ought to be theirs." Iowa's lawmakers, after all, "had been clubbing women" for years, and, since the futility of peaceable tactics was now clear to everyone, they were perfectly justified in resorting to other means, just as the men had been doing throughout history. Prominent feminists from out of state were called in to help fan this fire of militancy. Anna Shaw came frequently to urge the troops to forget about being so ladylike, to make themselves more conspicuous by staging noisy demonstrations so that the men would start paying attention to what they said. The English suffragette Emeline Pankhurst, in America on a speaking tour in the fall of 1909, also spent some time in Des Moines to encourage her sisters to start hounding lawmakers and show more force, even if this meant they might be arrested.[42]

In addition, from 1908 to 1910, Gordon's organization had a suffragette-in-residence to urge the workers on, thanks to a pulpit exchange between Mary Safford and Gertrude von Petzhold of Leicester, England. The first woman to have become a liberal minister in her adopted country, the Prussian-born Petzhold had been a cause célèbre in the women's movement in England even before becoming identified with the fight for political suffrage. She was a striking woman in her early thirties, with a thick German accent that added to her extremely dramatic effect and a wit that allowed her to scold without antagonizing her audience. Altogether, she was an engaging presence in the Unitarian pulpit and much in demand as a speaker out in the community.[43] The infusion of this fighting spirit from England, however, was not enough, or at least not enough of the right thing, to get the Iowa effort out of the doldrums.

If anything, Petzhold's stint in Des Moines set the cause back among many weary Unitarians, whose congregation had given the crusade its hard-core supporters and leadership from the start. Having already had four women ministers—Hultin, Safford, Jenney, and Gordon—the congregation was perfectly used to its pastors taking strong suffrage stands, but it was also accustomed to having them put the parish needs first. In Petzhold's case, her ties to the people were slight and her interest in politics all consuming, and, as the church work was left unattended and fell into disarray, the members began to complain that she was not earning her $150 a month. Of course, the church's historians brightened up the record as best they could, but Adele Fuchs's letters to Safford gave candid accounts of what it was actually like. By 1910, the visiting minister was so absorbed in writing a book that she rarely attended meetings, or made parish calls, or kept office hours. "The church suffers through lack of planning and management," Fuchs grumbled. With "nothing to hold the people together," all they could do was try to get through the year as best they could.[44] As an illustration not only of how easily a woman minister could extend her pulpit concerns to political activism but also of the perils of doing so while entrusted with running a church, the Petzhold experience made the Des

Moines people much more cautious about calling pastors with such absorbing political convictions.

Safford herself returned to her church only long enough to set things aright and then stepped down from the pulpit to follow her own growing passion for politics. Gordon was ready to make way for Safford at the head of the Iowa Equal Suffrage Association, having found her political foray invaluable as an education but still feeling called most strongly to the ministry of the church and eager to lead another household of faith.[45] It thus fell to Safford to try to revive the state's gasping suffrage crusade, and this she accomplished as skillfully as she had saved failing church congregations. The campaign launched under her leadership carried the bill through both houses in 1913, clearing the way for a referendum and ending a forty-year stretch of defeats. Safford also agreed to help orchestrate most of the follow-up campaigns in Iowa, though, after she moved to Florida and discovered that it had no movement at all, she devoted most of her energy to starting an organization there and serving as its president until 1918.[46]

Except for Helen Putnam, all these ministers who had crusaded for suffrage lived long enough to reach their destination or at least to see it assured in the very near distance. Yet their satisfaction in gaining the vote was tempered by their understanding that this legislation alone would not be enough to improve women's lives. From the start, they had viewed the political franchise as an essential instrument for "breaking into the human race," as Marie Jenney Howe described it, but they had no illusions about its being the comprehensive equality that would allow females to be their "whole, big, human selves."[47] Moreover, they knew that the real measure of their advancement was going to be how much society's views were changed since this was what would decide how much women were going to get with their votes. As Celia Woolley had written with great discernment in 1911, it made little difference if men like Teddy Roosevelt came out for suffrage since in the same breath they reminded their wives that their place was still in the home being mothers and maids, and the public elected men like these to be their national leaders![48] There was no better illustration of Woolley's point than the fact that Samuel Eliot's votes against suffrage had been overruled in both state and AUA referenda, and yet the majority of his compatriots still shared his attitude toward woman's public roles.

It came as no surprise to the feminist pastors that so many seemed to believe that the battle had been won when in truth only one outpost had been taken. Having found in the course of campaigning that many supporters, women as well as men, had never taken the movement seriously, the ministers' disillusionment had come well in advance of the suffrage "victory." Gordon remembered a state legislator telling her to her face that he would be glad to support her bill since it would merely "amuse the women and make no difference to the men." Now that they were starting to see that the women had really meant business, said Gordon in 1921, the men who gave them the vote were determined that they would get nothing more. As far as she could tell, the conviction that this was a man's world was just as pervasive as it had ever been.[49]

Even so, the suffrage effort repaid the loyalty of these crusaders. Exiled from their vocation in the church and scattered across the country, they found in the movement a surrogate network that affirmed their ideals and held them together. The suffrage conventions and lecture circuit replaced the ministerial meetings and pulpit exchanges that earlier kept their alliance intact and strong. The campaign for suffrage in California in 1910 reunited Wilkes, Murdock, and Buck, as the campaigns in Michigan, Iowa, and Illinois had brought others back together. The big demonstration that NAWSA staged in the late spring of 1916 to coincide with the Republican National Convention in Chicago saw Woolley, Fuchs, and Safford going about arm in arm to the speeches and caucuses, sitting together with Mrs. Catt at a luncheon for pioneer workers, and finally joining the rest of the delegates for a climactic parade, despite a cold wind and hard rain that eventually proved to be too much for Safford. Fuchs's journal account of how she stepped in for her friend and carried the Iowa banner undaunted "through the wind and storm and rain with no umbrella," and how she felt doubly proud to be marching for Safford as well as herself, shows poignantly how these experiences strengthened the sisterhood's solidarity.[50]

The enduring friendship between Anna Howard Shaw and Caroline Bartlett Crane was yet another testimonial to the suffrage crusade's binding force and its help to sister refugees from the parish ministry. Born of their shared aspirations and disillusionment in the church, and sustained by mutual sympathy through the trials germane to suffrage leadership, this relationship between Crane and Shaw continued for thirty years. Crane undoubtedly valued this well-placed connection but also appears to have felt a strong daughterly love and respect for the older woman, whom many others found difficult to work with and abandoned. It also meant a great deal to Shaw to have this long-term relationship in which she could let out her "whimpers and growls" and be assured comfort and reinforcement. When Anna Shaw died in 1919, she left her doctoral robe and the retirement watch that NAWSA had given her to her appointed disciple, and Crane, for her part, had the difficult honor of saying the benediction for Shaw at the NAWSA victory celebration in 1920.[51]

Yet, beyond preserving their network of relationships, the suffrage crusade provided the sisterhood with an affirming community that perpetuated their sense of "active ministry." Shunned by the Unitarian ministers' fellowship, among suffragists they were not only highly respected as females but courted as leaders and as women of the cloth and asked to represent their chosen profession. As in settlement work and public housekeeping, so in the fight for the vote the secular struggle never replaced but rather provided a new format for the women's religious commitment to symmetry, wholeness, and greater power for good in society. Even Marie Jenney Howe, who had moved the farthest away from religious structures, gave friends the distinct impression that she had been carried into her suffrage activity by the same "religious instinct which led her first to the Church."[52] The irony was that, as an alternative vehicle for their evangel, the crusade for suffrage sustained the sisterhood's practice of ministry in a way that the Nineteenth Amendment itself never did after finally being made law.

Chapter Seventeen

KEEPING THE PEACE

But let the blissful period haste,
When, hushed the canon's roar,
The sword shall cease mankind to waste,
And war shall be no more.
—Mary A. Livermore

I

Unlike the long fight for suffrage, which strengthened the sister-hood's ties to each other, the moral dilemma attached to the war that erupted in 1914 produced some divisions so great that they threatened to damage the network irreparably. The clergywomen had no disagreement, of course, about the importance of peace or their duty to help to preserve and defend it. Whether viewing themselves as the mothers of congregations or "Mothers of Civilization," all had been steadfast in their belief that more could be gained through cooperation than combat and that as ordained women, they had a rare chance to help promote harmony in the world. The difficulties among them arose when it came to choosing the method. Nei-ther Christianity's diverse responses to combat historically nor their liberal church's positions on war in the past provided the ministers with a simple, unassailable guide when the world went to war in Europe. While their early Unitarian and Universalist forebears had been strong peace advocates who preached the message of inclusive love and started the country's first peace periodicals and societies, their pacifism had had its limits. Unlike the Mennonites, Quakers, and Brethren, who refused to take arms under any conditions on the grounds that Jesus' message precluded it, the liberals chose peace only up to a point, drawing the line when it came to a threat to their country and all that it stood for. During the Civil War, most Unitarians and Universalists had been zealous crusaders, who saw themselves in a fight for the noble cause of abolition. Even the more ambivalent felt duty bound to help win this "just war" for the Union, viewing it as the necessary means of arresting and punishing evil and reinstating the good.[1]

In forming their own attitudes toward armed combat, the Western Conference's clergywomen were moved no less than their brothers by a fierce devotion to country that was deeply enmeshed in ancestral pride. Many could trace their family lines back to the Revolution. Most also carried through life stark impressions of the Civil War's trauma and of their families' material deprivations, grief, and fear for their kin and the nation. Gordon never forgot the homemade flag that her family had hung proudly from an upper window or the tears in her mother's eyes when the news came that Fort Sumter had been fired on. Almost seventy years afterward, she could still feel the dread that filled her when she heard that the country would be destroyed and later her family's unspeakable joy when, with her father still off in the South, they received word of Lee's surrender. Gordon wondered whether the flag and martial music could ever arouse the same feelings in men and women who were born after 1860, too late to have learned for themselves what "a just war" really meant.[2]

Unwilling to forget their debt to those who had fought to defend their rights as Americans, these women had always put patriotism close to the heart of their ministries. Safford and Gordon were proud to say in their Sioux City parish annual that their church "sought in every way . . . to awaken and renew the love of country." Patriotic services were among the highlights of the church year, with memorials for the Civil War's fallen heroes in the spring, parish picnics with prayers, speeches, and anthems on the Fourth of July, and Thanksgiving sermons that celebrated not only the blessings of their great land of liberty but also "the noble warriors" who had died defending it.[3] Safford's own "First Commandment," which she liked to recite at these times, gave the charge, "Love thy country, which has redeemed thee from tyranny and bondage." The wars that might follow from this would be "just wars" that taught people valuable lessons in sacrifice, self-reliance, and faithfulness to high ideals.[4]

While the pastors had always reminded their people that war was at best a necessary evil that should never be courted or glorified, only after public enthusiasm for doing so rose alarmingly did this became their pulpits' major emphasis. When expansionist appetites at the end of the century dragged the country into the Spanish-American War and later bloodied the Philippines, and when the British colonialists in South Africa worked their own horrors on the Boers, the pulpit sisterhood quickly locked step with the ecumenical movement to stop the gun-running imperialism and launch a new era of peace. Even before Samuel Eliot asked Unitarian clergy in 1904 to help the international peace effort, the sisterhood were airing the issues and trying to muster support. The previous year, Margaret Olmstead, summing up what her group had been preaching, wrote in *Old and New* that the recent "wars, just and unjust, sanctioned by Christian nations" showed a shameful "thirst for cheap glory," aggression, and greed that would not go away unless those who claimed to be Christians followed Jesus' teachings of love. America, Gordon suggested sardonically, would be much better equipped for world leadership if it would put as much effort into restoring its spiritual fiber as it did into building a superior force of brute manhood.[5]

After Germany's declaration of war in August 1914 broke up the first World Peace Congress and dashed all hopes of averting hostilities, most of America's clergy, liberal and orthodox, accepted President Wilson's position of sober disengagement. By 1915, however, the public's tolerance for neutrality was dissolving rapidly, and, as the people's outrage and condemnation started to churn, the pulpits began to close ranks with those who wanted to ready the country for combat. The Conference Committee on National Preparedness found a vigorous response when it called on American preachers to use their Thanksgiving Day sermons to build support for a righteous crusade. Only four of the women who had been connected with Safford's circuit a dozen years earlier—Gordon, Hultin, Morse Mann, and Padgham—still had congregations to preach to, but there were other ways of assisting the cause, and all but a few made the most of them.

The most visible on the national level was Caroline Bartlett Crane, whose knowledge of city support systems, sense of diplomacy, and platform charisma brought her numerous opportunities to contribute. In 1914, she was asked to go to the ruined cities of Belgium to aid in their reconstruction and then attend the peace conference in The Hague. In November of that year, Henry Ford telegrammed an appeal that she join his peace party of a hundred "representative Americans" who were going to sail to Stockholm in hopes of negotiating a just settlement. Uneasy about the personal risk of being so close to the fighting abroad, Crane excused herself from all such service and concentrated instead on redirecting the nation's woman power from suffrage and social work to stateside preparedness.[6]

Along with her deep love of country Crane brought to the war work a candid aversion to the smug chauvinism that was fast taking hold of her compatriots. Though proud enough of her native roots to have joined the

Daughters of the American Revolution or DAR, she had always appealed for a patriotism that was as alert to the dangers of corruption and weakness within as to the threats posed by forces outside.[7] With this understanding of patriotism, Crane joined the war effort thinking that she would be helping to keep America's house in order—which meant hardworking, honest, and praying for peace—while others were building its muscle. To this end, she served as chairman of Michigan's women's work, first for the State War Preparedness Board and later for the Council of National Defense, organizing the massive registration, training, and placement of 900,000 women for over a hundred different kinds of wartime occupations. She oversaw the state's enormous emergency programs for food production and marketing, conservation and thrift, child welfare, and news distribution, and coordinated these efforts with those of dozens of other state and federal agencies.[8]

For Mary Safford, as for Caroline Bartlett Crane, assisting the war effort did not replace as much as rephrase the kind of crusading that she had been doing since serving in parish ministry. More committed to suffrage than ever in 1914, Safford stood with the camp that insisted that women's rights and the nation's defense be treated as facets of a single struggle for freedom and democracy and not be split and prioritized. As Florida's representative to NAWSA's executive board, she was greatly relieved by her sisters' decision against deferring their special interests and letting up on pushing them forward even while, as loyal Americans, they were pledged to meeting their wartime obligations. As a matter of both principle and expediency, Safford unfailingly linked the two causes when asked to promote either one. "The ballot, the biscuit, and the bullet," she would say, were now "leagued together for national defense," and thoughtful men were beginning to see that women counted for more when staffing the Red Cross and tending the farms than when standing idly by on their "pseudo pedestals."[9] There could be little doubt of Safford's sincerity when she was one of Orlando's most active and charming patriots, one who helped lead the drive to sell Liberty Bonds, spoke at rallies and rode in parades, and even organized a women's reserve that she herself led in military drills to keep the sisters ready in case they were called to defend their families and homes.[10]

If this last show of patriotic fervor struck some people as out of character for a delicate, sixty-five-year-old retired woman minister, Captain Safford's identification with the cloth had the least to do with it. For, by 1917, the country's religious leadership was rallying to the war as a holy crusade against rampant autocracy. Once troops were actually sent overseas, the Federal Council of Churches, the National Catholic War Council, and the

Jewish Welfare Board started working closely with the armed forces to coordinate their services, and clergy sold war bonds, preached an aggressive patriotism, and enlisted as army chaplains and even as soldiers. Unitarians were among the most zealous in sounding the battle cry, as the *Christian Register,* justifying their fervor, assured them that Jesus himself would have rushed to take up the "bayonet and grenade and bomb and rifle [to] do the work of deadliness" had he been alive in 1918. It was clearly their duty as Christians, the *Register* swaggered, to vanquish a race that was "lusting to wrest away" their sacred freedoms.[11] Though most of the liberal clergy's rhetoric was more tempered, it was not uncommon for ministers to devote entire sermons to justifying the war on religious grounds, and the women with pulpits were just as quick as the men to enlist in this service. Rowena Morse Mann preached that Germany's use of force to gain world dominance was a "cardinal sin against the conscience of mankind" and that America must show its strength to help stamp it out.[12]

While not every minister had been eager for intervention or was comfortable preaching a gospel of violence, open dissent became increasingly difficult. The religious liberals, whose comradeship with the British Unitarians had undermined early attempts at nonpartisanship, were as quick as any to close off opposing points of view. When they met for their national conference in the fall of 1917 and the issue of the war effort came to the floor, the moderator, former president William H. Taft, had no trouble leading the hawks to an overwhelming victory over the handful of doves who dared speak for disengagement. John Haynes Holmes from New York, a leading Unitarian pacifist minister who had preached nine consecutive sermons on "Non-resistance" and published widely to urge "a ministry of reconciliation," was given the platform just long enough to state his well-known positions. Then Taft stepped up to deliver a scathing rebuttal to Holmes's "insidious document," and the vast majority of the delegates gave him a standing ovation. The sense of the body, as put forth by Taft in a resolution, placed Unitarians solidly in favor of fighting for freedom. The following year, the AUA silenced any remaining clergy who were not "earnest and outspoken" supporters of the war by moving to discontinue aid to their churches. Holmes's reply to this was to sever his ties to the Unitarians and form a new movement of community churches.[13]

The Holmes affair and the general muzzling of dissenters were doubtless disturbing to ordained women who regarded as sacred the right to freedom of speech, but more disturbing still was the fate of Jenkin Lloyd Jones, who was one of the very few ministers to continue to speak out for peace. The heartbreaking vilification of their closest brother compelled them to face as never before the inherent ethical problems of patriots. From his days as a young soldier who had enlisted to fight for his hero, Abraham Lincoln, Jones had carried the knowledge of war's real horror and depravity. As his thinking matured and assimilated the ideas of Darwin, he reached the conclusion that organized slaughter of human beings was an aberrant form of behavior, some remnant from a lower evolutionary stage that should have been shucked off but somehow was not. With the Spanish-American War, Jones emerged as one of the country's most outspoken critics of militarism, as broadcasted by the white-bordered flag that flew over his Abraham Lincoln Center. The material waste of war was bad enough, he raged, but immeasurably worse was "the moral cost—the murder of the innocent, the degradation, the inebriety, the gambling and sensuality" that followed the army wherever it went. Though others said almost nothing about these things in 1914, Jones vowed that he would never be part of their shameful "conspiracy of silence." [14]

Unlike Crane, Jones accepted the invitation from Ford to sail on the peace ship in 1914 and, when Ford had to leave, agreed to serve as the head of the mission. Because he was well anchored in a pulpit that had always been fiercely independent and drew its support from a left-of-center constituency, Jones was able to hold his appointment after the AUA took steps to purge its ranks of his kind, but the widespread condemnation by colleagues and banishment from once hospitable pulpits forced him into a lonely exile. Then, in the spring of 1918, the postmaster of Chicago began to hold up the mailings of Jones's *Unity,* which was the only religious journal besides the fledgling *New World* that was still providing a voice for the doves. Jones, who was laboring under a heart condition, spent his waning energies fighting to get the paper back in the mails. It was his last stand, for the strain and heartbreak soon overtook him, and in September he died believing that most of his friends had abandoned him. [15]

While Eleanor Gordon had never approved of Jones's insistence on disengagement, it had not been the first time that they had disagreed, and she had not lost her affection for him. As always, she had respected his courage and high-mindedness and felt that despite their differences they could still love each other as brother and sister. She was pained by the public abuse heaped on him and outraged by the government's censorship of *Unity.* But she had been slow to send him a sisterly word of encouragement when he most needed it, and it caused her great anguish after his death that she had let him down. As she told his widow, she had actually had a letter "partly written when the sad news came," but by then it was too late to let him know that she had not deserted him. [16]

Celia Woolley was one of the few liberal clergy whom Jones was able to count on to the end. Because she agreed with Jones's view of the war, as Gordon could not, she was able to back him up while assuring him of her abiding friendship. While other old friends closed their doors, she made sure that he knew hers was open for him and that he would always be able to find a receptive ear at the Douglass Center. "No war talk," she promised him gently, on a reminder that she was expecting him there, "you need not be afraid." [17] This sister's loyalty, Jones told her husband, meant all the more to him at a time when "so many 'friends' had turned their backs." [18]

Jones was not the only one in the sisterhood's clan to be hurt by the wartime hysteria. Another of its victims, this one silent in her suffering, was Adele Fuchs, whose German ancestry and ties to kin in the old country made her feel like an alien everywhere. In the diary to which she now turned more and more for an understanding confidant, she admitted to having lost faith in "this free land" to which her father had come as a young man expecting to find a better life for his family. "Now seventy years later I, the American child," she wrote bitterly, "feel conditions for the future intolerable." Wherever she went, she was bruised by a battering of "hatred for the 'Huns'" and a "maligning of everything German." [19] For a long time, it looked as if she would also be stripped of her livelihood by being forced out of her job teaching German in the Des Moines public schools.

The worst of it was that not even good friends who had comforted Fuchs in the past seemed able to give her much comfort now. If not altogether caught up in the madness themselves, they were too accustomed to it to appreciate its full effect on someone of German descent. Fuchs saw her own isolation and disillusionment mirrored in Gertrude von Petzhold, whom she looked up while visiting family in Germany in the fall of 1915. Since her pulpit exchange in Des Moines five years earlier, Petzhold had gone back to England only to be deported to her country of origin when the two powers went to war. "Poor woman, she is in rather a hard place," Fuchs remarked in a letter to Safford. "All her personal interests are in England, while her family interests are in Germany, so that at present she doesn't fit very well in either place." [20] That Fuchs might as easily have been writing about her own sense of displacement apparently never occurred to Safford, whose insensitivity opened a gulf that made their relationship, painful enough in the best of times, sheer torture in this period of war. Despite her obvious hatred of Germany, Safford still asked for the younger woman's affection, while Fuchs, her own feelings mixed, hardly knew how to answer when she could not speak openly without drawing the other woman's abuse. It was to the broad and discerning Gordon that Fuchs had to turn for solace when neighbors and coworkers questioned her loyalty, or when Safford, not ever thinking to spare her, had her over for dinner and then promptly got herself "finely worked up" on the "Huns," or, again, when it looked as if Fuchs's school board was going to follow the national trend of dropping German from the curriculum, jeopardizing her job and the pension that meant some future security.

Fuchs apparently waited until 1921 to speak to Safford directly about the wedge that the war put between them, not risking the confrontation until she was on the ship sailing abroad to check up on relatives after the armistice. Safford had asked her to write, and so she was writing, but what did she want her to write about? Certainly not of how happy she was to be back with her German kin and acquaintances or of her sympathy for these "enemies" who had been brutalized by American patriots. Out of what materials were she and Safford to build and sustain communication? While there is no record of Safford's reply, it was clear to Fuchs, as she noted in her journal, that, in order "to be near to one another," people "must have common interests" and congenial points of view, and Safford neither shared her German sympathies nor in wartime provided "much stimulus of the radical, liberal kind" that had first brought them together.[21] Fuchs's visit in 1919 with Murdock and Buck, who still impressed her as "two fine women . . . so loving and loyal and generous" but also as ardent Wilsonites and therefore unable to understand her unhappiness, was "another example," she noted, "of just how intricate" old connections could become in time of war and "how divided" people were likely to be.[22]

Mary Collson was forced to the same conclusion when, seeking to reestablish her ties with the liberal church and her old sisterhood, she found her way blocked by the militancy that had captured the Unitarian fold. After trying for years to create the perfect society through Christian Science, a bitterly disillusioned Collson had wrenched herself free of the Eddy movement and hoped again to experience the "immediate contact with life" that she had enjoyed in the liberal ministry. Having heard that the AUA was placing women as temporary supplies for pulpits left empty when preachers enlisted in the military services, she submitted an application to the Ministerial Union and gave the names of Jane Addams and Florence Buck as her references. Collson stressed her interest in social work and tried to play down her political views, but the letters from Addams and Buck were enough to raise questions about her patriotism. Though Addams's letter said only that Collson had done a commendable job at Hull House some fifteen years earlier, in 1917 any association with the now notorious pacifist Addams was suspect, and Buck's letter to the committee as much as confirmed these doubts by noting that, while the applicant stood "with the government for the war," she was an "avowed Socialist" whose "somewhat radical views" might "tend to cause division in a congregation."[23] Whatever action the screening committee decided to take, the case became moot when, as Buck had imagined, Collson's dislike of the war propaganda and her interest in starting a program of "moral rearmament" in the church were met with at least mild hostility and she abandoned her plans for returning to the Unitarians. Shocked to hear liberals with whom she had once identified as a sister in faith now speak of the war so approvingly and to see the women "smugly . . . keeping 'the home fires burning'" by folding bandages and singing "songs of hate in a deluded sense of patriotism," Collson had beaten a lame retreat back to the bastion of Christian Science.[24]

II

The postwar years in America were a sobering time for idealistic progressives, who presumed when they joined in their nation's crusade that defeating the forces of evil would leave the righteous to rule the earth. Even before the terms of the peace in Europe were finally settled on, the reformers and church leadership came to see that their expectations had been naive and their trust misplaced and abused. Once the troops were back home, the earnest high-mindedness that had been propped up by war work gave way to a mood of moral suspension that seemed to engulf the entire society. Even worse, there now surfaced persuasive evidence of the warmongering and corruption that critics like Jones and Holmes had alleged, and students of propaganda and international relations presented a new picture of the war that looked less like a noble crusade to save democracy than a sordid scramble for power by grasping imperialists. Seeing that they had been duped, progressive evangelists entered the new decade of the 1920s filled with remorse for their weakness and pledged to return to the gospel of peace.[25]

In Chicago, Rowena Morse Mann, having joined with the city's other ministers in a public expression of penitence, vowed never again to sanction war as a holy crusade. Anxious to make amends, especially when it enhanced her platform exposure, she seized on the chance to fill the vacancy left by the death of Anna Shaw on a nationwide speaking tour that was promoting Wilson's peace plan and the League of Nations. In her church, she put a ban on any remnant of militancy and enforced it so strictly that a young and unthinking Sunday School pianist never forgot her rebuke when she heard him pounding out "Onward Christian Soldiers." Acknowledging that the minister's task was to use the "weariness" of the times to return to the social gospel and thereby restore the national conscience, she once again used her sermons to plead for the socialistic ideal commonwealth in which altruism replaced the pure profit motive.[26]

Caroline Bartlett Crane also had good cause to feel betrayed by the government. Always deeply repulsed by the human slaughter that was the essence of war and genuine in her belief that her first duty was to encourage world peace, she had tried early on, without much success, to help Addams rally support in the state for the work of the Women's Peace Party. But she could not reconcile this disapproval of violent destruction with her love of liberty and her concern for her country's safety. She therefore had tried to defer the problem, refusing, when the press interviewed her, "to mix up the peace issue in Europe with the preparedness issue at home" and concentrating her energies on the latter. Besides bringing up this unresolved moral dilemma, the postwar disclosures about the profiteering and graft—which she had dismissed when first rumored as but the "astounding aspersions of irresponsible pacifists"—compromised Crane's reputation as a defender of ethics in government.[27] To make what reparation she could, Crane agreed to head up the women's work in the state and national reconstruction efforts, helping convert the stateside defense apparatus to peacetime machinery. At the same time, with other reformers who still had hopes of salvaging their ideals, Crane returned to the platform and conference table to explore the causes for war and find its cure.[28]

Ironically, Crane's greatest insight into the wartime mentality came when her peace studies opened her up to the same sort of viciousness that had worked its brutality earlier on Jones and other pacifists. The public hysteria had by now shifted from a hatred of Germans to a hatred of anyone thought to have possible communistic sympathies, and Crane's radical connections and antiestablishment reputation had made her a likely target even before her alliance with the peace movement brought her directly into the red-baiters' line of fire.

The irony was deepened by the fact that it was some of Crane's sisters in the Michigan DAR who targeted her—along with Jane Addams, Carrie Chapman Catt, John Haynes Holmes, and others who dared criticize the government's conduct in any way—and put her name on a list of "disloyal Americans," which they circulated all over the state among public and private organizations. Crane had been a member of the Daughters for many years and had valued her association with this select group as an affirmation of her deeply rooted national pride and loyalty. As a woman who like many idealists never spent too much time weighing the consequences of actions that she felt compelled to take as a matter of principle, she had never imagined that her reform work, however disturbing to some, would be seen as unpatriotic. Indeed, many Daughters had shared her progressive ideals and reform activities. The appearance of an arch conservative force and the organization's failure to put a stop to its mischief promptly were therefore a rude disappointment for Crane as well as a sad validation of what she had always known about national feeling in general: it was bound to miscarry when people uprooted it from its ground of tradition. Of all groups, she pointed out, the DAR should have honored free speech and dissent, for these were the principles for which the Revolution was fought in the first place, but, in its benighted nationalism, it had lost sight of the founders' ideals. Having never been one to yield a point of honor, and hardly ready to now, Crane sent exposés of the blacklisting to all the major papers in Michigan and a number of national magazines. Then she sent off a letter withdrawing her membership from the organization, which unwittingly had done as much as any to make her a radical patriot.[29]

While Crane's disillusionment after the war was typical of her reform generation, her resilience was not. Most of the old crusaders were tired radicals by the 1920s.[30] They were all growing old, Marie Howe told Fuchs, and practically "no one" seemed to have the fight "to reform the world anymore."[31] Like Fuchs, Crane, and Jones, Howe had suffered personally from the mass hysteria fed by the war. She had seen her charmed circle of Heterodoxy, which normally thrived on debate, ripped apart by the ragged issue of the government's role in the conflict and lose valued members like Charlotte Perkins Gilman and Rheta Childe Dorr. Then, after her close friend and club member Fola LaFollette's father, Senator Robert La Follette, cast one of the few votes against America's entry into the war, Marie had been one of a number of Heterodites, both hawks and doves, to be harassed indiscriminately because of their unorthodox life-styles or views. The Howes were especially vulnerable to the red-baiting because of Fred's tough stand, as commissioner of immigration of the Port of New York, against deportations without due process. On one occasion, Marie was seized in front of her New York apartment and held for some time by the Secret

Service without being able to contact a lawyer or Fred.[32] Life became quieter for Marie after 1919, and, though much of this reprieve was forced on her by poor health, she was ready, she said, to step back and watch the world from the sidelines.[33]

Adele Fuchs was also enjoying the relative calm that followed the war and gloated that the terrible greed and brutality were now "admitted by everyone." Personally, this meant that, in her immediate circle of friends, Marion Murdock had put aside her hatred of Germany and was once again a rational woman whose warmth and goodwill insisted that Fuchs forgive her "wartime madness."[34] It also meant that Mary Safford was no longer the zealous captain of Orlando's Home Defenders and was better company now that she was giving her time to raising fruit, promoting the arts, and, after a boycott of more than a decade, working for liberal religion again.

Safford's return to religious reform in the wake of the war was motivated by a concern, shared by virtually all the women who had served in the ministry with her, about the revival of Reformation theology, a revival that was shaking the very foundations of liberal religion. Emphasizing the deeply felt sinfulness of humanity, its proponents—most notably Barth, Brunner, and the young Niebuhr—were teaching that God's grace, not any human solutions, was the only hope for society. As the war had shown, they said, even the people with best intentions were weak and corruptible and thus incapable of detaching themselves or others from evil. Most leaders in the religious community found this assessment more realistic in the 1920s than the notion that people were basically good. But, for the sisterhood's remnant, not even the cataclysmic evidence of the war was enough to uproot them from an idealistic belief in humanity, a faith that, having survived the stresses of wartime, still kept them together.[35]

Epilogue

LEGACY

I will come forward and sing from memory songs they will need once more to hear.
—Alice Walker

I

No chapter of the sisterhood's story was more of a struggle for them than the last, for there, in their old age, society tried more than ever to force them into the closure—the passive acceptance of things as they were, the end to their questing and hopes—that they had defied all their lives. These women intended to live by their own measure, not the biblical three score and ten, since anyone's life, as Crane pointed out, could be "nearly over" at any time and to number the days of those who were well on in years was counterproductive and cruel.[1] Taking the very idea of retirement as an affront, they did their best to hold their ground as contributing citizens in the community and, most important, to make their presence there known. Except for Marie Jenney Howe, who had lost all faith in the great cosmic order she longed for, these women, incurable evolutionists, fully expected their souls to move on from this earthly phase to new stages of growth, enfolded and protected in divine love. It was not, then, the fear of death that caused them to hold onto life so tenaciously but a compelling desire to drain their earthly portion, to "accept life and try to use it" to the end.[2]

To be sure, it was not at all easy coming to terms with the process of growing old. Adele Fuchs wrote privately of her anger when she saw its "decided traces" on the women she had always looked to as pillars of strength and invincibility. Eleanor Gordon had grown quite deaf by her early seventies, and, with her frustration at being cut off from so much of the conversation she loved, her former "peculiarities"—"her nervous, jerky

224

movements, her emphatic manner"—had become more pronounced and even rather bizarre. To make matters worse, in a valiant effort to stay in touch with the times, she had bowed to fashion and bobbed her hair, which her sisters had always considered "the crowning glory of her physique." On the other hand, Marion Murdock, though still "light of step and alert of mind" and altogether "quite wonderful" for a woman of eighty in 1929, had "toned down . . . a good deal" under the weight of her age and loneliness in the four years since Florence Buck's death. Mary Safford looked frail and quite pitiful as she hobbled around on crutches and in constant pain after falling and breaking a hip. There was also the shock of seeing Marie Jenney Howe at fifty-nine, swearing that she did not feel her age, but visibly weakened by heart problems and wearing glasses to read, a jolt to the youthful image that still came to mind whenever Fuchs thought about her. Altogether, it hurt "to see old age set in, often so relentlessly," and those who had been "at the front" now ill and weak and "pushed into the background."[3]

Still, for all longevity's liabilities, in the balance these women felt blessed by it. What made their lives hardest was not their real disabilities but being treated as if they had outstayed their welcome and were in the way. Healthy and active at seventy, Crane was indignant enough to write a strong letter of reprimand to her young preacher when something he said from the pulpit seemed to imply that people her age were not useful and "had nothing to do but wait now and die."[4] For women like Crane who never stopped seeing themselves as pastors, it was insufferable to hear such things coming from the men who had taken their place in the pulpits, though this was not even the worst of it. The most painful part of these messages was that the ministry still saw itself as a brotherhood and was doing its best to disown them and delete their past from its record.

To be sure, the women in Safford's group had been lingering largely unnoticed on the far reaches of their profession ever since their network had lost its influence in the Western conference and could no longer help women secure churches that would pay them enough to live on. Local church boards were so well aligned with the attitude of the AUA that, from 1906, when Rowena Morse was ordained at Geneva, Illinois, until 1917, not one other female was brought into the active Unitarian ministry. Clara Cook Helvie, who broke the hiatus, was able to find a position only because her cousin happened to be William Howard Taft, the former president and a prominent Unitarian lay leader, who was willing to use his clout on her behalf.[5] Few were this fortunate, and, when they had to rely on their own incomes and service records, they had virtually no chance of finding a permanent pastorate that they could afford to take.

By accepting a series of low-paying churches after returning from settlement work, Mary Leggett had managed to stay in the parish ministry fifteen years longer. But, in 1917, with her church in Revere, Massachusetts, verging on bankruptcy, she voluntarily tendered her resignation and lost her toehold. As she was not yet sixty and felt that she had many more years of service to give, she appealed to the AUA to help her find another position, but, as she had feared, the word was sent down that it had nothing to offer, and she was "tenderly . . . laid on the shelf" though still in her "vigorous prime." Almost twenty years later, Leggett still spoke bitterly with her sisters about the needless and tragic curtailment of their careers.[6] Granted, Leggett did not have the strongest credentials to offer the settlement office. Her long history of poor health and shaky congregations and mawkish way of expressing herself could only have reinforced the prevailing view— however unfair—that women were too weak, unbusinesslike, and sentimental to succeed in professions. Yet the fate of Rowena Morse Mann, who was forced out of active service in her early fifties, showed that not even a woman with outstanding qualifications could get the backing she needed from Boston to keep her secure in the ministry.

Mann's pulpit at the Third Unitarian Church on Chicago's West Side had been on shaky ground even before she arrived in 1911, an influx of European immigrants having changed the neighborhood culture and largely displaced the market for liberal religion. The few Unitarians who had stayed on in the parish were happy to see how "the place brightened up" after "Dr. Morse" took over, and how her rare pulpit eloquence brought a sizable block of commuters back in from the suburbs on Sundays.[7] Insiders also appreciated the benefits of the minister's marriage soon after she came to them, knowing that Newton Mann's income not only allowed her to work for a pittance, but, that in the interest of advancing his wife's position, he pledged a fourth of her yearly salary, upping the ante in the society's dealings with the AUA and helping them get larger annual subsidies.

Not even the preacher's holding power was able to block the damage, however, when race riots during the summer of 1919 set off a mass exodus of Chicago's white middle class to the suburbs. The congregation was nearly wiped out, and the remnant of fifty members voted unanimously to move downtown to the Loop, where they felt that a central church with Mann preaching would quickly become the biggest liberal draw in the city. Nor would this distinction be hard to achieve, they noted ironically, given the fact that the city's three Unitarian churches combined did not have a weekly attendance of more than 250—and that when the weather was good.[8] Despite the plan's obvious merits, however, the AUA's Eliot showed little interest when congregational leaders asked for the needed financial backing, though he offered instead to put money into converting the failing society into an institutional church, using the present site and placing it under another minister, a man whom his men had recommended highly.

Stunned by the very suggestion, the members replied that they were not about to put good money into a program of neighborhood outreach for people who had their own orthodox ministries, and, as for calling new leadership, that was "the last thing to meet the problem." They had studied his record, they said, and had found the AUA's man to be "unaccept-able . . . to put it mildly," a ludicrous replacement for the present pastor, who was a rare talent and their only possible hope of survival.[9] Chicago's pulpits were already "filled with men of no ability." The South Side had an "eccentric" and the North Side someone no better, a "nothing." "If you have found a *real* minister, keep her and sustain her," was their remedy.[10] All discussion stopped there, and, without Boston's help, the dream of a central church died, and with it a future for Mann in the ministry. Part of the membership splintered off, and, although what was left of it moved to a hall near the University of Chicago campus and gave Mann a forum for several more years, it was clear that the AUA still wanted Third Church to have other leadership and had no interest in helping its popular preacher get resettled anywhere.[11]

There had been warning signals of this as early as 1919, when the West Side attendance had dropped to fewer than forty people a week and the preacher, starting to search for a new pulpit, noticed that all the openings had a way of closing as soon as she tried to look into them. When she sent out the word through her husband that she was available to fill the empty pulpit in Palo Alto, California, where her Ph.D. would surely appeal to the large university crowd, Samuel Eliot notified them that the post was being held for a young man who was still in seminary but close to graduation and already well known in the California churches. When she inquired about an open position in Brooklyn, New York, she was told that the chairman of the Supply Committee did not accept applications from females, and he was not expected to change his ways.[12]

Mann's defeat and forced early retirement during the mid-1920s was just one more case of what Gordon was thinking of when she decried the denomination's insidious bias against women clergy after the First World

War. The powers were no longer nearly as candid as they had been earlier in
the century, when one of Boston's emissaries, speaking ex cathedra in Iowa,
not only frankly admitted to the opposition to females in ministry but
defended it. Enough was still said behind the scenes, however, to remove
any doubt that the feeling was stronger than ever.[13] For this we have, in
addition to settlement patterns, not just the women's word but also the
words of the men who gloated at their sister colleagues' decline and took
swipes at them quite gratuitously.[14]

George Badger, who took over Gordon's pastorate in Orlando when she
retired, crowed in his letters to Eliot that their female colleagues no longer
had any real clout. Not seen as a forceful presence himself, Badger was eager
to let Boston's higher command know how well he was holding their ground
in the Florida field, despite Safford's effort to regain her former influence
through the Southern Unitarian Association. He recounted with relish
how he had kept her in check at the recent Southern association meetings,
when she had seemed to be making a comeback with "an impassioned
speech" on future mission work climaxed by a motion to form a state
organization "duplicating her darling Iowa Conference . . . and with herself as Master," Badger suspected. This had long been her "pet dream," he
said, and fortunately he had moved in at once "to snatch [it] out of her
hands as deftly and graciously as possible." Although one "impetuous"
Universalist seconded Safford's proposal and actually moved to make her
president of the new body, Badger had coolly suggested that the vote be
deferred and then had "a little personal talk" with the man that "straightened things out." Badger, of course, had been happy enough to accept
Safford's fund-raising expertise and financial assistance to make improvements on the church property in Orlando, and he had certainly not discouraged her when she had recently "robbed her will" to raise what was needed
to build the parish house. Yet accepting her money was one thing; accepting her leadership was something else. What the liberal movement needed,
he and Eliot agreed, was more "resolute men," not more women.[15]

Elizabeth Padgham picked up the ominous signs of the movement's
conspiracy to rid the ministry of its old women when she noticed that the
letter *R*—for *retired*—which was to have followed her name in the *AUA
Year Book,* had changed mysteriously to an *N,* ostensibly for *nonparochial
service.* Whatever was really behind it, and whatever the *N* really meant,
this tampering with her professional status caused Padgham enormous
anguish, and, for the first time ever, she turned on the AUA furiously. Why
should she be described any differently from all the other "retired minis-

ters," few of whom had even been active in the profession as long as she? She had always referred to herself as one of them, and it hurt her, she wrote, that her colleagues would now try to disconnect her from the field that had shaped her identity and meant more in her life than anything else.[16]

Even knowing that no one was listening, these women had been in the business of speaking out far too long to withdraw quietly. Crane set about in these later years compiling a record of women's exclusion in various denominations and publishing at least one exposé of the churches' neglect of their female talent.[17] Gordon persisted in sending off caustic complaints to 25 Beacon Street, even after her eyesight became so bad that she had to pay for the writing with a great deal of effort and pain. In 1939, just two years before her death, she was still castigating the AUA for its use of the words *man* and *men* and the obvious meaning: "There is not room on top for both of us," she translated plainly, "so you must climb down." As Gordon told Boston, old women like her would continue to register their complaints even without an audience because their integrity gave them no choice in the matter.[18]

II

Protest, of course, was not the only register in which the elderly could voice their pride and try to preserve their place in history's record. Those with material means could also articulate what they had aimed for in life, what their ideals had been and what they had contributed, by passing on "living monuments" that would speak to those who came after them. Mary Safford, who had the financial resources, chose to make such a statement by building a high school auditorium in her hometown to honor her mother and the other pioneer women who had inspired her girlfriends in Hamilton. As fate would have it, this eloquent tribute achieved even greater resonance when it turned out to be her last public gesture and thus the grand summation of her entire prophetic ministry.[19]

It was 1927 when Safford took a train back to Illinois to dedicate the Louisa Hunt Safford Memorial Auditorium. Still recovering from her broken hip and unable to walk without crutches, she asked Adele Fuchs to go with her. Eleanor Gordon, who had moved back to the family homestead in Hamilton some years earlier, was at the station to meet her friends and assist them. As Fuchs later reconstructed the fateful chain of events in her journal, Safford had started to run a high fever soon after they reached Hamilton but, ignoring the protests from every side, insisted on taking part in the ceremonies that she had so carefully planned. On top of everything else, as in so many banner days in the past, there was a hard rain, and a mote of mud had formed all around the construction site. By the time her party got into the school and up on the stage, Safford was too weak to say more than one or two words. Fuchs had had to read the speech, while through sheer determination her friend remained standing silently by her side, "so slender and delicate and yet so indomitable in her one idea, her fight for the recognition of women." Safford suffered a stroke on the trip back to Florida, and death came within a matter of days. Fuchs stayed with her constantly until the very last morning, when "a slight pressure of the hand" let her know that this was to be the final good-bye. At noon, Fuchs wrote later, the person whom she "had loved best in all the world" died in her arms.

The sisterhood's guiding spirit was quickly encircled by those who had loved her. Friends and family came aboard to join the bereaved as the funeral train wound its way back up North along the Mississippi River. Eleanor Gordon again was at the station in Hamilton when they pulled in and took the body home with her for the viewing, and the following day at the funeral, speaking as pastor to sister pastor, she gave a blessing that put the final seal on a pledge of partnership that two bold young girls had made to each other half a century earlier.

III

An educated historical sense had always had much to do with the way Safford's sisterhood thought about life and themselves. As descendants of America's Revolutionary heroes, and as daughters of pioneers whose country was still young and making its way, they acquired the habit of turning backward for ratification early on and grew up with the feeling of being carried into the future on the current of a powerful national legacy. As religious liberals, too, their inspiration had come as much from life stories as from the myths of the Bible, and their first bits of abstract thinking tended to be set off by events that crystallized the idea of time's continuity.

Caroline Bartlett Crane, for example, remembered standing alone as a child on the deck of her father's small passenger steamboat as it moved slowly up the Mississippi and watching a dramatic projection of wooded landscape ahead flatten out magically, become nothing more than a commonplace shoreline as the boat passed alongside, and then regain its prominence as it receded into the distance behind her. In this stroke of wizardry, the girl had suddenly grasped the deceptive nature of the distinctions that people made between their tomorrows, todays, and yesterdays, and the epiphany cautioned her ever after against thinking that she could see the shape of the present until it became a part of the longer view.[20]

Women who had such a feeling for history were not content to leave only brass plaques on old churches to let posterity know that they had been there. They wanted to witness to their past in their own living prose and then find a permanent place for their testimonials. Most of these women, in fact, had started preparing to enter the annals much earlier, having kept careful logs and records of their daily activities, and carrying notebooks around by habit, as other women brought baskets of needlework. Later, when they had been forced to concede that their ideals were too far advanced for the times to be implemented any time soon, they had started publishing *Old and New* as a means of preserving their conference proceedings, parish calendars, sermons, and editorials for society's use when it had caught up enough to appreciate them. They imagined that, when the time came, historians would be grateful to have these archives and would reconstruct the record of their noble work for a ready readership.[21] Thirty years later, however, with society having progressed very little and the church caring less than ever to hear of the sisterhood's role in its growth, these elderly women could wait no longer and took up the task of writing their way into history on their own.

Yet becoming a visible part of the past by producing memoirs and autobiographies proved to be just as difficult as commanding an audience. For one thing, the sheer economics of getting one's words onto paper and into the public view presented enormous obstacles for those living close to the poverty line. In 1934, Mary Collson, with no steady income or savings to speak of, had to move out of her modest apartment and into a tiny garret, sell most of her books, and pawn her furniture to support herself while writing a book about her life's search for a better world. For her sacrifice, she ended up with only some typescript that no one would publish and the humiliation of having to sign herself onto the welfare roles.[22] At about the same time, Collson's mentor Eleanor Gordon also began to write down her memories of her group's experience, though being more circumspect, on a less ambitious scale. What she planned was to bring out the story in a series of short "chapters," each printed separately and circulated the way she had sometimes distributed sermons before her retirement. It seemed to her well worth the $25 to give her story the dignity and mobility gained through this printed format. Yet, here again, even this minimal cost was barely affordable, and, when she was no longer able to handle the business details without family assistance, well-meaning relatives put an end to the printing.[23]

Even without the problem of money, society's lack of respect for its women's experience was enough to discourage the pastors from writing about it or taking the risk of saving the records for other writers to use as they would. The sisterhood's worst imaginings of what could happen by leaving their lives open for others' scrutiny and interpretation came to pass in 1927, when Safford died and her papers, a number of them quite intimate, were literally dumped in her yard and pried into by strangers.[24] Later, Mary Collson, hospitalized but not "done for," as people assumed, suffered the same violation when her personal things were "picked . . . and scattered about by other people." Stripped of all palpable ties to her past, she spent her last six years on the faded margins of society;[25] not surprisingly, when the end came, the death warrant finished the job of effacement by stating that she—who had taught in the schoolrooms and served in the slums, preached in the pulpits and marched in the picket lines—had spent her life doing "housework at home."

Such lessons were not lost on Gordon, who promptly began sorting through her own papers, rereading and burning great stacks of old letters, diaries, notes, sermons, and manuscripts, preferring that her record be sacrificed than left in its entirety for unappreciative readers to desecrate.[26] The "awful accidents [that] happened to letters" also had their effect on Marie Jenney Howe, who became all the more reticent about getting herself into print after hearing about them. If the Safford incident did not prompt her to destroy her paper trails, and it may have, it at least made her all the more leery of candor in private correspondence and all the less given to writing her life's story for the public's perusal.[27]

Yet it might be argued that none of these problems was more of a block to recording the story than the subjects' own inability to speak for themselves, to tell the truth about what their lives had been from their own perspective instead of from the establishment's. For today's biographer, searching for writings by these gifted women in hopes of bringing them their well deserved recognition, it is disheartening to discover how readily some of them falsified or concealed their experiences as they knew them. One of the most disconcerting examples of this is Rowena Morse Mann, a brilliant orator, scholar, and Ph.D., who accomplished more than enough to warrant, if not to attain, the kind of respect and acceptance she craved from her field. When these rewards were withheld because what a woman did counted for less, she fabricated yet other credentials that she thought would impress the world more. Not only did she delete the fact of having grown up in Iowa under the tutelage of a dubious group of liberal women ministers, but she claimed academic affiliations that never existed and authorship of books she never wrote. Thus "compensating for being a woman," she spent her rare command of words pretending to be what she never had been when instead she might have used it to write a biography that expressed womanly pride in real victories as well as justified anger and pain brought on by unfair defeats. Discredited now for this futile distortion, Mann was already notorious among her closer contemporaries for what Fuchs and Gordon called her "insincerity" and indulgence in spinning outrageous tales.

Ironically, Mann was aware of the pathos of people who put on facades to "puff themselves up" and had once remarked to her mother that putting on airs was often a way of coping with one's "accumulated discontentments" in life. "Sometimes we try to cheat ourselves into at least thinking we are big in this world because we want to be a little something and have not succeeded." [28] What all the motives behind her own masquerading were and how conscious she was of them can only be guessed, but, plainly, revising the record in part reflected her wanting to be the exceptional female by seeking success outside any recognizably female scenario. As a consequence, not only Mann's individual tale but the larger story was lost when she tried to deny the role the sisterhood played in shaping her life.

Mary Collson's recounting of what she had learned in the ministry, settlement work, and mind cure was yet another compromising exercise in concealment. Fearing, with cause, that she might be sued for denouncing the Christian Scientists, she had simply left out such specific details as people's names, places, and dates to minimize the risk of full disclosure. Thus she spoke with affection and gratitude of the women who had been her mentors but never identified them by name or location or put in the pigment that might have saved much of their story from fading away irretrievably. More disturbing still was Collson's effort to soften her anger and bold indictments by assuming a self-deprecating narrative posture. By presenting herself in this way, she relinquished the power that the autobiographer has to control her protagonist's destiny, and she ended up playing the part of a battered and belittled victim instead of a proud survivor.

It was only after the publishing circuit rejected the life that she presented, rudely dismissing the manuscript as the biography of a weak and self-pitying female who squandered her years seeking ways to escape the world as it was, that Collson bolted from their point of view and broke through to what was authentically hers. Her "greatest weakness in life," she acknowledged and now told a friend in all candor, had been "a desire always to please and to be what somebody else wanted" her to be. In her memoir, she said, by force of this unconscious habit, she had made herself seem to be weaker than she knew she actually was, accepting far more than her share of responsibility for her problems and covering up for those who were really to blame. Having paid the price, she resolved to be "through with the smoke screens of human invention" and, speaking truthfully now, thundered, "I am not whining. I am to myself the heroine of my own adventures," a proud woman who with Browning's Sir Roland could say, "I saw them and I knew them all. And yet / Dauntless the slug-horn to my lips I set, / And blew." [29] Here, finally, Collson's story of how she had failed to be "a successful lady in life" was retold as a testament to her courage and honesty, though it would be many years after her death before the public would hear it.

Though some will persist in reading the record of Collson's mentors and colleagues through the patriarchal lenses that suppressed it in its own time, this history has in fact triumphed over the silencing of the past, in part precisely because its principals had to struggle so hard to preserve it. For surely no story cries out more insistently for restoration of justice than that which has been violated or rudely abridged and denied its entire hearing. Walking behind this pioneer band and singing their song for them now, we hear in its text an ongoing narrative telling of shared destinies and discern that its subjects were not stray eccentrics or characters who moved through plots that were theirs alone. Indeed, these women themselves understood that theirs was a fluid community with a common experience that transcended time and place. This was what Marie Howe was referring to when, after finally writing a book, a successful biography of the iconoclastic George Sand, she told Adele Fuchs that the story had simply "welled up" from the depths of her sense of a shared female fate. [30] Finally, the record of these prophetic sisters serves to remind us that, even where there is much to mourn in our past, there may be much to celebrate also, for where women have cast their lives in the terms that they and not others have set for them, their stories of struggle will speak to us of inspiring human achievement and bravery. As a legacy, then, this shared history has no conclusion but only takes pause, defying the kind of closure that the world has too long imposed on the female destiny and bidding us all to create a freer, authentic narrative for the future.

THE SISTERHOOD'S BIOGRAPHIES

FLORENCE BUCK (1860–1925)

Florence Buck entered the feminist ministry on the frontier through the influence of Marion Murdock and Caroline Bartlett, who were pastoring at the Unitarian Church in Kalamazoo when she started attending services there in 1890. Buck and Murdock became inseparable and spent the rest of their lives together as co-ministers and domestic companions. Buck was ordained in 1893 and received a B.D. from Meadville Theological School the following year. In 1912, after almost two decades in parish ministry in Ohio, Michigan, Wisconsin, and California, the couple resettled in Boston, where Buck had been offered the job of associate secretary of religious education for the American Unitarian Association. She held this position until her death.

MARY EDITH COLLSON (1870–1953)

This daughter of poor pioneers in Humboldt, Iowa, was groomed for the feminist ministry by the Unitarian women who ran the town's liberal church and public school in the 1880s. With her mentors' encouragement and the financial support of Eleanor Gordon, Collson went on to college and theological school and dutifully took her first church in rural Iowa in 1897. Soon restless in parish ministry, and hoping for greater rewards, Collson passed up ordination and moved to Hull House in Chicago, where she served as probation officer for the city's new Juvenile Court. When this ministry in the urban slums also disappointed her hopes for reform, she abandoned the new sociology and rational theology and spent the next thirty years as a Christian Science mind-cure practitioner. Collson never returned to the liberal church after leaving the Eddy movement in 1932, but she did renew old friendships with some of the women clergy who had been her colleagues.

CAROLINE JULIA BARTLETT CRANE (1858–1935)

Known as Carrie Julia until she was almost thirty, this hometown acquaintance of Eleanor Gordon and Mary Safford changed her name to Caroline in 1889, when she was ordained by the First Unitarian Church of Kalamazoo, Michigan. With Bartlett's marriage to A. Warren Crane, a physician, in 1896, her named changed again, as did her ideas about having both a career and a family. On her husband's advice that a rest from her work would improve her chances of pregnancy, she gave up her pulpit in 1899, but remained childless. When she tried to return to the parish ministry two years later, she found it almost impossible for a woman to get her own pulpit. Seeking other channels for her reform zeal and talents as writer, speaker, and organizer, Crane carved out new ministries for herself in the secular fields of public health and municipal housekeeping, woman's suffrage, and peace.

ADELE FUCHS   (1872–ca. 1956)

Though not herself an ordained minister but a public school teacher of German, Fuchs's passionate love for Mary Safford and active involvement in Safford's churches placed her in the sisterhood's inner circle. From her position behind the scenes, she was able to keep a rare journal record of what went on among the network of women in the Western Unitarian ministry for the fifty years from the 1880s to the 1930s.

ELEANOR ELIZABETH GORDON   (1852–1942)

Eleanor Gordon, a farmer's daughter from Hamilton, Illinois, spent most of her life fulfilling an early pledge that she and her best friend, Mary Safford, had made to work as a team for enlightened religion. Though she started out teaching and let Safford preach, Gordon soon saw the greater need for good pastors and in 1889 was ordained as Safford's associate minister in the Unitarian Church of Sioux City, Iowa. Gordon moved off to serve pastorates independently for a while, but shortly after the turn of the century, when Safford suffered a nervous collapse, she returned to her friend and filled in for her at the church in Des Moines. In the early 1900s, Gordon also joined forces with sister clergy in leading the state's woman's suffrage campaign. Her greatest calling, however, remained the church ministry, and, in 1912, she returned to a full-time pastorate with the newly formed church in Orlando, Florida, where Safford and other old Unitarian friends had gone to retire.

MARIE HOFFENDAHL JENNEY HOWE   (1870–1934)

Carrying forward a family tradition of liberal religion and female equality, Marie Jenney earned a B.D. from Meadville Theological School and went to Sioux City to be Mary Safford's associate pastor in 1897. When Safford moved on to the church in Des Moines, Jenney went with her, but she soon became disillusioned by the sluggish response to her radical gospel and disaffected by the denomination's neglect of its women. Much to her sister colleagues' distress, she resigned from her post in 1903 and married an old suiter, Frederick C. Howe. As her cohort feared, the marriage turned out to be a disappointment, and Marie eventually turned again to a female community for support and companionship. When the Howes moved to New York City, Marie organized her feminist friends into the Heterodoxy Club and eventually formed an intimate bond with sister Heterodite Rose Young. In the 1920s, Marie Jenney Howe gained literary acclaim when she published two best-selling books on the writer George Sand.

IDA C. HULTIN   (1858–1938)

Ida Hultin entered the Iowa circuit of sister ministers in 1882 when she took her first Unitarian church in Algona. Here, as a neighbor of Eleanor Gordon and Mary Safford, the pastor in Humboldt, she worked to recruit such young girls as "Minnie" Rowena Morse for the future ministry. Several years later, she answered a call from the church in Des Moines and was there ordained in 1886. Hultin remained in the Midwest until the turn of the century, serving as pastor in Moline, Illinois, from 1891 to 1898 and playing a prominent role in the Western Unitarian Conference. Hultin's last two parishes were in Massachusetts, where she settled after retiring from active ministry in 1916.

MARY L. LEGGETT   (1856–1938)

A preacher's daughter from New York State, Mary Leggett entered the network of women ministers on the frontier in 1888 when she answered a call from a floundering congregation of Unitarians in Beatrice, Nebraska. Although there was never much cause for encouragement, save for a brief flirtation with settlement work at the turn of the century, Leggett persisted for almost three decades in trying to salvage ailing societies in the Midwest and New England and would have stayed at it longer if given the chance. But, by 1916, when Leggett resigned from her last pastorate in Revere, Massachusetts, to keep the church from bankruptcy, it was almost impossible for a woman to find a new pulpit anywhere. The denomination's indifference to her loss of anchorage was a deep sorrow and source of bitterness which she carried to her death.

ROWENA MORSE MANN   (1870–1958)

This last of the women to be ordained and considered a part of the frontier sisterhood married her former pastor Newton Mann in 1912, shortly after being called to the Third Unitarian Church in Chicago. Given to misrepresenting the facts of her life to acquire prestige, she claimed to have spent all her formative years going to school in the East but actually moved with her family to Iowa even before she had reached her teens and grew up under the influence of the sister ministers there. If she hoped to gain greater distinction by proving herself an exceptional female rather than making the case for her sex's equality through an alliance with other women, she learned in due course that she was as subject as any female to sexist bias when, with most of the ministry's sisterhood, she was forced into an early retirement.

MILA TUPPER MAYNARD   (b. 1864)

The younger sister by twenty years of one of the first frontier women to preach, Mila Tupper prepared to carry on the family tradition of feminist ministry by attending Cornell University and spending summers helping to organize new liberal congregations in the Midwest in the late 1880s. She received her degree in 1889 and was ordained in La Porte, Indiana, the following year. In 1893, however, after taking a church in Grand Rapids, Michigan, she resigned and married another Unitarian minister, Rezin A. Maynard, who shared her interest in urban problems. The couple spent six months in settlement work in Chicago and then moved West, settled in Denver, and joined the Broadway Temple Movement of Myron Reed. This radical redefinition of liberal religious identity led the Unitarian settlement office to drop the Maynards' names from its list of ministers, and the couple moved on to writing and lecturing.

AMELIA MURDOCK WING   (1852–1949)

In the later 1880s, Amelia Murdock was the parish assistant in Humboldt, Iowa, where her older sister Marion had replaced Mary Safford as minister. Though she also spent time in the summers helping to organize new congregations, she did not seek ordination, feeling a stronger pull toward teaching young children. When her sister left Humboldt, Amelia enrolled in a Kindergarten College in Chicago and, on graduation, was asked to head up the kindergarten at Hull House. It was a flattering offer, but needing a rest, she declined, went back to Iowa, and put her training to use in the smaller communities there. For a decade or so, Amelia was happily married to a widowed minister and, after his death in 1910, settled in California, where Marion joined her in 1929.

MARION E. MURDOCK   (1850–1943)

Raised by parents who fostered their daughters' expectations of equal opportunities, Marion Murdock announced her intention of being a preacher when she was a girl and reached her goal after earning a B.D. from Meadville Theological School. Called to be pastor in Humboldt, Iowa, in 1885, Murdock succeeded Mary Safford, who with Eleanor Gordon helped ordain her. Though Marion brought in her sister Amelia to be her assistant, the work in the frontier parish proved too much and damaged her health, forcing her to look for a less demanding position elsewhere. In 1890, she moved to the church in Kalamazoo to help Caroline Bartlett, and there she met Florence Buck, the woman with whom she spent the rest of her life as domestic companion, copastor, and sister suffragist. In 1912, still in unstable health and semiretired, Murdock accompanied Buck to Boston and remained there until 1929, four years after her companion's death. She then went to live with Amelia in California.

ANNA JANE NORRIS   (1851–1925)

One of the first women to attend Meadville Theological School and be ordained to the Unitarian ministry in the 1880s, Norris was claimed by her feminist colleagues as one of the Iowa conference's sisterhood, though she appears to have been but a marginal figure. Indeed, by the 1890s, the stresses of having to work all alone in Nebraska and farther west, trying to plant liberal congregations on what she described as "poor soil," had so undermined her confidence and desire to do parish ministry that she turned instead to social settlement work.

MARGARET TITUS OLMSTEAD   (1860–1950)

Brought up as a Hicksite Quaker until her family became Universalists, Margaret Titus was ordained to the Universalist ministry in 1894 and shortly thereafter married Rett Olmstead, a fellow minister. The two worked successfully as a team and, after 1900, joined with the Unitarian women in leading small churches in Iowa. After a son was born, the problems of trying to tend to both family and church became increasingly difficult and eventually too much for Margaret. Feeling that she had been failing at both and was now also letting the sisterhood down, she resigned from the parish ministry in 1908 and left the state with her family.

ESTELLA ELIZABETH PADGHAM   (1874–1952)

Raised as a Unitarian in Syracuse, New York, Padgham was inspired to enter the ministry by an older church friend, Marie Jenney. After graduating from Smith College and Meadville Theological School, she answered a call from Mary Safford's organization in Iowa to care for the small congregation in Perry. In 1901, with Jenney and Safford beside her, Padgham became ordained "in serene confidence that it was a woman's right." Padgham left the sisterhood's territory in 1904 when she moved back East to accept the church in Rutherford, New Jersey. She remained there as pastor for twenty-two years, until she retired in 1926.

GERTRUDE VON PETZHOLD   (b. 1876)

As the first woman ever to pastor a Unitarian church in England and an articulate suffragette in the feminist movement there, it was inevitable that Gertrude von Petzhold would join forces with her American counterparts in the early 1900s. Eager to broaden their view of the women's rights movement, Petzhold and Mary Safford exchanged churches with each other from 1908 to 1910. Members of the church in Des Moines complained that the visiting pastor neglected the parish to campaign for suffrage, and, when after Safford's return Petzhold sought to secure yet another American pulpit, few were willing to put in a good word for her, and she went back to England.

HELEN GRACE PUTNAM   (1840–95)

Helen Putnam had grown up near Boston and spent her early adulthood as a music teacher and editor before she decided in middle age to enter the Unitarian ministry. Enrolling in Meadville Theological School in 1886, she joined the Western sisterhood in their work the following year. Her ordination in 1889 was performed with the help of Eliza Tupper Wilkes and Marion Murdock.

MARY AUGUSTA SAFFORD   (1851–1927)

A consummate organizer and brilliant fundraiser, Mary Safford was recognized as the driving force behind the network of women who dominated the liberal ministry on the frontier in the late nineteenth century. In addition to pastoring churches in

Humboldt, Sioux City, and Des Moines—with Eleanor Gordon, Marie Jenney, and Helen Wilson assisting—Safford organized seven more and made them self-supporting so as to be independent of Eastern patronage. In the 1900s, her lifelong pursuit of equal rights led to a two-year pulpit exchange with the suffragette Rev. Gertrude von Petzhold of England. On her return, she retired from parish ministry, moved to Orlando, and took on the leadership of the suffrage campaigns in Iowa and Florida.

ELIZA TUPPER WILKES   (1844–1917)

Ordained as a minister almost ten years before Mary Safford, Eliza Wilkes was a strong mentor figure as well as an active collaborator among the women who carried the message of liberal religion along the frontier. With the faithful support of her husband, Wilkes spent forty years, in the upper Great Plains, starting new churches that opened positions for women who wanted to preach and pastor.

HELEN WILSON   (1883–1926)

Helen Wilson began attending Mary Safford's church in Des Moines when she was barely out of her teens and apparently without family. The minister soon took her under her wing, introducing her as her "adopted daughter," and groomed her to be her parish assistant and right hand in suffrage work. When Safford retired and moved to Florida, Helen went with her. There she met and married Victor Starbuck and became the mother of a daughter, Mary Helen. Tragically, Helen contracted tuberculosis and died in 1926, a year before Mary Safford, and Mary Helen Starbuck was killed in an automobile accident ca. 1932.

CELIA PARKER WOOLLEY   (1848–1918)

Celia Woolley's feminist views and leadership in the Western conference brought her into the network of women ministers on the frontier well in advance of her own ordination in 1894; indeed, with Adele Fuchs and Mary Safford, she became one of an inner circle that playfully spoke of themselves as "the Super Six." As a wife and mother whose children were nearly grown by the time she took her first parishes in and around Chicago, Woolley experienced far less conflict in trying to care for both family and church than she did in trying to preach the social gospel to people who paid no attention. Unwilling to compromise what she believed, she left her church work after just four years and in 1904 forged a new ministry far away from the privileged parishes. To promote better race relations and serve the disadvantaged, she set up a neighborhood house called the Frederick Douglass Center, moved in with her husband, and lived there until her death.

ABBREVIATIONS

AUA   American Unitarian Association Archives, Andover Library, Harvard Divinity School, Cambridge, Mass.

BHL   Jabez and Eliza Sunderland Papers, Bentley Historical Library, University of Michigan, Ann Arbor.

CBC   Caroline Bartlett Crane Papers, Western Michigan University Archives, Kalamazoo, Mich.

CHS   Chicago Historical Society, Chicago

DMUC   Des Moines Unitarian Church Records, Des Moines, Iowa

DMPL   Des Moines Public Library, Des Moines, Iowa.

DPL   Western History Department, Denver Public Library, Denver, Colo.

GP   Gordon Family Papers, private holdings of Donald R. Gordon, Hamilton, Ill.

HHJ   Adele Fuchs Papers, private holdings of Helen Hoagland Johnson, Orlando, Fla.

HHP   Hull House Papers, University of Illinois at Chicago

IHI   Inez Haynes Irwin Papers, Schlesinger Library, Radcliffe College, Cambridge, Mass.

ISHD   Iowa State Historical Department, Des Moines, Iowa

JPA   Juvenile Protective Association Papers, University of Illinois at Chicago

JLJ   Jenkin Lloyd Jones Papers, Joseph Regenstein Library, University of Chicago

LFP   La Follette Family Papers, Library of Congress, Manuscript Division, Washington, D.C.

MFP   Murdock Family Papers, Garnavillo Historical Society, Garnavillo, Iowa.

MTS   Jenkin Lloyd Jones and Western Unitarian Conference Papers, Meadville-Lombard Theological School Library and Archives, Chicago

MVC   Mississippi Valley Collection, Memphis State University, Memphis

NMS   Private papers of Nora McNeill Staton, Orlando, Fla.

OPL   Orlando Public Library, Orlando, Fla.

OUC   Records of the Orlando Unitarian Church, Orlando, Fla.

PC   Records of People's Church, Kalamazoo, Mich.

RMM   Rowena Morse Mann Papers, Schlesinger Library, Radcliffe College, Cambridge, Mass.

SCPC   Swarthmore College Peace Collection, Swarthmore, Pa.

SHSI   State Historical Society of Iowa, Iowa City, Iowa

UHSP   Universalist Historical Society Papers, Andover Library, Harvard Divinity School, Cambridge, Mass.

UUA   Unitarian Universalist Association Papers, Andover Library, Harvard Divinity School, Cambridge, Mass.

WMC   Women's Ministerial Conference Records, Andover Library, Harvard Divinity School, Cambridge, Mass.

NOTES

INTRODUCTION

1. See, e.g., the essays collected in Janet Wilson James, ed., *Women in American Religion* (Philadelphia, 1980); Rosemary Radford Ruether and Rosemary Skinner Keller, eds., *Women and Religion in America,* vol. 1, *The Nineteenth Century* (San Francisco, 1981); and Leonard I. Sweet, *The Minister's Wife* (Philadelphia, 1983).
2. Ann Douglas describes the effect on the liberal clergy in *The Feminization of American Culture* (New York, 1977).
3. The manuscript, Mary E. Collson's "My Search for an All Right World," was completed in 1934 and discovered among the Edward J. Meeman Papers when they were given to Memphis State University in 1973.
4. "Comparative Statistics," Association of Theological Schools in the United States and Canada, New York, National Council of Churches, 1988; figures for 1976–88 provided by the Unitarian Universalist Association, Ministerial Settlement Office, Boston.
5. See Joy Charlton, "Women in Seminary: A Review of Current Social Science Research," *Review of Religious Research* 28 (1987): 305–18.
6. Diane Tennis, "We Don't Need Any More Pronouncements," *Presbyterian Survey* (May 1988): 17.
7. Judith Walker-Riggs, "Cleaning Up the Kitchen and the Theology," *Transforming Thought: Position Papers on Feminist Theology* (Boston, 1988), 1:59.

CHAPTER ONE *The Entering Wedge*

1. Dr. Adele Fuchs to Pearl Avis Gordon Vestal, 1934, in "Rev. Mary Augusta Safford, 1851–1927: Biographical Notes" (hereafter cited as "Safford Notes"), compiled by Pearl Avis Gordon Vestal, Hamilton, Ill., May 1949, ISHD, 10; Abbie Safford Wiesecke, Safford's niece, to Pearl Avis Gordon Vestal, 14 April 1942, ibid., 13; Virginia Safford Bristow, Safford's niece, to Pearl Avis Gordon Vestal, 1942, ibid., 13.
2. "Safford Notes," 4; unpublished typescript by Mary Polasky, ca. 1928, ISHD.

3. Outline of Personal History of Reverend Mary Augusta Safford, Biographical Records of the Iowa Memorial Commission, ISHD.

4. Eleanor Elizabeth Gordon, *A Little Bit of a Long Story* (n.p., n.d.).

5. Ibid.

6. Ibid.

7. Nora McNeill Staton, interview with Cynthia G. Tucker, 8 March 1985, Orlando, Fla.

8. "Safford Notes," passim.

9. Ibid., 14.

10. Gordon, *Long Story*.

11. Outline of Personal History . . . Safford; Gordon, *Long Story*.

12. Gordon, *Long Story*.

13. Charles D. Cashdollar, "European Positivism and the American Unitarians," *Church History* 45 (1976): 490–506.

14. Hawthorne Literary Society, Secretary's Record Book, 1871–77, Hamilton, Ill., excerpted in "Safford Notes," 14.

15. Charles H. Lyttle, *Freedom Moves West: A History of the Western Unitarian Conference, 1852–1952* (Boston, 1952), 118–19.

16. Arthur M. Judy, "Rev. Oscar Clute in Iowa," *Old and New* 10 (1902): 4.

17. Excerpted from an unidentified news clippings in "Safford Notes," 6.

18. H. H. Hunting, Western secretary's report, cited in Clara C. Helvie, "Unitarian Women Ministers" (1929, typescript, in UHSP).

19. Thomas Graham, "The Making of a Secretary: Jenkin Lloyd Jones at Thirty-One," *Proceedings of the Unitarian Universalist Historical Society* 19, pt. 2 (1982–83): 36–55.

20. *Unity* 82 (1918): 148.

21. *Unity* 3 (1879): 105, 201, 300.

22. Eleanor E. Gordon, *The Second Chapter of a Long Story* (Hamilton, Ill.: privately printed, 1935).

23. *History of Kossuth and Humboldt Counties, Iowa* (Springfield, Ill., 1884); Stephen H. Taft, *The History of Humboldt Iowa* (Humboldt, Iowa, 1934).

24. A. D. Bicknell, "S. H. Taft: A Sketch," *Old and New* 14 (1906): 33.

25. C. W. Garfield, "The Old Church," in *Centennial History of Humboldt*, ed. Oliver DeGroote (Humboldt, 1963), 194–95.

26. "A Pentacostal Feast," *Christian Register* 59 (24 July 1880): 478.

27. Frank W. Bicknell, "The Conference of 1880, Its Spirit and Its Influence" (read at the fiftieth anniversary of the Iowa Unitarian Association, Davenport, Iowa, September 1927, DMUC).

28. Mrs. C. T. Cole, "Charge Given at Mary Safford's Ordination," *Unity* 5 (1880): 160–61.

29. "The First Secretary of the Iowa Unitarian Association" (biographical tribute to Mrs. Cordelia Throop Cole), *Old and New* 7 (1904): 1–2.

30. *Unity* 5 (1880): 160–61; *Services at the Ordination and Installation of Rev. Phebe A. Hanaford* (Boston, 1870).

31. *Compendium of the Tenth Census (1880)*, pt. 2 (Washington, D.C., 1883),

1640; the Western secretary's report for 1872 (cited in Helvie, "Unitarian Women Ministers," 19) suggests that men would accept salaries of from $800 to $2,000 a year.

32. Mary E. Collson, "My Search," 27.
33. Garfield, "The Old Church," 195.
34. "Experiencing Religion," handwritten sermon, Safford file, SHSI.
35. Gordon, *The Second Chapter.*
36. Eleanor E. Gordon, "The Story of a Long Life, Part 3" (ca. 1942, typescript, GP), 9.
37. "On Unity Clubs," *Unity* 18 (1887): 264.
38. Gordon, *The Second Chapter.*
39. Ibid.; *Unity* 13 (1884), and 19 (1887): 30.
40. *Unity* 13 (1884): 229.
41. Elizabeth Cady Stanton, *History of Woman's Suffrage* (hereafter cited as *HWS*), 6 vols. (New York: Fowler & Wells, 1969), vol. 1; see also William Leach, *True Love and Perfect Union* (New York, 1980), 156.
42. Gordon, *The Second Chapter.*
43. *Unity* 13 (1884): 134.
44. *History of Humboldt County* (Chicago and Cedar Rapids, 1901), 461.
45. *Fifty Years of Unity Church* (Sioux City, 1935) 18.

CHAPTER TWO   *Lengthening Cords and Strengthening Stakes*

1. Gordon, *The Second Chapter.*
2. Charles E. Snyder, "Unitarianism in Iowa," *Palimpsest* 30 (1949): 369.
3. Gordon, *The Second Chapter.*
4. Carroll Smith-Rosenberg, "The Female World of Love and Ritual: Relations between Women in Nineteenth-Century America," *Signs* 1 (1975): 16–17.
5. Jessie Vaupell Bicknell, "Rev. Eleanor Gordon's Teaching Years," in Vestal "Gordon Notes," 6–7, SHSI; F. W. Bicknell, "The Conference of 1880."
6. Collson, "My Search," 1–2.
7. Mary A. Safford to Jenkin Lloyd Jones, 18 May 1882, MTS.
8. "Band of Women Ministers," *Boston Herald,* 5 May 1890, clipping, WMC.
9. Ibid.
10. Ida C. Hultin to Jenkin Lloyd Jones, 22 November 1881, 7 December 1881, MTS.
11. Hultin's reputation as an independent worker is referred to in Anna J. Norris to Jenkin Lloyd Jones, 21 April 1890, MTS.
12. Mary A. Safford to Jenkin Lloyd Jones, 7 July 1885, MTS.
13. Ida C. Hultin to Jenkin Lloyd Jones, 13 March 1886, MTS.
14. Ibid.
15. Rowena Morse Mann, incomplete draft of biography and biographical notes, n.d., typescript, RMM.
16. Ibid.; Rowena Morse's school records, RMM.

17. This immensely popular lecture circuit is described in Hubert H. Hoeltje, "Notes on the History of Lecturing in Iowa, 1855–1885," *Iowa Journal of History and Politics* 25 (1927): 62–131.
18. Rowena Morse Mann, autograph book, 1878–83, RMM.
19. The entry on Rowena Morse Mann in Catherine F. Hitchings, *Unitarian and Universalist Women Ministers*, 2d ed. (Boston, 1985), 100–102, describes how Mann misrepresented her record of achievements.
20. As Amelia Murdock (Wing) explained to Charles Aldrich in a letter dated 30 November 1897, MFP, the family had different ways of spelling their last name, some preferring *Murdock* and others *Murdoch*. Amelia and Marion tended to stick with the former.
21. Samuel Murdock to his wife, Louisa Patch Murdock, 9 January 1870, MFP.
22. Amelia Murdock Wing, "Early Days in Clayton County," *Annals of Iowa*, 3d ser., 27 (1946): 257–96, passim.
23. Ellen and Marion Murdock to the editor of the *North Iowa Times*, 24 December 1866, MFP.
24. Wing, "Early Days in Clayton County," 281.
25. Marion Murdock to Jenkin Lloyd Jones, 4 May 1884, MTS; Rev. Marian [*sic*] Murdock, "Women at Meadville," an address at the semicentennial of the Meadville Theological School, June 1894, MTS; see also Francis A. Christie, *The Makings of the Meadville Theological School, 1844–1894* (Boston, 1927).
26. Lyttle, *Freedom Moves West*, 119–25, describes the climate that Jones found at Meadville and how he weathered it.
27. Marion Murdock to Jenkin Lloyd Jones, 4 May 1884, MTS.
28. Recollection of John Howland Lathrop, sent to Jessie E. Donahue, ca. 1940, typescript, UUA.
29. *Unity* 19 (1887): 30.
30. Marion Murdock to Rev. Grindall Reynolds, AUA secretary, 29 February 1888, AUA.
31. Marion Murdock to Jenkin Lloyd Jones, 30 June 1887, MTS.
32. Marion Murdock to Jenkin Lloyd Jones, 2 June 1888, MTS.
33. Marion Murdock to Jenkin Lloyd Jones, September 1889, MTS.
34. Marion Murdock to Jenkin Lloyd Jones, 2 June 1888, MTS.
35. Marion Murdock to Jenkin Lloyd Jones, 27 May 1889, MTS.
36. Marion Murdock to Jenkin Lloyd Jones, 6 July 1887, MTS.
37. Marion Murdock to Rev. Grindall Reynolds, 2 February 1888, AUA.

CHAPTER THREE   *A Happy Company*

1. Caroline Bartlett Crane, "Early Religious Struggle," autobiographical notes, CBC.
2. Caroline Bartlett Crane, "The Story," autobiographical notes, 7, CBC.
3. Ibid.; Caroline Bartlett Crane, "Memories of 'C.C.,'" *Carthage College Bulletin* 9 (1925): 5 (available in CBC).
4. Letters from Virginia Safford Bristow to Pearl Avis Gordon Vestal, 1942, excerpted in "Safford Notes," 14.

5. Caroline Bartlett, "Press, Pulpit and Penates," *Carthaginian* 4 (1881): 101−103 (available in CBC).
6. Crane, "Early Religious Struggle," 12.
7. Ibid., 8.
8. Untitled columns, written under the pseudonym "Nell Hudson," *Minneapolis Tribune,* ca. 1885, clipping file, CBC.
9. Crane, "Early Religious Struggle," 9.
10. See Conrad Wright, *A Doctrine of the Church for Liberals* (Boston, 1983).
11. Carrie J. Bartlett to Oscar Clute, 8 October 1886, CBC.
12. Crane, "Early Religious Struggle," 11.
13. Eliza Tupper Wilkes to Jenkin Lloyd Jones, 2 August 1881, MTS.
14. Eliza Tupper Wilkes to Grindell Reynolds, 31 March 1887, AUA.
15. Eliza Tupper Wilkes to Grindell Reynolds, 17 March 1887, 31 March 1887, AUA.
16. Eliza Tupper Wilkes to Jenkin Lloyd Jones, 28 February 1888, MTS.
17. "Clergywomen. They Meet for a Conference in Boston," *Boston Daily Globe,* 3 June 1889, WMC; *Old and New* 4 (1895): 5.
18. Crane, "Early Religious Struggle," 12.
19. Carrie J. Bartlett to Jenkin Lloyd Jones, 26 December 1887, MTS.
20. Crane, "Early Religious Struggle," 14; People's Church Secretary's Book, 1883−94, p. 51, PC.
21. Clipping from *Minneapolis Tribune,* 25 May 1889, p. 1, CBC.
22. Crane, "Early Religious Struggle," 14; People's Church Secretary's Book, 1883−94, pp. 54−56.
23. Clipping from *Grand Rapids, Mich., Telegram-Herald,* 21 October 1889, CBC.
24. People's Church Secretary's Book, 1883−94, p. 76.
25. Carrie J. Bartlett to Lorenzo Dow Bartlett, September 1889, CBC.

CHAPTER FOUR   *Coming to the Front*

1. For a succinct survey of women's entry into the teaching profession in the nineteenth century, see Sheila M. Rothman, *Woman's Proper Place* (New York, 1978), 56−60.
2. Catherine Beecher, *Suggestions Respecting Improvements in Education* (Hartford, Conn., 1829), 46.
3. Catherine Beecher to Horace Mann, *Common School Journal* 5 (Boston, 1843): 356.
4. Mida F. Doan, "Recollections of First School Days," in *History of Humboldt* (Humboldt, Iowa, 1963), 106; F. W. Bicknell, "The Conference of 1880"; Gordon, *The Second Chapter.* 2.
5. Collson, "My Search," 10.
6. Gordon, *The Second Chapter.*
7. Collson, "My Search," 7.
8. Gordon, "The Story of a Long Life," 7.
9. Gordon, *The Second Chapter.*
10. Snyder, *Unitarianism in Iowa,* 355ff.

11. Gordon, *The Second Chapter.*
12. Eleanor E. Gordon to Jenkin Lloyd Jones, 8 December 1885, MTS.
13. Ibid.
14. Eleanor E. Gordon to Jenkin Lloyd Jones, 12 April 1886, MTS.
15. Eleanor E. Gordon to Jenkin Lloyd Jones, 16 December 1887, MTS.
16. *Fifty Years of Unity Church,* 18.
17. Eleanor E. Gordon to Jenkin Lloyd Jones, 12 April 1886, MTS.
18. *Ten Years of the First Unitarian Church of Sioux City* (Sioux City, Iowa, 1895), 13–14.
19. Eleanor E. Gordon to Jenkin Lloyd Jones, 27 October 1888, MTS.
20. Gordon, "The Story of a Long Life," 3.
21. Gordon, *Long Story.*
22. The available information on Putnam has been collected in Hitchings, *Unitarian and Universalist Women Ministers,* 123–25.
23. Anna Jane Norris to Cordelia Throop Cole, 17 July 1883; Eliza Tupper Wilkes to Jenkin Lloyd Jones, 28 February 1888, MTS.
24. Helen G. Putnam to Jenkin Lloyd Jones, 8 October 1889, MTS.
25. Anna Jane Norris to Cordelia Throop Cole, 17 July 1883; Anna Jane Norris to Jenkin Lloyd Jones, 21 April 1890; Helen G. Putnam to Jenkin Lloyd Jones, 18 March 1890, 8 October 1889, MTS.
26. "Women Ministers at Mrs. Howe's," clipping from *Woman's Journal,* 11 June 1904, WMC.
27. Estella Elizabeth Padgham, autobiographical essay, 7, handwritten manuscript, UUA.
28. Safford identified one of the thorny differences in a letter to AUA secretary Charles E. St. John, 18 March 1902, AUA, in which she said that she had some hopes of starting a church in a Quaker community in her district, "but knowing the Quakers," it would "take time to educate those interested in the services to *pay* for them." For an excellent history of American Quaker women and their involvement in nineteenth-century reform, see Margaret Hope Bacon, *Mothers of Feminism* (San Francisco, 1986).
29. For the sisterhood's objections to Christian Science, see Cynthia Grant Tucker, *A Woman's Ministry* (Philadelphia, 1984), esp. 64–65.
30. Letter from Celia Parker Woolley to Jenkin Lloyd Jones, 15 September 1894, MTS. Lyttle, *Freedom Moves West,* 11–16, discusses the reasons for the lack of greater fellowship and cooperation between the Unitarians and the Universalists.
31. H. K. Carroll, *Religious Forces of the United States* (New York, 1893), 392.
32. "Record of the Woman's Ministerial Conference," 84, WMC.
33. Marie Jenney, "Women in the Ministry," *Meadville Portfolio* 1 (1894): 21.
34. Reprinted in unidentified newspaper clipping dated 19 April 1891, CBC.

CHAPTER FIVE   *Tending Church Families*

1. William R. Alger, "Women and Religion," *Unitarian* 12 (August 1897): 352.

2. Reflections by nine clergywomen on this and other aspects of their ministries were published in the *Unitarian* 2 (1907): 96–101.

3. As Mary Safford told AUA secretary Samuel A. Eliot—in a letter dated 16 February 1898, AUA—her conference's societies had raised more money than any other.

4. For example, Mary Safford to Samuel Eliot, 14 July 1899, AUA.

5. Eleanor E. Gordon to Jenkin Lloyd Jones, 3 March 1897, MTS.

6. Estella Elizabeth Padgham, autobiographical essay, 7–8, UUA.

7. Carrie J. Bartlett to Lorenzo Dow and Louise N. Babcock Bartlett, 22 September 1890, CBC.

8. *Old and New* 9 (1900): 8.

9. Nora M. Staton, telephone interview with Cynthia G. Tucker, 1 June 1986.

10. Amelia Murdock to Louisa Patch Murdock, 11 May 1888, MFP.

11. This conclusion is based on the data provided for over a hundred ministers in the relevant time frame in Hitchings, *Unitarian and Universalist Women Ministers*.

12. Susan B. Anthony to Caroline Bartlett Crane, 21 January 1897, CBC.

13. Anna Howard Shaw to Caroline Bartlett Crane, 26 April 1916, CBC.

14. Caroline Bartlett Crane to Joanne Blanenfeldt, 9 February 1927, CBC.

15. Caroline Bartlett Crane to Augustus Warren Crane, 16 September 1920, CBC.

16. Caroline Bartlett Crane to Augustus Warren Crane, 14 February 1920, CBC.

17. Margaret Titus Olmstead to Eleanor E. Gordon, 15 January 1907, 2 June 1907, DMUC.

18. "Woman as Minister," *Woman's Standard* 8 (1893): 3; Celia Parker Woolley, *Unitarian* 4 (1909): 229.

19. The marriage was given extensive press coverage; see clippings file, CBC.

20. Nora M. Staton, telephone interview with Cynthia G. Tucker, 20 March 1988.

21. Gordon, "The Story of a Long Life," 3.

22. Marion Murdock, "Home" (poem), in *History of Clayton County, Iowa* (1882), 628. See also Colleen McDannell, *The Christian Home in Victorian America* (Bloomington, Ind., 1986).

23. *Old and New* 5 (November 1896).

24. *Old and New* 1 (December 1891).

25. *Old and New* 4 (May 1895).

26. Eleanor E. Gordon to Jenkin Lloyd Jones, 30 August 1900, MTS.

27. Interview with Nora M. Staton at her home in Orlando, Fla., 9 March 1895.

28. Letter from Mary A. Safford to "My Friends" (found with her will), excerpted in "Safford Notes," 12.

29. Eliza Tupper Wilkes to Jenkin Lloyd Jones, 28 February 1888, MTS.

30. Clipping from the *Woman's Journal* (11 June 1904), WMC.

31. Jabez Sunderland, "The Liberal Christian Ministry as a Calling for Young Women," *Woman's Standard* 3 (July 1889): 3.

32. "'Parish Calls' from the Lay-Woman's Point of View" (a symposium), *Unitarian* 2 (May 1907): 170–75; Jenney, "Women in the Ministry," 23.

33. Padgham, autobiographical essay, 14.
34. This phenomenon has been explored in Nancy Chodorow, *The Reproduction of Mothering* (Berkeley, 1978).
35. "The Ethical Implications of the Organic Theory of Society," *Old and New* 10 (November 1901): 2.
36. Mary A. Safford, "Liberal Religious Leadership in Our Day," *Old and New* 10 (November 1901): 3.

CHAPTER SIX   *Special Friendships*

1. In a tribute to one of her parish families, Caroline Bartlett Crane recalled, "As a Thanksgiving Day guest at the home of Mr. and Mrs. Kleinsteuck, I looked up and down the long table filled with happy home-coming people and then, quite unconscious of my own status, whispered to my nearest neighbor, 'We are all relatives but Eddie!'" ("The Life of Caroline Irene Hubbard Kleinsteuck," 38, typescript, CBC).
2. Eleanor E. Gordon to Jenkin Lloyd Jones, 23 March 1898, MTS.
3. Eliza Tupper Wilkes to Miss Jones, 8 February 1887; Eliza Tupper Wilkes to Jenkin Lloyd Jones, 2 February 1887, MTS.
4. Eliza Tupper Wilkes to Jenkin Lloyd Jones, 1 January 1887, MTS.
5. J. H. Woolley to Jenkin Lloyd Jones, 15 April 1918, MTS.
6. J. H. Woolley to Jenkin Lloyd Jones, 9 April 1918, MTS.
7. A journal entry made by Caroline fifteen years after the marriage shows the couple's enduring romance: "Warren and I had our most beautiful Sunday morning hour together. He read Van Dyke's 'The Mansion,' while I sat on a low stool beside and *against* him, and our 'Mignouette' played 'O, that we two were maying.' . . . I think to sit silent by him, while he reads something I have read . . . and to know just what he is reading—and to play for him—is the sweetest of all. . . . He was so moved by the beautiful story—he said—'We have had our service this morning,' and his dear eyes were smiling but *wet!* O, how blest I am!" 16 February 1913, CBC).
8. I am much indebted to O'Ryan Rickard of Western Michigan University, who has worked extensively with the Crane papers, for sharing his insights into the Cranes' relationship and pointing out that, thanks to Warren, Caroline was made an honorary member of the city's all-male medical society, whose meetings she proudly attended.
9. A letter that Caroline wrote to Warren's medical partner on 25 May 1920, CBC, proposing a financial reorganization of the practice that would be more favorable to the Cranes, shows her to be the family's business and financial manager. As for Warren's willingness to let his wife take center stage, relatives later maintained that he had little choice in the matter, so intolerant was Caroline of being upstaged by him. Reportedly, she insisted on getting rid of the family piano because he could play it as well as she even without having had formal lessons ("Caroline Bartlett Crane: A Preliminary Sketch," typescript, CBC).

10. Augustus Warren Crane to Caroline Bartlett Crane, 29 October 1911, CBC.

11. A letter from Eleanor E. Gordon to Jenkin Lloyd Jones, 3 March 1909, MTS, shows that word of an impeding marriage began to circulate several years before it actually took place.

12. These poems, which I and several other scholars were able to see before the Rowena Morse Mann Papers were processed by the Schlesinger Library, are now in a restricted file that remains closed until 1 January 2000.

13. Helen Bullard, "Personal Notes on Dr. Rowena Morse Mann," 24 June 1974, typescript loaned by the author; phone interview with Bullard, 25 April 1987; Newton Mann to Jenkin Lloyd Jones (postcard), 5 June 1913, MTS.

14. Bullard, "Personal Notes."

15. Rowena Morse Mann to Sarah Flichette Morse, 23 December 1912.

16. Newton's "padding of the figures" is mentioned in a letter from Western Unitarian Conference secretary Ernest C. Smith to Henry Wilder Foote, 12 February 1914, AUA.

17. Frederick C. Howe, *The Confessions of a Reformer* (New York, 1925), 233.

18. Adele Fuchs to Mary A. Safford, 8 June 1903, HHJ.

19. For this information I am indebted to Mary-Ella Holst, independent scholar at All Souls Unitarian Church, New York City, who is working on a fuller biography of Marie Jenney Howe.

20. Marie Hoffendahl Jenney to Charlotte Perkins Stetson, 12 August 1899, reproduced in Zona Gale, *The Living of Charlotte Perkins Gilman* (New York, 1935), xx–xxii.

21. Howe, *The Confessions of a Reformer,* 66–67.

22. Marie Hoffendahl Jenney to Charlotte Perkins Stetson, 12 August 1899.

23. Mary Ella Holst, who told me about the Howes' baby, learned of it from a nephew of Marie's. For a good account of Marie's life in New York, see Judith Schwarz, *Radical Feminists of Heterodoxy* (Lebanon, N.H., 1982).

24. In a journal entry dated September 1929, HHJ, Adele Fuchs, a former parishioner and longtime friend who had found Marie alone and depressed when she visited her, summed up the situation this way: "She does not enthuse over her husband. There has been a let-down there, but who shall criticize a man of F. C. Howe's gifts running a summer hotel and a lecture Chautauqua?"

25. Marie Jenney Howe to Fola La Follette, n.d., LFP.

26. Hutchins Hapgood, *A Victorian in the Modern World* (New York, 1939), 232–33.

27. Mabel Dodge Luhan, *Intimate Memories,* vol. 3, *Movers and Shakers* (New York, 1936), 143–44.

28. In a letter to Fola La Follette dated 22 March 1933, LFP, Marie wrote, "Rose has just finished her biography and Fred (thank goodness) has just finished his book on banking. I have heard nothing but banking for 10 years and I would like to have a change of subject at the dinner-table. But to my despair he has immediately started another book—on banking. Any other subject would interest me more."

29. Adele Fuchs, diary entry, 18 June 1934, HHJ.
30. For explicit analogies between Marie's church ministry and stewardship of the Heterodoxy Club, see "Heterodoxy to Marie," especially the entry by Mabel Potter Daggett, scrapbook, IHI.
31. Adele Fuchs, *Diary, 1913–1917*, 4 January 1917, HHJ.
32. Eleanor E. Gordon, "The Great Opportunity," *Unity* 23 (1899): 101.
33. *Old and New* 11 (April 1903): 2; "Charge Given at Mary Safford's Ordination," *Unity* 5 (1880): 160–61.
34. Adele Fuchs, *Diary 1923–1934*, 11 September, 1929, HHJ.
35. Mary E. Collson to Edward Meeman, 30 December 1932; Emily Greene Balche, quoted in Ray Ginger, *Altgeld's America* (Chicago, 1965), 140–41.
36. "Friendship between Girls," *Old and New*, vol. 4 (May 1895).
37. As a positive term affirming the wide spectrum of women's love for women, the term *lesbian*, which came into currency only around the turn of the century, might well be applied to these alliances, though historians have not yet reached a consensus on whether to assign the term retroactively or to use the "native categories" the women themselves would have used. This ongoing issue is debated in Judith Schwarz, "Questionnaire in Lesbian History," *Frontiers* 4 (Fall 1979): 4–5. Lillian Faderman's introduction to *Surpassing the Love of Men* (New York, 1981) helps put the term *lesbian* into historical perspective.
38. Marion Murdock to Jenkin Lloyd Jones, 2 August 1890, MTS.
39. People's Church Secretary's Book, 1883–94; People's Church Ladies Society Records, 1890–92, DMUC.
40. Amelia Murdock Wing to Joseph Crosby, 1 January 1911, 4 September 1911, GHS.
41. Marion Murdock to "The Friends of Florence Buck and Marion Murdoch," [1925], UUA.
42. Rev. George Badger, "Contemporary Portraits," *Unitarian* 2 (1907): 91–92.
43. Samuel A. Eliot to A. W. Gould, 19 September 1898; George Batchelor to Joseph Scammon, 23 October 1897, AUA.
44. Eleanor E. Gordon to Jenkin Lloyd Jones, 21 November 1898; George Batchelor to Joseph Scammon, 21 October 1898, AUA.
45. Eleanor E. Gordon to Jenkin Lloyd Jones, 11 February 1900, MTS.
46. Adele Fuchs, *Diary 1918–1922*, 22 August 1919, HHJ.
47. Fuchs's diary entries make repeated reference to this trait.
48. Eleanor E. Gordon, "The Early History of the Orlando Unitarian Church, 1911–1918," n.d., 1, 3, mimeographed pamphlet, NMS.
49. Mary A. Safford to Eleanor E. Gordon, 9 September 1911, quoted in ibid., 3.
50. Interview with Nora M. Staton at her home in Orlando, Fla., 8 March 1985.
51. Gordon, "The Early History of the Orlando Unitarian Church," 7.
52. Eleanor E. Gordon, "History of the Round Table," 1913–15, handwritten notes, NMS; Record of the Orlando Unitarian Church, OUC.
53. Samuel A. Eliot to Eleanor E. Gordon, 18 April 1927, AUA.
54. Adele Fuchs, *Diary, 1923–1934*, 11 August 1928, HHJ.
55. Adele Fuchs, "A Vagabond's Wanderings," 14–15, ca. 1950, typescript carbon copy, HHJ.

56. Ibid., 21; Fuchs, *Diary, 1923–1934,* 1 January 1932, HHJ.
57. Fuchs, *Diary, 1885–1892,* entries for 1885, HHJ.
58. Fuchs, *Diary, 1923–1932,* September 1929, 1 January 1932, HHJ.
59. Adele Fuchs to Mary A. Safford, ca. 1899, HHJ.
60. Adele Fuchs to Mary A. Safford, 28 January 1899, HHJ.
61. Adele Fuchs to Mary A. Safford, 4 July 1899, HHJ.
62. Adele Fuchs to Mary A. Safford, ca. 1899, HHJ.
63. Interview with Nora M. Staton at her home in Orlando, Fla., 8 March 1985.
64. *Old and New* 14 (November 1906): 59; Record Book of the Young People's Religious Union, 1907–13, First Unitarian Church, Des Moines, Iowa, DMUC.

CHAPTER SEVEN   *The Pastor as Teacher*

1. Gordon, *The Second Chapter,* 5.
2. Eleanor E. Gordon, "Giving What We Have: A Christmas Sermon," *Old and New* 10 (December 1901): 5.
3. Catherine E. Beecher and Harriet Beecher Stowe, *The American Woman's Home* (New York, 1869), 456.
4. Lawrence Buell, "The Unitarian Movement and the Art of Preaching in 19th Century America," *American Quarterly* 24 (1972): 170.
5. Lyttle, *Freedom Moves West,* 128–31.
6. Padgham, autobiographical essay, 12.
7. Gordon, "The Story of a Long Life," 6–7.
8. For example, Cora Stockman, "Our Nursery," *Kindergarten* 3 (1891): 337; for a good survey of this movement, see also Rothman, *Woman's Proper Place,* 99ff.
9. Rothman, *Woman's Proper Place,* 103.
10. Caroline Bartlett Crane, "The Story of an Institutional Church in a Small City," *Charities* (6 May 1905): 5.
11. Snyder, *Unitarian in Iowa,* 362; *Unity* 13 (1884): 118, 134.
12. For example, Margaret T. Olmstead, "Spiritual Education. . . ," *Old and New* 14 (November 1906): 61–62.
13. Gordon, "The Story of a Long Life," 3.
14. *Old and New* 13 (September 1905): 3.
15. Rothman, *Woman's Proper Place,* 65; see also Karen J. Blair, *The Clubwoman as Feminist* (New York, 1980).
16. People's Church Ladies Society Records, 1890–1892, PC.
17. *New Unity* 17 (1898): 9.
18. Jones's talk on "Modern Slavery" before the Chicago Woman's Club in April 1906 summed up his concerns and hopes for the club movement (reported in the *Grand Rapids, Mich., Herald,* 15 April 1906, clippings file, MTS).
19. "The Meaning of Life: A Problem in Proportion," *Old and New,* vol. 4 (December 1895).
20. *Unity Circle History,* Des Moines Unitarian Church, 8, DMUC.
21. Ibid., 4–9.

22. George Eliot, who was the great favorite among nineteenth-century feminists and appeared repeatedly on the Unity Circle calendars, was acclaimed by the ministers as a "source of moral strength and inspiration" and valued especially for her uplifting portraits of ministrant women (*Old and New* 11 [January 1903]: 6); their lists of the "noblest novels" written in English were dominated by Eliot (*Unity* 13 [1884]: 229). One issue of *Old and New* (12 [November 1904]: 6) describes a typical eight-month course on Eliot.

23. Woman's Section of Unity Club, Des Moines Unitarian Church, Secretary's Book, 1892–1893, p. 21, DMUC.

24. See the report from Des Moines on the Unity Circle's programs in "Notes from the Field," *Old and New,* vol. 4 (March 1895).

25. Marie Jenney Howe, "American League for Civic Improvement," *Old and New* 11 (September 1902): 4.

26. *Old and New* 8 (January 1900): 5.

27. Mrs. T. J. Bowlker, "Woman's Home-making Function Applied to the Municipality," *American City* 6 (1912): 863.

28. Nettie F. Bailey, "Significance of the Women's Club Movement," *Harper's Bazaar* (1905): 204; Women's Educational and Industrial Union Report, 1 May 1885, quoted in Blair, *The Clubwoman as Feminist,* 74.

29. Caroline Dall, *College, Market, and Court,* memorial ed. (Boston, 1914), 233–36.

30. *Unity* 13 (1884): 134.

31. Gordon, "The Story of a Long Life," 1.

32. *Unity* 44 (1899): 447.

33. *Old and New* 8 (June 1900): 7, and 11 (May 1903): 7.

34. *Old and New* 11 (October 1903): 7.

35. Caroline Bartlett Crane, "Early Religious Struggle," 18.

CHAPTER EIGHT   *The Church Home*

1. For an excellent study of domestic religion, see McDannell, *The Christian Home in Victorian America.*

2. Clara C. Helvie, "Unitarian Women Ministers," 110.

3. William Channing Gannett, *The House Beautiful* (River Forest, Ill., 1897).

4. This lecture, a modified sermon, is paraphrased in an undated clipping, ca. 1904, in clippings scrapbook, MTS; also see sermons file, MTS.

5. Caroline Bartlett Crane, *Everyman's House* (New York, 1925).

6. Caroline Bartlett Crane, "Naming the Home," 23 August [ca. 1893], CBC.

7. Caroline Bartlett Crane, "Dedication of The New Home of Walter R. and Ella E. Taylor," Kalamazoo, Mich., 21 December 1895, CBC.

8. Caroline Bartlett Crane, "Dedication of the Home of Henry Holcomb and Lizbeth Vaupel Griffiths," 25 October 1901, DMUC; *Old and New* 10 (November 1901): 7.

9. Eleanor E. Gordon to Jenkin Lloyd Jones, 8 October 1886, MTS.

10. *Ten Years of the First Unitarian Church of Sioux City,* 21; "Dedication of The First Unitarian Church, Des Moines," 30 April 1905, DMUC.

11. Beecher and Stowe, *The American Woman's Home,* 456.

12. Lyttle, *Freedom Moves West,* 158.

13. "The Ideal Church," quoted in ibid., 158–59.

14. *Old and New* 11 (November 1903): 3. See also Rev. Von Ogden Vogt, *Art and Religion* (New Haven, Conn., 1921). Vogt was a leading advocate for more beauty in worship.

15. *Old and New* 11 (November 1903): 3.

16. Caroline Bartlett Crane, "The Story of an Institutional Church," 4.

17. *Ten Years of the First Unitarian Church of Sioux City,* 11; *Fifty Years of Unity Church,* 18. Mary Collson followed Sioux City's example when she was called to Ida Grove and found that this town of only two thousand already had seven sanctuaries. Instead of "inflicting" another on it, Collson encouraged the people to purchase an empty theater and turn it into a "seven day church" and community cultural center. Mary Collson to Samuel A. Eliot, 7 November 1898, AUA; Collson, "My Search," 25.

18. Eliza Tupper Wilkes to Jenkin Lloyd Jones, 1 December 1887, MTS.

19. Eliza Tupper Wilkes to Jenkin Lloyd Jones, ca. 1887, MTS.

20. *Ten Years of the First Unitarian Church of Sioux City,* 91.

21. Crane, "The Story of an Institutional Church," 4.

22. *Ten Years of the First Unitarian Church of Sioux City,* 91–92.

23. "Unitarians to Build Church in This City," *Orlando Reporter-Star,* 20 January 1912; "Attractive Little Church Costs Modest Sum," *Popular Mechanics,* May 1917, p. 800.

24. H. H. Griffith, "History of Unitarianism in Iowa and Nebraska," June 1924, 7, typescript, DMUC.

25. Robert S. Loring to Eleanor E. Gordon, 21 June 1917, 8 September 1907, 19 December 1907, DMUC; Mary Bell Glick, *Furnishings and Friends* (Iowa City, 1983).

26. "Unitarian Church Was Dedicated Last Evening," *Iowa City Republican,* 26 October 1908, p. 1.

27. *Christian Register* (8 May 1823).

28. Mrs. William I. Nichols, "The Architecture of Liberal Churches," *Unitarian* (September 1907): 301, 304.

29. Mary A. Safford to Grindall Reynolds, 5 March 1889, AUA.

30. Mary Safford to Samuel A. Eliot, 16 February 1898, AUA.

31. "Forward's the Word," *Kalamazoo Daily News,* 20 December 1884.

32. Eleanor E. Gordon to Samuel A. Eliot, 7 October 1912, 29 November 1912, AUA.

33. Eleanor E. Gordon to Samuel A. Eliot, 4 January 1913, AUA.

34. "Orlando: History of Its Church Homes," *Orlando Sun,* 14 July 1968, clippings file, OPL.

35. Gordon, "The Early History of the Orlando Unitarian Church," 9–10.

36. See Nichols, "The Architecture of Liberal Churches," 302–3.

37. *Old and New* 8 (December 1899): 5; "Laying of Des Moines Church Cornerstone," *Old and New* 12 (September 1904): 3.

38. Jenkin Lloyd Jones to Eleanor E. Gordon, 22 March 1898, MTS.

39. Eleanor E. Gordon to Jenkin Lloyd Jones, 7 January 1904, MTS.

40. *Kalamazoo Daily News,* 9 December 1894, clippings file, CBC.
41. Caroline Bartlett to Jenkin Lloyd Jones, 30 January 1893, MTS.
42. Crane, "The Story of an Institutional Church," 4.
43. Ibid.
44. Leach, *True Love and Perfect Union,* 65.
45. Crane, "The Story of an Institutional Church," 8.
46. "Dedicatory Sermon by Rev. Jenkin Lloyd Jones," *Kalamazoo Daily News,* 20 December 1894, clippings file, CBC.

CHAPTER NINE   *East and West*

1. Caroline Julia Bartlett to Jenkin Lloyd Jones, 19 June 1889, MTS.
2. See William Thurston Brown, "The Problem of Liberal Religion in the West," *Unitarian* 5 (April 1910): 116–17.
3. Jenney, "Women in the Ministry," 21; see also W. M. Bakus, "Western Unitarianism," *New Unitarian* 1 (February 1906): 36–37.
4. "The Western Women's Unitarian Conference," ca. 1901, handwritten manuscript, MTS.
5. "The Story of the Post Office Mission," ca. 1886, handwritten manuscript, MTS.
6. *Unity* 82 (November 1918): 148.
7. "The Story of the Post Office Mission."
8. Lyttle, *Freedom Moves West,* 202.
9. A note on "Lay Leaders" in the *Unitarian* (2 [August 1887]: 203) tells of the women's conference helping to underwrite Amelia Murdock's congregational development in Rock Rapids; a letter from Licinia E. Hilton to Eliza Sunderland (23 June 1882, BHL) mentions the conference pledging $50 to help Ida Hultin attend college classes.
10. Memoir of Rev. Charles Lowe, quoted in George William Cooke, *Unitarianism in America* (Boston, 1902), 370.
11. Ibid., 232.
12. Mary A. Safford to Grindall Reynolds, 23 March 1887, AUA.
13. Mary A. Safford to Grindall Reynolds, 5 April 1889, AUA.
14. Ibid.
15. Eliza Tupper Wilkes to Grindall Reynolds, 29 October 1889, AUA.
16. Mary A. Safford to Miss Close, 5 April 1889, AUA.
17. Mary A. Safford to Grindall Reynolds, 30 April 1890, AUA.
18. Eliza Tupper Wilkes to Jenkin Lloyd Jones, 2 August 1881, MTS.
19. Eliza Tupper Wilkes to Grindall Reynolds, 21 January 1894, AUA.
20. "The Story of the Post Office Mission."
21. *Unity* 19 (1887): 30.
22. Eleanor E. Gordon to Samuel A. Eliot, 25 March 1888, AUA.
23. Murdock, "Women at Meadville."
24. Gordon, *The Second Chapter.*
25. Padgham, autobiographical essay, 6.
26. John Tunis, "Women in the Ministry: An Appeal to Fact," *Unity* 15 (1885): 92–94.

27. Marion Murdock, "What Did Phoebe Do?" 1893, typescript, UUA.
28. Eleanor E. Gordon, "Amongst Ministers," *Unitarian* 2 (March 1907): 96–101.
29. Ida Hultin, "Woman in the Ministry," *Woman's Standard* 3 (January 1889): 3.
30. Murdock, "What Did Phoebe Do?" 1.
31. Eleanor E. Gordon, "Just Like a Woman," *Woman's Standard* 17, (December 1904): 1–2, and (January 1905): 1–2.
32. Hultin, "Woman in the Ministry," 3; Mary A. Safford, *The Woman's Standard* 8 (October 1893): 3.
33. Gordon, "Just Like a Woman" (1904), 1–2.
34. Caroline Bartlett Crane, "The Liberal Minister: His Equipment and Place," reprint of address given before the Western Unitarian Conference, 1892, CBC, and abridged as "The Woman Minister," *Parthenon* 1 (June 1892): 1–2.
35. Ibid.

CHAPTER TEN   *The Economics of Power*

1. Elizabeth Cady Stanton, "Anniversary of the American Equal Rights Association," *Revolution,* 13 May 1869.
2. Jenkin Lloyd Jones to Eleanor E. Gordon, 16 November 1894, MTS.
3. Mary A. Safford to Grindall Reynolds, 5 March 1889, AUA.
4. Eleanor E. Gordon to Jenkin Lloyd Jones, 14 September 1890, JLJ.
5. Mary Leggett to Grindall Reynolds, 28 April 1890, 23 December 1890, AUA.
6. Eliza Tupper Wilkes to Grindall Reynolds, 28 December 1893, 21 January 1894, AUA.
7. Eliza Tupper Wilkes to George Batchelor, 12 November 1897, AUA.
8. Eliza Tupper Wilkes to George Batchelor, 28 January 1896, AUA.
9. Eliza Tupper Wilkes to George Batchelor, 29 January 1897.
10. Mary A. Safford to Grindall Reynolds, 10 October 1890, AUA.
11. Mary A. Safford to George Batchelor, 5 August 1895; Mary A. Safford to Grindall Reynolds, 12 October 1892, AUA.
12. *Ten Years of the First Unitarian Church,* 67.
13. Eleanor E. Gordon to Jenkin Lloyd Jones, 11 May 1897, MTS.
14. Eleanor E. Gordon to Jenkin Lloyd Jones, 4 December 1891, 3 January 1892, MTS.
15. Eleanor E. Gordon to Samuel A. Eliot, 6 May 1899, AUA.
16. Eleanor E. Gordon to Jenkin Lloyd Jones, 4 April 1898, MTS.
17. Eleanor E. Gordon to Samuel A. Eliot, 10 October 1900, AUA.
18. Eliza Tupper Wilkes to George Batchelor, 2 March 1897, AUA.
19. Mary A. Safford to Charles St. John, 30 January 1901, AUA.
20. Eleanor E. Gordon to Jenkin Lloyd Jones, 9 February 1898, MTS.
21. Arthur Cushman McGiffert, Jr., *Pilot of a Liberal Faith: Samuel Atkins Eliot, 1862–1950* (Boston, 1976), chap. 4.
22. *Christian Register,* 8 February 1900, p. 175.
23. Conrad Wright, "A Wave at Crest: Administrative Reform . . . ," in *The Stream of Light: A Sesquicentennial History of American Unitarianism,* ed. Conrad

Wright (Boston, 1975), 97; Board of Directors Minutes, 10 March 1903, 14 March 1911, AUA.

24. Mary A. Safford to Samuel A. Eliot, 6 June 1898, AUA; "The 75th Anniversary of the American Unitarian Association," *Old and New* 8 (May 1900): 1.
25. Mary A. Safford to Samuel A. Eliot, 24 November 1898, AUA.
26. Mary A. Safford, "The Hard Test Being Put Upon Our Conference," *Old and New* 8 (June 1900): 1.
27. Statement by Arthur Judy, IUA president, in ibid.
28. "Is Local Self-Government Desirable?" *Old and New* 9 (October 1900): 23.
29. Mary A. Safford to Samuel A. Eliot, 16 February 1898, AUA.
30. Eliza Tupper Wilkes to George Batchelor, 28 January 1896, AUA.
31. Eleanor E. Gordon to Samuel A. Eliot, 1 December 1898, AUA.
32. Mary A. Safford to Samuel A. Eliot, 30 January 1901, AUA.
33. Eleanor E. Gordon to Samuel A. Eliot, 14 November 1898, AUA.
34. Mary A. Safford to Samuel A. Eliot, 30 January 1901, AUA.
35. Mary A. Safford to Charles E. St. John, 30 June 1902, AUA.
36. Mary A. Safford to Charles E. St. John, 14 November 1900, 6 December, 1900, AUA; "Our Denominational Polity," *Old and New* 9 (May 1901): 1.
37. Florence Buck to Samuel A. Eliot, 25 March 1899, 2 April 1899, 12 May 1899, AUA.

CHAPTER ELEVEN   *Religious Divisions*

1. For example, Cooke, *Unitarianism in America,* 225ff.; Lyttle, *Freedom Moves West,* 163ff.; Conrad Wright, ed., *A Stream of Light* (Boston, 1975), 62ff.
2. See Stow Persons, *Free Religion: An American Faith* (Boston, 1963).
3. Lyttle, *Freedom Moves West,* 176–81.
4. Eleanor E. Gordon, "Chapter IV," handwritten fragment, GP.
5. Ibid.
6. Eleanor E. Gordon to Jenkin Lloyd Jones, 18 May 1886, MTS.
7. Eleanor E. Gordon to Jenkin Lloyd Jones, 8 October 1886, MTS.
8. Francis Abbot, "Modern Principles of Free Religion," *Index,* 7 January 1871.
9. Eleanor E. Gordon to Jenkin Lloyd Jones, 8 October 1886, MTS.
10. Ibid.
11. Marion Murdock to Jenkin Lloyd Jones, 26 April 1887, MTS.
12. The proposed text was printed in the *Christian Register,* 29 March 1894, p. 194.
13. "Our National Conference," *Unitarian* 9 (1894): 459.
14. Griffith, "History of Unitarianism in Iowa and Nebraska."
15. Eleanor E. Gordon to Jenkin Lloyd Jones, 2 April 1896, MTS.
16. Eleanor E. Gordon to Jenkin Lloyd Jones, 4 May 1896, MTS.
17. Jenkin Lloyd Jones to Eleanor E. Gordon, 7 April 1896, MTS.
18. Eleanor E. Gordon to Jenkin Lloyd Jones, 9 October 1897, MTS.
19. Eleanor E. Gordon to Jenkin Lloyd Jones, 12 May 1897, MTS.
20. Eleanor E. Gordon to Jenkin Lloyd Jones, 9 February 1898, 23 April 1898, MTS.

21. Eleanor E. Gordon to Jenkin Lloyd Jones, 1 January 1900, MTS; Eleanor E. Gordon to Samuel A. Eliot, 11 May 1900, AUA.

22. Celia Parker Woolley to Jenkin Lloyd Jones, 15 September 1894, 4 April 1895, MTS. See also Woolley's address to the Western conference in *Old and New* (June 1898): 1. Caroline Bartlett Crane also counseled against the state conferences merging with the Liberal Congress. Such actions, she feared, might suggest to the AUA that the West's undisciplined liberals had let their associations "go to pieces" and now were trying clumsily to sweep up the remnants. Caroline Bartlett Crane to Mr. Udell, 24 June 1905, MTS.

23. Jenkin Lloyd Jones to Eleanor E. Gordon, 16 November 1894, MTS.

24. Eleanor E. Gordon to Jenkin Lloyd Jones, 11 November 1894, MTS.

25. Jenkin Lloyd Jones to Mary A. Safford, 24 June 1896, MTS.

26. Eleanor E. Gordon to Jenkin Lloyd Jones, 4 May 1896, MTS.

27. Unidentified Eastern member of the National Women's Alliance to Mrs. Richardson, 2 January 1889, MTS.

28. "The History of the Western Women's Unitarian Conference," 13ff., MTS.

29. Marion Murdock to Jenkin Lloyd Jones, 8 October 1895, JLJ.

30. Jenkin Lloyd Jones to Eleanor E. Gordon, 26 November 1896; Eleanor E. Gordon to Jenkin Lloyd Jones, 16 November 1898, MTS.

31. Eleanor E. Gordon to Jenkin Lloyd Jones, 21 November 1898, MTS.

32. Eleanor E. Gordon to Jenkin Lloyd Jones, 21 November 1898, MTS.

33. Mary E. Collson to Jenkin Lloyd Jones, 19 November 1899, MTS.

34. Jenkin Lloyd Jones to Mary A. Safford, 24 June 1896, MTS.

CHAPTER TWELVE   *Woman's Place in a "Manlier" Ministry*

1. Samuel A. Eliot to Mary A. Safford, 5 November 1898, 5 December 1898, AUA.

2. *Old and New* 9 (April 1901): 1; Griffiths, "History of Unitarianism in Iowa and Nebraska," 7ff.

3. Helvie provides a detailed profile of this decline in "Unitarian Women Ministers."

4. James H. Madison, "Reformers and the Rural Church, 1900–1950," *Journal of American History* 73 (1986): 649–50.

5. Griffiths, "History of Unitarianism in Iowa and Nebraska."

6. Eleanor E. Gordon to Jenkin Lloyd Jones, 3 March 1909, MTS.

7. See Douglas, *The Feminization of American Culture.*

8. James Elliot Cabot, *A Memoir of Ralph Waldo Emerson* (Boston and New York, 1887), 105, 167, 329.

9. D. Roy Freeman, responding to a survey in the *Unitarian* 2 (July 1907): 248–49.

10. John Haynes Holmes, "The Unitarian Ministry: The Problem of Withdrawals Again," *Unity* 68 (1911): 229–31.

11. George Batchelor to J. M. O. Hewitt, 4 October 1897, AUA.

12. Samuel A. Eliot to Dr. Fay, 3 February 1898, AUA.

13. Samuel A. Eliot to George Latimer, 25 November 1898, AUA.

14. Samuel A. Eliot to William W. Fenn, 4 February 1898; Samuel A. Eliot to Abram Wyman, 5 February 1898, AUA.

15. George Batchelor to Coburn, 30 November 1897, AUA.

16. Samuel A. Eliot to Miss Marshall, 6 January 1898, AUA.

17. Samuel A. Eliot to W. W. Fenn, 11 November 1898, AUA.

18. McGiffert, *Pilot of a Liberal Faith,* 146–47.

19. Mary A. Safford to Charles E. St. John, 11 November 1901, AUA.

20. Mary A. Safford to Charles E. St. John, 6 December 1900, AUA.

21. Mary A. Safford to Samuel A. Eliot, 15 March 1901, AUA.

22. Mary A. Safford to Charles E. St. John, 28 November 1901, AUA.

23. The affable Buck pointed out in a letter to Eliot (22 February 1899, AUA) that he and his officers seemed to "scold" the membership constantly and might get better results for the movement by taking a gentler and more appreciative approach.

24. Florence Buck to Charles E. St. John, 16 October 1900, AUA.

25. *Unitarian* 2 (March 1907): 97.

26. Ibid., 98.

27. *Old and New* 13 (June 1905): 7.

28. Margaret T. Olmstead to Eleanor E. Gordon, 15 January 1908, DMUC.

29. Eleanor E. Gordon to Samuel A. Eliot, 19 November 1898, AUA.

30. Eleanor E. Gordon to Jenkin Lloyd Jones, 24 November 1900, MTS.

31. *Old and New* 13 (February 1909): 7.

32. George Albert Coe, *Education in Religion and Morals* (Chicago and New York, 1904), 335.

33. Alger, "Woman and Religion," 352–53.

34. "Work for All," *Unitarian* 5 (August 1910): 288.

35. *New Unitarian* 1 (June 1906): 201–2.

36. Samuel A. Eliot to Mrs. W. Scott Fitts, 15 September 1906, Tuckerman School File, AUA. As part of this trend, the liberals' Pacific School of Religion and Canton Theological School also encouraged women to take courses training them to be parish assistants rather than ministers.

37. *Christian Register* 87 (28 February 1908): 6–7, 86 (21 March 1907): 6.

38. See Mary Graves's comments to this effect in the *Unitarian* 2 (March 1907): 99.

39. "Introductory Address by Dr. Eliot," 1912, typescript; Minutes of the Board of Directors, 26 November 1907, Tuckerman School File, AUA.

40. Samuel A. Eliot to Mrs. W. Scott Fitts, 15 September 1906; Minutes of the Board of Directors, 26 November 1907, Tuckerman School File, AUA.

41. "Address of Prof. L. P. Jacks," 23 May 1912, typescript, Tuckerman School File, AUA.

42. Minutes of the Board of Directors, 28 January 1908, Tuckerman School File, AUA.

43. Louise Henderson to Clara T. Guild, 30 September 1920, 15 June 1921, Tuckerman School File, AUA.

44. Eleanor E. Gordon to Jenkin Lloyd Jones, 3 March 1909, MTS.

45. "The Young Woman and the Church," *Old and New* 13 (September 1905): 3–5; Crane, "The Church and the Women," 14, CBC.

CHAPTER THIRTEEN   *Preaching Reform*

1. See Conrad Wright, "The Minister as Reformer" in *The Liberal Christians* (Boston, 1970), 62ff.; Peter Raible, "The Historical Myth Tensions of American Unitarianism," in *Unitarianism Universalism 1984: Selected Essays* (Boston, 1985), 78–79.
2. William Ellery Channing, *The Works of William Ellery Channing* (Boston, 1898), 1013.
3. Theodore Parker, *Theodore Parker's Experience as a Minister* (Boston, 1859), 133, and *Theodore Parker's Works*, vol. 7 (London, 1864), 16.
4. Quoted in Wright, *The Liberal Christians*, 72.
5. Parker, *Theodore Parker's Experience as a Minister*, 132.
6. The argument is developed in typical fashion in Samuel J. Niccolls, "Woman's Position and Work in the Church," *Presbyterian Review* 10 (April 1889): 267–79.
7. *Ten Years of the First Unitarian Church of Sioux City*, 13.
8. Caroline Julia Bartlett to the editor of the *Chicago Tribune*, 28 January 1896.
9. Rowena Morse Mann, undated sermon with text from Heb. 5:11 ("We have many things to say, seeing you have become dull of hearing"), handwritten and typescript, RMM.
10. John Howard Lathrop, recollection of Marion Murdock, typescript, n.d., ministers' files, AUA.
11. Marion Murdock, "The Ninetieth Psalm," typescript, ISHD.
12. Marion Murdock, "The Growth of the Hebrew People" (Humboldt, Iowa: printed by the congregation 1889), MTS.
13. Eleanor E. Gordon, "The Meaning of Life: A Problem in Proportion," *Old and New* 4 (December 1895).
14. *Old and New* 4 (April 1895); "Religion and Science," *Old and New* 5 (July 1896).
15. Mary A. Safford, "The Glory of the Imperfect," *Old and New* 12 (February 1904): 2–4.
16. Rowena Morse Mann, "Punishment of Sin," 18 November 1906, handwritten, RMM.
17. Eleanor E. Gordon, "The Glory of the Imperfect."
18. Spencer Lavan and George Huntston Williams, "The Unitarian and Universalist Traditions," in *Caring and Curing* (New York, 1986).
19. *Unity* 44 (1899): 449.
20. B. F. Underwood, "Mental Healing," *Old and New* 6 (November 1897).
21. Caroline Bartlett Crane, "Christian Science," *Unity* 47 (1901): 53.
22. See Tucker, *A Woman's Ministry*, esp. 80–85.
23. Eleanor E. Gordon, editorial, *Old and New* 13 (January 1905): 2.
24. Gordon, *The Second Chapter*, 1–2.
25. Charles Howard Hopkins, *The Rise of the Social Gospel in American Protestantism, 1865–1915* (New Haven, Conn., 1940), 4–5.
26. G. S. Garfield, "What I Like to Hear from the Pulpit," delivered at Ida Grove, Iowa, 1897, and reprinted in *Unity* 41 (1898): 42–43.

27. William Bos and Clyde Faries, "The Social Gospel: Preaching Reform, 1875–1915," in *Preaching in American History,* ed. Dewitte Holland (Nashville, 1969), 223–38.

28. *Old and New* 8 (June 1900): 7; *Old and New* 9 (November 1900): 4; Marie H. Jenney to Charlotte Perkins Stetson, 12 August 1899, *The Living of Charlotte Perkins Gilman,* xx–xxii.

29. Rowena Morse Mann, "None of Us Liveth to Himself," Keokuk, Iowa, 1906, handwritten sermon, RMM.

30. Caroline Bartlett Crane, "Solid Chunks of Truth," reprint of a sermon on "Sullivanism," ca. 1896, unidentified clipping, CBC.

31. Mary A. Safford, "Your Work and Mine," *Old and New* 4 (May 1895), and "Ships that Pass in the Night," *Old and New* 4 (May 1895).

32. Eleanor E. Gordon, "The House of Mirth," *Old and New* 14 (February 1906): 12–13, and "The Worth of Sympathy," *Old and New* (June 1907): 43–44.

33. Clipping from the *Des Moines Leader,* 6 June 1900, DMUC.

34. Rowena Morse Mann, "I Came Not to Judge the World," Keokuk, Iowa, 7 October 1906, handwritten sermon, RMM.

35. Mary A. Safford, "Editorial," *Old and New* 12 (April 1904): 1.

36. Eleanor E. Gordon, "The Good Part," *Old and New* 14 (December 1906): 69–70.

37. Eleanor E. Gordon, "Impressions of the Sioux City Conference," *Old and New* 8 (April 1900): 2.

38. Collson, "My Search," 25.

39. *Unity* 45 (1900): 302.

40. See typical letters from Samuel A. Eliot to Dr. Fay, 3 February 1898, D. W. Morehouse, 11 November 1898, and James C. Hodgins, 5 October 1898, AUA.

41. Statement by Maxwell Savage, *Unitarian,* n.s., 2 (July 1907): 247.

42. *Unitarian,* n.s., 2 (July 1907): 245.

43. Statement by D. Roy Freeman, *Unitarian,* n.s., 2 (July 1907): 248.

CHAPTER FOURTEEN *Blessed Neighborliness*

1. *Unity* 45 (1900): 262–64.

2. Caroline Bartlett Crane, Journal, 1891, 2:27–28, CBC.

3. Wing, "Early Days in Clayton County," 289.

4. Kathryn Kish Sklar ("Hull House in the 1890s," *Signs* 10 [1985]: 663) points out that this was not quite as true of the settlements' female leadership, whose primary impetus was their political goals, not religious motives. This difference in orientation between the leadership and the rank-and-file staff, who were carried into the settlements by the force of the social gospel movement, contributed to the disappointments that pastors like Collson and Leggett experienced when they spent some time as Hull House residents.

5. "The Settlement and Religion," reprinted from the *Churchman* in *Readings in the Development Work,* ed. Lorene M. Pacey (New York, 1950), 140–41.

6. These views were expressed in a discussion on "Religion as the Basis of Social

Ideals" at the annual Iowa conference meetings in 1901, as reported in *Old and New* 10 (November 1901): 3.

7. See Allen F. Davis, *Spearheads for Reform* (New York, 1967), 18–19; and also William Matthews, "The Settlement House Is Not a Charity," in *The Meaning of the Settlement Movement* (Pittsburgh, 1909), 13–31; Vida Scudder, *Socialism and Character* (Boston, 1912), 16–18; Robert Hunter, "Relations between Social Settlements and Charity Organizations," *National Conference of Charities and Correction* (1902): 302–14.

8. Mary L. Leggett to Jenkin Lloyd Jones, ca. February 1902, MTS.

9. Mary Kingsbury Simkhovitch, *Neighborhood: My Story of Greenwich House* (New York, 1938), 80–82.

10. Ministerial files, UUA.

11. Samuel A. Eliot to J. M. Mariott, 12 January 1898; a general overview of the movement can be obtained from "Recollections of Myron W. Reed," scrapbook, DPL.

12. *Old and New* 12 (November 1904): 2.

13. *Bulletin of Roadside Settlement, Des Moines, 1914*, ISHD; Eleanor E. Gordon to Jenkin Lloyd Jones, 3 December 1906, MTS.

14. Jane Addams, "The Settlement as a Factor in the Labor Movement," in *Hull House Maps and Papers* (Boston, 1895).

15. "Miss Addams' Idea of Citizenship," *Old and New* 8 (December 1899): 2.

16. Dall, *College, Market and Court*, 233–36.

17. "Hull House, Chicago: Its Work and Workers," *Unitarian* 8 (September 1893): 400; Eleanor E. Gordon, "Why Young Women Do Not Go to Church," *Old and New* 13 (October 1905): 3.

18. Edith Kendall, "Warren Goddard House," *Unitarian* 3 (April 1908): 126–35; Roadside Settlement House Association Records, DMPL.

19. *Unity* 41 (1898): 192.

20. *Unity* 45 (1900): 302.

21. *Old and New* 10 (November 1901): 3.

22. Collson, "My Search," 25; Mary E. Collson to Jenkin Lloyd Jones, 19 November 1899, MTS.

23. Collson, "My Search," 35.

24. *Hull-House Bulletin* 4 (January–May 1901): 12, HHP.

25. Collson, "My Search," 37.

26. Sara L. Hart, *The Pleasure Is Mine* (Chicago, 1947), 133. See also Mrs. Joseph T. Bowen, "The Early Days of the Juvenile Court," in *The Child, the Clinic and the Court* (New York, 1925), 300ff.

27. "Report of a Committee, 1912: The Juvenile Court of Cook County, Ill.," 7, 31, CHS.

28. Case Studies—Supplement I, folder 9 (November 1899–August 1901), 295, 211, 197, 239, 241, 211, 207–8, 219, JPA. For the optimistic report, see the Chicago Woman's Club, Club Meetings, 1900–1901, pp. 222–23, CHS.

29. Case Studies—Supplement I, 161, 235, 191.

30. This scandal is recounted by Robert L. Reed, "The Professionalism of Public

School Teachers: The Chicago Experience, 1895–1920" (Ph.D. diss., Northwestern University, 1968).

31. Collson, "My Search," 29–30.
32. Ibid., 31, 37–38.
33. Alzina Stevens, "As For Trade Unions," *Commons* 4 (June 1897): 12.
34. Collson, "My Search," 30.
35. H. Augusta Howard, "Woman Considered as a Human Being," *Social Democratic Herald*, 29 December 1900, p. 3.
36. See Sklar's discussion of the settlement's independence from male structures in "Hull House in the 1890s," 670ff.
37. For a good account of the movement's attitude toward women at the turn of the century, see Ira Kipnis, *The American Socialist Movement, 1897–1912* (New York, 1952), 261–65.
38. Collson, "My Search," 35.
39. Mary E. Collson to Edward Meeman, ca. September 1934, MVC.
40. Collson, "My Search," fragment, MVC.
41. Mary L. Leggett to Jenkin Lloyd Jones, ca. January 1901, MTS.
42. Alice Hamilton to Agnes Hamilton, 8 August 1900, quoted in Barbara Sicherman, *Alice Hamilton: A Life in Letters* (Cambridge, Mass., 1984), 140.
43. *Woman's Standard*, n.s., 21 (April 1908): 4, and (February 1908): 1.
44. *Woman's Standard*, n.s., 18 (December 1905): 3.
45. Eleanor E. Gordon to Jenkin Lloyd Jones, 3 March 1909, MTS.
46. Eleanor E. Gordon to Jenkin Lloyd Jones, 3 December 1906, MTS.
47. Eleanor E. Gordon to Jenkin Lloyd Jones, 3 March 1909, MTS.
48. See Jessie Shears-Carnovale's tribute to Celia Parker Woolley in *Unity* 81 (1918): 118.
49. Celia Parker Woolley to Jenkin Lloyd Jones, 5 January 1894, MTS.
50. Celia Parker Woolley to Jenkin Lloyd Jones, 4 October 1897, 5 January 1894, MTS.
51. Jenkin Lloyd Jones to Celia Parker Woolley, 8 June 1896, MTS.
52. Her husband, J. H. Woolley, explained the circumstances of her resignation in a letter to Jenkin Lloyd Jones, 5 April 1918, MTS. Her cohort's position on gambling is well represented in Jones's sermon 1071, MTS.
53. "The Frederick Douglass Center," *Unity* 81 (1918): 334; Fannie Barrier Williams, "The Frederick Douglass Center," *Southern Workman* 35 (June 1906): 334.
54. *The Chicago Record-Herald*, 19 May 1904; Celia Parker Woolley, "The Frederick Douglass Center, Chicago," *Commons* 9 (July 1904): 328.
55. Woolley, "The Frederick Douglass Center," 329.
56. Williams, "The Frederick Douglass Center," 336.
57. Ibid., 336–37; weekly programs in *Broad Ax*, 2 December 1905–10 February 1906; Celia Parker Woolley to Jenkin Lloyd Jones, 5 April 1905, and 14 August 1905, MTS.
58. For example, Thomas Lee Philpot, *The Slum and the Ghetto* (New York, 1978), 316ff.
59. "Mrs. Crane Discusses Luncheon," *Kalamazoo Daily Telegraph*, undated clipping, ca. 1905, CBC.

60. Caroline Bartlett Crane to an unidentified friend, 18 April 1927, CBC.

61. *Association of Commerce and Industry: Contributors' Handbook* (Chicago, 1915 [published annually]).

62. *Unity* 81 (1918): 121, 118.

CHAPTER FIFTEEN   *Ministering to Municipalities*

1. Frances Willard, *Minutes of the National WCTU at Its 11th Meeting* (Chicago, 1884), 51–52.

2. Eleanor E. Gordon, *Woman's Standard*, n.s., 20 (February 1908): 1.

3. Jenney's talks on municipal housekeeping as reported in the *Woman's Standard*, n.s., 14 (May 1901): 3.

4. "Caroline Bartlett Crane: Minister to Municipalities," *Review of Reviews* 42 (October 1910): 485–87.

5. Caroline Bartlett Crane, "The Work for Clean Streets," pamphlet reprinted from the *Woman's Forum* (September 1905), CBC.

6. Crane described this experience in *Teacher's Sanitary Bulletin* (Michigan State Board of Health) 6 (February 1903): 10–12.

7. Caroline Bartlett Crane to Lorenzo D. and Louise N. Babcock Bartlett, 17 May 1903, CBC.

8. Samuel Hopkins Adams, "U.S. Inspected and Passed," *Survey* 30 (6 September 1913): 695–98.

9. Crane, "Early Religious Struggle," 23.

10. Caroline Bartlett Crane, "Questions about Your City," CBC.

11. Caroline Bartlett Crane to Mrs. Atwood, 16 September 1910, CBC.

12. Caroline Bartlett Crane to Mrs. Atwood, 13 August 1910, CBC.

13. Caroline Bartlett Crane to Mrs. Barrows, 23 September 1910, CBC.

14. See, e.g., *Kentucky Medical Journal*, vol. 7 (August 1909), which was almost entirely devoted to Crane's reports; *A Sanitary Survey of Rochester* (Rochester, N.Y., 1910); *A Sanitary Survey of Uniontown, Pennsylvania* (Uniontown, Pa., 1914), CBC.

15. Caroline Bartlett Crane, "The Story and the Results," CBC.

16. Helen C. Bennett quotes Crane as saying that she was a home woman "first of all" but was fondest of her title "Minister to Municipalities" (*American Women in Civic Work* [New York, 1919], 44, 45). *Unity* (66 [1910]: 52) suggested that Crane was "creating a new functionary, which might be called a *civic engineer*, not a *civil engineer*." See also "Woman Doctor of City Ills," *Literary Digest* 44 (17 February 1912): 350; and "Caroline Bartlett Crane: Minister to Municipalities," *Review of Reviews* 42 (October 1910): 485–87.

17. Helen C. Bennett, "Women of the Hour," *La Follette's* 3 (20 May 1911): 10.

18. Bennett, *American Women in Civic Work*, 45.

19. Henry F. May, *Protestant Churches in Urban America* (New York, 1949), 216. Alan S. Brown ("Caroline Bartlett Crane and Urban Reform," *Michigan History* 61 [1972]: 290) calls attention to her sociology course notebooks as guides to what she was reading at this time.

20. While still pastor of People's Church, Crane expressed this conviction in

introducing a series of Sunday School lessons that she had prepared to give the children a simplified "sociology" of the city's problems and thereby teach them the essence of liberal religion ("Everyday Religion; or Studies in Good Citizenship," *Sunday School Helper* [Western Unitarian Sunday School Society, Chicago], vol. 2 [September 1897], CBC).

CHAPTER SIXTEEN   *Crusading for Suffrage*

1. *Record of the Woman's Ministerial Conference,* 78, AUA.
2. Outline of Personal History . . . Safford.
3. Mary Safford, *Des Moines Register and Leader,* 23 November 1908.
4. *Record of the Woman's Ministerial Conference,* 79.
5. Louise Noun, *Strong-Minded Women* (Ames, Iowa, 1969), 12–20.
6. Ibid., 147; Gwendolyn B. Willis, "Olympia Brown," *Journal of the Universalist Historical Society* 4 (1963): 1–76.
7. Robert V. Morse, text written for his aunt's obituary, typescript, RMM.
8. George W. Kingsbury, *History of Dakota Territory* (n.p., 1915), 3:765.
9. Padgham, autobiographical essay, 8.
10. *Woman's Standard* 1 (December 1886): 4, and 5 (March 1891): 2; *Unity* 81 (1918): 117.
11. *Unity Circle History,* 4.
12. *Woman's Standard* 1 (September 1886): 1.
13. *Woman's Standard* 4 (May 1890): 2.
14. *Woman's Standard,* n.s., 10 (December 1904): 1–2.
15. Safford's sermon at NAWSA's 1904 convention as reported in the *Woman's Standard,* n.s., 17 (March 1904): 2.
16. *Woman's Standard,* n.s., 12 (January 1900): 3, and 5 (1891): 5.
17. Jane Addams, "Women and Public Housekeeping," tract, DMUC.
18. *Pennsacola Journal,* Suffrage edition, 7 September 1914.
19. Cooke, *Unitarianism in America,* 350–51; Taft, *The History of Humboldt, Iowa.*
20. Gordon, *The Second Chapter.*
21. Clipping from the *Grand Rapids Telegram Herald,* n.d., CBC.
22. Eliza Tupper Wilkes to Jenkin Lloyd Jones, 17 September 1901, MTS.
23. Noun, *Strong-Minded Women,* 254; see also Carrie Chapman Catt, "The Iowa Story," in *Woman Suffrage and Politics,* ed. Carrie Chapman Catt and Nettie Rogers Shuler (New York, 1923), 211–26; Celia Parker Woolley, "Our Friendly Critic," *Unity* 68 (26 October 1911): 117.
24. "The Universality of Democracy," *Unity* 68 (1911): 232.
25. See Flavia Alaya, "Victorian Science and The Genius of Woman," *Journal of the History of Ideas* 38 (1977): 261–80.
26. *Unitarian Advance* 5 (1915): 263, 339–40.
27. Jones's suffrage work in his last years is documented by numerous clippings in his scrapbook, MTS.
28. *Boston Herald,* 14 February 1885.
29. Samuel A. Eliot to Mr. Smith, 10 January 1898.

30. For example, Gordon, "The Story of a Long Life," 6; Howe, "The Young Woman and the Church"; Crane, "The Church and the Women."

31. Padgham, autobiographical essay, 16.

32. For a concise statement of Wells's views, see *Woman's Journal*, (16 February 1884): 53; see also *HWS*, 4:704; *Unitarian Advance*, n.s., 2 (July 1912): 339–40.

33. Celia Parker Woolley, for one—in a letter to Jenkin Lloyd Jones, 25 March 1909, MTS—deplored the clubwoman's "cardinal principle" that she must "dress well and look good" at any expense as slowing the progress of the woman's movement.

34. Eleanor E. Gordon to Frederick May Eliot, 4 February 1938, AUA. The dynamics of the female opposition to suffrage are explored in Jane Jerome Camhi, "Women against Women: American Antisuffragism, 1880–1920" (Ph.D. diss., Tufts University, 1983).

35. Gordon to the Sioux City Suffrage Convention, 30 November 1898, reprinted in *Woman's Standard*, n.s., 11 (January 1899): 2; Catt quoted in Noun, *Strong-Minded Women*, 241.

36. Catt and Shuler, eds., *Woman Suffrage and Politics*, 211.

37. *Woman's Standard*, n.s., 21 (March 1908): 1, 4.

38. Eleanor E. Gordon, "Suffrage Parade—Boone, Iowa," typescript, ISHD; *Woman's Standard*, n.s., 21 (November 1908): 2.

39. *Woman's Standard*, n.s., 21 (December 1908): 1.

40. *Woman's Standard*, n.s., 22 (April 1909): 1–2; and, n.s., 22 (December 1909): 2; Gordon, "Letter to Readers" and "Report to IWSA," *Woman's Standard*, n.s., 22 (April 1909): 1, 2.

41. *Woman's Standard*, n.s., 22 (January 1909): 2; and 22 (February 1909): 2.

42. *Woman's Standard*, n.s., 22 (December 1909): 4, 1; n.s., 22 (November 1909): 3; and, n.s., 22 (December 1909): 1.

43. Keith Gilley, "Women and the Unitarian Ministry," 1985, typescript, loaned by the author; *Woman's Standard*, n.s., 22 (April 1909): 2, and, n.s., 23 (May 1910): 4.

44. Adele Fuchs to Mary A. Safford, 23 May 1910, HHJ.

45. Eleanor E. Gordon to Jenkin Lloyd Jones, 3 March 1909, MTS.

46. Clippings and leaflet on men's suffrage leagues, Safford's notes for report to IESA in 1911, *Suffrage Scrapbook, 1911–1912*, ISHD; Catt and Shuler, eds., *Woman Suffrage and Politics*, 216ff.; Eleanor E. Gordon to Jenkin Lloyd Jones, 14 December 1912, MTS.

47. "Feminist Meeting at Cooper Union," *New York Times*, 21 February 1914, p. 18.

48. *Unity* 68 (1911): 117; McGiffert, *Pilot of a Liberal Faith*, 146–47.

49. "The Woman Minister," *Unity* 88 (1921): 92–92.

50. Fuchs, *Diary, 1913–1917*, 7 June 1916, HHJ.

51. Anna Howard Shaw to Caroline Bartlett Crane, 14 September 1912, CBC; Helvie, "Unitarian Women Ministers," 53; *HWS*, 4:764.

52. Hutchins Hapgood, *A Victorian in the Modern World*, 332–33.

CHAPTER SEVENTEEN   *Keeping the Peace*

1. Roland H. Bainton, "The Churches' Shift on War," in *Christian Unity and Religion in New England* (Boston, 1964), 187–200; Cooke, *Unitarianism in America,* 343ff.

2. Gordon, *Long Story.*

3. *Ten Years of the First Unitarian Church of Sioux City,* 71; *Old and New* 16 (December 1908): 74.

4. Eleanor E. Gordon, "Lessons Learnt from the War," *Old and New* 6 (July 1897): 196.

5. Charles S. Macfarland, *Pioneers for Peace through Religion* (New York, 1946), 34–35; *Old and New* 12 (September 1904): 5, and 11 (December 1903): 2; "The Final Basis of Independence," *Old and New* 12 (November 1904): 1.

6. "Mrs. Crane Refuses to Go on Ford Peace Trip," *Kalamazoo Telegraph-Press,* 30 November 1915, p. 1.

7. The "Twentieth Century Patriot," Crane had stressed in the 1890s, would have to keep the nation free and great by applying its founders' high standards of moral conduct to the running of government and business (clipping from the *Hawkeye* [ca. 4 July 1894], CBC).

8. Caroline Bartlett Crane, *History of the Work of the Women's Committee (Michigan Division), Council of National Defence during the World War* (n.p., [ca. 1922]).

9. *Tampa Tribune,* 20 November 1911, p. 5; *Woman Citizen,* 11 May 1918.

10. Eve Bacon, *A Centennial History of Orlando* (Chuluota, Fla., 1975), 288, 290–91; Outline of Personal History . . . Safford."

11. *Christian Register* 97 (1918): 775; Ray H. Abrams, *Preachers Present Arms* (New York, 1933), 193, 201.

12. Rowena Morse Mann, "The Moral Issue of the War," September 1918, handwritten manuscript, RMM.

13. Wright, *A Stream of Light,* 102–4. Holmes had already laid out his views before the denomination repeatedly in such journals as the *Unitarian Advance; Unity* 81 (9 May 1918): 160; John Haynes Holmes, *I Speak for Myself* (New York, 1959), chap. 16.

14. *Cleveland Plain Dealer,* 9 August 1914; for much of my information about Jones's pacifism, and about Jones in general, I am indebted to Professor Thomas Graham of the University of Winnipeg.

15. *Unity* 82 (1918): 29.

16. Ibid., 192.

17. Celia Parker Woolley to Jenkin Lloyd Jones (postcard), n.d., MTS.

18. Jenkin Lloyd Jones to J. H. Woolley, 10 April 1918, MTS.

19. Fuchs, *Diary 1918–1922,* 14 February 1919.

20. Adele Fuchs to Mary A. Safford, 18 October 1915, HHJ.

21. Adele Fuchs to Mary A. Safford, 31 January 1921; Fuchs, *Diary 1913–1917,* 1 January 1915; Fuchs, *Diary 1918–1922,* 24 September 1919.

22. Fuchs, *Diary 1918–1922,* 15 August 1919.

23. Jane Addams to Rev. Harry Lutz, Committee on Supply of Pulpits, 28 April 1917; Florence Buck to Rev. Harry Lutz, 28 April 1917, UUA.

24. Collson, "My Search," 111–12.

25. Harry Elmer Barnes, *Revisionism: A Key to Peace* (San Francisco, 1980), 4–12;
    Sherwood Eddy and Kirby Page, *The Abolition of War* (New York, 1924), 193;
    Jess Yoder, "Preaching on Issues of War and Peace," in *Preaching in American
    History,* ed. Dewitte Holland (Nashville, 1969), 248.
26. Rev. Donald Wheat cited this incident as told to him by the guilty party,
    parishioner Gunnar Helsing, in a sermon delivered at Third Unitarian Church
    in Chicago, ca. 1974.
27. *The Kalamazoo Progressive-Herald,* 1 January 1916, p. 1.
28. *Report on the Michigan Reconstruction Committee* (Lansing, 1919), CBC.
29. Elaine Goodale Eastman brought this out by analyzing the other societies that
    Daughters belonged to ("Are D.A.R. Women Exploited?" *Christian Century*
    [11 September 1929]). The correspondence contained in the Crane papers
    thoroughly documents this episode.
30. See William E. Leuchtenburg on the "Tired Radicals" after the war in *The
    Perils of Prosperity 1914–32* (Chicago, 1958), 120ff.
31. Fuchs quotes Marie in her *Diary 1923–1934,* 6 January 1923.
32. Robert La Follette to his wife, 12 January 1919, in Bella Casa La Follette and
    Fola La Follette, *Robert La Follette,* 2 vols. (New York, 1953), 2:938.
33. Marie Jenney Howe to Fola La Follette, 22 March 1933, LFP.
34. Fuchs, *Diary 1923–1934,* 1 January 1925, July and August 1930.
35. Yoder, "Preaching on Issues of War and Peace," 248–49.

EPILOGUE   *Legacy*

1. Caroline Bartlett Crane to Rev. W. H. Gysan, 7 May 1928. Crane also let
   the younger generation know that older folks did not exist merely to experience life vicariously through them ("If I Were Twenty Again" [Boston,
   n.d.], 9, CBC).
2. Marie Jenney Howe to Fola La Follette, 22 March 1933, LFP; letter left by
   Mary A. Safford for her heirs, quoted in full by Fuchs in a letter to friends
   of Mary Safford, 22 November 1927, DMUC; Mary E. Collson to Jane
   Addams, 17 June 1932, SCPC.
3. Fuchs, *Diary 1923–1934,* 22 February 1926, 6 and 7 July 1929, 10–23
   September 1931.
4. Caroline Bartlett Crane to Rev. W. H. Gysan, 7 May 1928.
5. Hitchings provides a good account of Helvie's experience ("Unitarian Women
   Ministers," 84–86).
6. Mary L. Leggett to Louis C. Cornish, 10 October 1916; Mary L. Leggett
   Cooke to Clara Cook Helvie, 27 March 1937, AUA.
7. Robert L. Thompson to Minot Simmons, 10 January and 23 April 1921;
   Stanley Heymar to Minot Simmons, 4 October 1921, AUA.
8. Earnest C. Smith to Henry Wilder Foote, 12 February 1914, AUA.
9. Robert L. Thompson to Minot Simmons, 23 April 1921; Minot Simmons to
   Rowena Morse Mann, 11 June and 13 October 1921, AUA.
10. Gertrude Briggs to Minot Simmons, 30 September 1921; Stanley Heymar to
    Minot Simmons, 4 October 1921; Martha Dahm to Minot Simmons, 4
    October 1921, AUA.

11. Phone interview with Helen Bullard in Sparta, Tenn., 25 April 1987; Samuel A. Eliot, "Report on the Chicago Situation," ca. 1923, typescript, AUA.

12. Newton Mann to Samuel A. Eliot, 26 November 1921; Minot Simmons to Rowena Morse Mann, 12 December 1921, AUA.

13. "The Woman Minister," *Unity* 85 (20 October 1921): 92–93; Eleanor E. Gordon to Frederick May Eliot, 4 February 1938, AUA.

14. The Western secretary, Ernest C. Smith, e.g., commented casually on the basis of long-distance observations—in a letter to Samuel A. Eliot dated 17 June 1919, AUA—that Crane's opinions were no longer worth very much as they seemed to be "heavily discounted not only in the church group but also in the community."

15. Samuel A. Eliot to E. Q. S. Osgood, 13 June 1908; George H. Badger to Samuel A. Eliot, 24 April 1926, 6 February and 6 December 1923. In an interview with Cynthia G. Tucker in Orlando, Fla., 8 March 1985, Nora M. Staton recalled the popular Badger as a mild-mannered pastor whose wife was the more commanding of the two.

16. E. Elizabeth Padgham to Frederick May Eliot, 29 October 1948, AUA.

17. For example, "Women Ascend the Pulpit," *Woman's Journal* 14 (December 1929): 16, 46.

18. Eleanor E. Gordon to Frederick May Eliot, 2 February and 29 November 1939, AUA.

19. This experience was recorded by Fuchs in her journal (*Diary 1923–1934,* pp. 176–79) and in a letter she wrote to friends of Mary A. Safford, (22 November 1927, DMUC).

20. "The Story and the Results," 1925, typescript autobiography, 3–4, CBC.

21. *Old and New* 12 (December 1904): 1, and 13 (June 1905): 2.

22. See Tucker, *A Woman's Ministry,* 155ff.

23. Gordon's sympathetic niece, Avis Gordon Vestal, explained afterward—in a letter to Mary Hunter, 3 March 1942, ISHD—that the best she could do for her aunt was to type up a half-dozen copies of the final installment and put them into binders for the relatives.

24. Fuchs, *Diary 1923–1934,* "Feb. & March & April, 1931" [p. 47]; 25 October 1927 [pp. 178–79].

25. Mary E. Collson to Edward Meeman, 24 June 1947, MVC.

26. Avis Gordon Vestal to Mary Hunter, 3 March 1942, ISHD.

27. See Pauli Jakobi's inscription in "Heterodoxy to Marie," album, IHI.

28. Rowena Morse Mann to Sarah Filchette Morse, 7 March 1902, RMM.

29. Mary E. Collson to Edward Meeman, 11 October 1934, MVC.

30. When the Sand biography, *A Search for Love,* appeared in 1927, critic Percy Hutchinson called it a "one-sided, prejudiced" defense of Sand's failings; but Howe's sister Heterodite and psychobiographer Katherine Anthony praised it as "the tribute of one much revered woman to the memory of another." Howe told Fuchs about the book's emerging "from the unconscious" almost without her knowing it, in a lengthy inscription written on the frontispiece of the copy she sent her, HHJ.

BIBLIOGRAPHY

MANUSCRIPT COLLECTIONS

Addams, Jane. Papers. Swarthmore College Peace Collection, Swarthmore, Pa.

American Unitarian Association. Letter Books. Andover Library, Harvard Divinity School, Cambridge, Mass.

American Unitarian Association. Presidential Papers of Samuel Atkins Eliot, 1900–1927. Andover Library, Harvard Divinity School, Cambridge, Mass.

Annals of the Chicago Woman's Club. Chicago Historical Society, Chicago.

Biographical Records of the Iowa Memorial [Suffrage] Commission. Iowa State Historical Department, Des Moines, Iowa.

Collson, Mary Edith. Papers. Meadville-Lombard Theological School Library, Chicago.

Crane, Caroline Bartlett. Papers. Regional History Archives. Western Michigan University Library, Kalamazoo, Mich.

Hull-House Association Papers. University of Illinois at Chicago.

Irwin, Inez Haynes. Papers. Schlesinger Library, Radcliffe College, Cambridge, Mass.

Jones, Jenkins Lloyd. Papers. Meadville-Lombard Theological School Library, Chicago.

Juvenile Protection Association Papers. Case Studies, November 1899–August 1901. University of Illinois at Chicago.

"Ladies Society Secretary's Report, 1890–1892." First Unitarian Church of Kalamazoo [later People's Church], Mich.

Mann, Rowena Morse. Papers. Schlesinger Library, Radcliffe College, Cambridge, Mass.

Meeman, Edward J. Papers. Mississippi Valley Collection, Memphis State University, Memphis.

National American Woman Suffrage Association Records, 1850–1960. Library of Congress, Washington, D.C.

National Woman's Party Records, 1911–1936. Library of Congress, Washington, D.C.

Records of the Chicago Woman's Club Meetings, 1900–1901. Chicago Historical Society, Chicago.

Records of the Unitarian Church of Iowa City, Iowa. State Historical Society of Iowa, Iowa City, Iowa.

Roadside Settlement House Association. Records, 1913, 1914, DMPL.

Rosenwald, Julius. Papers. Regenstein Library, University of Chicago.

Sunderland, Jabez and Eliza. Papers. Bentley Historical Library, University of Michigan, Ann Arbor, Mich.

Unitarian Universalist Association. Church Records. Archives. Boston and Cambridge, Mass.

Unitarian Universalist Association. Department of Ministry Files. National Headquarters, Boston.

Western Unitarian Conference Papers. Meadville-Lombard Theological School, Chicago.

Woman's Ministerial Conference Records, 1882–96, 1904, 1909–13. Andover Library, Harvard Divinity School, Cambridge, Mass.

The Woman's Standard. 1886–1911. State Historical Library, Des Moines, Iowa.

Woman's Suffrage Records. State Historical Library, Des Moines, Iowa.

PRIMARY SOURCES

Beecher, Catherine E. *A Treatise on Domestic Economy: For the Use of Young Ladies at Home and at School.* New York: Harper, 1849.

—————. *Suggestions Respecting Improvements in Education.* Hartford, Conn.: Packard & Butler, 1829.

Beecher, Catherine E., and Harriet Beecher Stowe. *The American Woman's Home.* New York: J. B. Ford, 1869.

Bicknell, A.D. "S. H. Taft: A Sketch." *Old and New* 14 (May 1906): 1, 35.

Bicknell, Frank W. "The Conference of 1880, Its Spirit and Its Influence." Typescript read at the fiftieth anniversary meeting of the Iowa Unitarian Association, Davenport, Iowa, 1927. DMUC.

Buck, Florence. *Religious Education for Democracy.* Boston, 1919. AUA.

Bullard, Helen. "Personal Notes on Dr. Rowena Morse Mann." 24 June 1974. Transcript loaned by the author.

Bullard, Helen. Telephone interview, 25 April, 1987.

Bulletin of Roadside Settlement, Des Moines, 1914. ISHD.

Cabot, James Elliot. *A Memoir of Ralph Waldo Emerson.* Boston: Houghton Mifflin, 1887.

Channing, William Ellery. *The Works of William Ellery Channing.* Boston: The American Unitarian Association, 1898.

Coggeshall, Mary Jane. "History of the Polk County Women Suffrage Association (1870–1895)." Manuscript in the Woman Suffrage Collection, ISHD

Collson, Mary E. "My Search for an All Right World." Typescript. MVC.

Crane, Caroline Bartlett. "The Church and the Women." Typescript. CBC.

—————. "Dedication of the New Home of Walter R. and Ella E. Taylor." Printed order of service, Kalamazoo, Mich., 21 December 1895. CBC.

—————. "Early Religious Struggle." Typescript autobiographical notes. CBC.

—————. *Everyman's House.* New York: Doubleday, Page, 1925.

—————. "Everyday Religion; or Studies in Good Citizenship." *Sunday School Helper,* vol. 2 (September 1987).

———. *History of the Work of the Women's Committee (Michigan Division), Council of National Defence during the World War.* N.p., [ca. 1922].

———. *If I Were Twenty Again.* Boston: James H. West, n.d.

———. "The Liberal Minister: His Equipment and Place." Abridged and reprinted as "The Woman Minister." *Partheon* 1 (June 1892): 1–2.

———. "The Life of Caroline Irene Hubbard Kleinsteuck." Typescript. CBC.

———. "Memories of Caroline Bartlett Crane." *Carthage College Bulletin* 9 (September 1925): 4–6.

———. "Naming the Home." Printed order of service, Kalamazoo, Mich., 23 August 1893. CBC.

———. "Press, Pulpit and Penates." *Carthaginian* 4 (1881): 101–3.

———. *A Sanitary Survey of Rochester.* Rochester, N.Y., 1910.

———. *A Sanitary Survey of Uniontown, Pennsylvania.* Uniontown, Pa., 1914.

———. "The Story." Typescript autobiographical notes. CBC.

———. "The Story of an Institutional Church in a Small City." *Charities* 15 (6 May 1905): 1–8.

———. "Women Ascend the Pulpit." *Woman's Journal* 14 (December 1929): 16, 46.

"Dedication of the Home of Henry Holcomb and Lizabeth Vaupel Griffiths." Printed order of service, Des Moines, Iowa, 25 October 1901. DMUC.

"Dedication Sermon by Rev. Jenkin Lloyd Jones." *Kalamazoo Daily News,* 20 December 1894.

"Editorial." *Old and New* 12 (April 1904): 1.

Eliot, Samuel A. "Introductory Address by Dr. Eliot." 1912. Typescript. Tuckerman School File, AUA.

———. "Report on the Chicago Situation." Ca. 1923. Typescript. AUA.

"Feminist Meeting at Cooper Union." *New York Times,* 21 February 1914.

Fifty Years of Unity Church. Sioux City, Iowa: First Unitarian Church of Sioux City, 1935.

"The First Secretary of the Iowa Unitarian Association." *Old and New* 7 (September 1904): 1–2.

"Forward's the Word." *Kalamazoo Daily News,* 20 December 1884.

"Friendship between Girls." *Old and New,* vol. 4 (May 1895).

Fuchs, Adele. Diaries, Dec. 1884–Dec. 1891, 1913–1916, 1918–1922, 1923–1935.

Gannett, William Channing. *The House Beautiful.* River Forest, Ill.: Auvergne, 1897.

Garfield, G. S. "What I Like to Hear from the Pulpit." *Unity* 41 (1898): 42–43.

Gordon, Eleanor E. "The Early History of the Orlando Unitarian Church, 1911–1918." N.d. Mimeographed pamphlet. NMS.

———. "The Final Basis of Independence." *Old and New* 12 (November 1904): 1.

———. "Giving What We Have: A Christmas Sermon." *Old and New* 10 (December 1901): 4–5.

———. "The Glory of the Imperfect." *Old and New* 12 (February 1904): 2–4.

———. "The Good Part." *Old and New* 14 (December 1906): 69–70.

———. "The Great Opportunity." *Unity* 23 (23 May 1889): 101.

———. "History of the Round Table." 1913–15. Handwritten notes. OUC.

———. "The House of Mirth." *Old and New* 14 (February 1906): 12–13.

———. "Just Like a Woman." *Woman's Standard,* vol. 17 (December 1904, January 1905).

———. "Lessons Learnt from the War." *Old and New* 6 (July 1897): 196.

———. *A Little Bit of a Long Story for the Children.* Hamilton, Ill.: privately printed, 1934.

———. "The Meaning of Life: A Problem in Proportion." *Old and New,* vol. 4 (December 1895).

———. *The Second Chapter of a Long Story.* Hamilton, Ill.: privately printed, 1935.

———. "The Story of a Long Life, Part 3." 1942. Typescript. GP.

———. "Why Young Women Do Not Go to Church." *Old and New* 13 (October 1905): 3.

———. "The Woman Minister." *Unity* 85 (1921): 92–93.

———. "The Worth of Sympathy." *Old and New* 15 (June 1907): 43–44.

Griffith, H. H. "History of Unitarianism in Iowa and Nebraska." June 1924. Typescript. DMUC.

Helvie, Clara Cooke. "Unitarian Women Ministers." Typescript. 1929. UHS.

"Heterodoxy to Marie." Club photograph album, Christmas 1920. IHI.

Holmes, John Haynes. "The Unitarian Ministry: The Problem of Withdrawals Again." *Unity* 68 (1911): 229–31.

Horack, Frank E. "Equal Suffrage in Iowa." In *Applied History,* vol. 2, ed. Benjamin F. Shambaugh. Iowa City: State Historical Society of Iowa, 1914.

Howard, H. Augusta. "Woman Considered as a Human Being." *Social Democratic Herald* 29 December 1900.

Howe, Frederic Clemson. *The Confessions of a Reformer.* New York: Scribner's, 1925.

Howe, Marie Jenney. "American League for Civic Improvement." *Old and New* 11 (September 1902): 4.

———. *George Sand: The Search for Love.* New York: John Day, 1927.

———. *The Intimate Journals of George Sand.* New York: John Day, 1929.

———. "Women in the Ministry." *Meadville Portfolio* 1 (1894): 21–23.

———. "The Young Woman and the Church." *Old and New* 13 (September 1905): 3–5.

"Hull House, Chicago: Its Work and Workers." *Unitarian* 8 (September 1893): 400.

Hultin, Ida C. "Woman in the Ministry." *Woman's Standard* 3 (January 1889): 3.

Hunter, Mrs. Fred, et al. "Iowa Suffrage Memorial Commission." *Annals of Iowa,* ser. 3, vol. 14 (April 1924).

Hunter, Robert. "Relations between Social Settlements and Charity Organizations." *National Conference of Charities and Correction* (1902): 303–14.

"Impressions of the Sioux City Conference." *Old and New* 8 (April 1900): 2.

"Is Local Self-Government Desirable?" *Old and New* (October 1900): 23.

Jones, Rev. Jenkin Lloyd. "The Frederick Douglass Center." *Unity* 55 (1905): 163.

———. "House Building." Typescript sermon series. JLJ.

———. "A Noble Work: A Neglected Opportunity." *Unity* 72 (23 October 1913): 117.

Judy, Arthur M. "Rev. Oscar Clute in Iowa." *Old and New* 10 (February 1902): 4.

Kendall, Edith. "Warren Goddard House." *Unitarian* 3 (April 1908): 126–35.

Knowles, Jane. Taped interview with Rowena Mann Lanzer, 5 April 1985, Cambridge, Mass. RMM

Lathrop, Julia C. "The Background of the Juvenile Court in Illinois." In *The Child, the Clinic and the Court*. New York: New Republic, 1925.

"Laying of Des Moines Church Cornerstone." *Old and New* 12 (September 1904): 3.

Malkiel, Theresa. "Where Do We Stand on the Woman Question?" *International Socialist Review* 10 (1909): 159.

Mann, Rowena Morse. "I Came Not to Judge the World." Handwritten sermon, Keokuk, Iowa, 7 October 1906. RMM.

———. "The Moral Issue of the War." September 1918. Handwritten manuscript. RMM.

———. "None of Us Liveth to Himself." Keokuk, Iowa, 1906. Handwritten sermon. RMM.

———. Untitled sermon based on Heb. 5:11. N.d. Handwritten and typed. RMM.

Matthews, William. "The Settlement House Is Not a Charity." In *The Meaning of the Settlement Movement*. Pittsburgh: Kingsley House, 1909.

Meadville Theological School Catalogue, 1895–1896. Meadville, Pa., 1896.

"Memorial Exercises for Susan Charlotte Lloyd Jones." *Unity* 68 (9 November 1911): 147–49.

Minutes of the Board of Directors, 1907–23. Tuckerman School File, AUA.

"Mrs. Crane Refuses to Go on Ford Peace Trip." *Kalamazoo, Mich., Telegraph-Press*, 30 November 1915.

Murdock, Ellen, and Marion Murdock. "To the Editor." *North Iowa Times*, 24 December 1866.

Murdock, Rev. Marion. "The Growth of the Hebrew People." Humboldt, Iowa: Unity Church, 1889.

———. *Helpfulness, or How the World Moves: A Sermon by Rev. Marion Murdock*. Humboldt, Iowa: Unity Church, 1888.

———. "The Ninetieth Psalm." Typescript. ISHD.

———. "What Did Phoebe Do?" 1893. Typescript. UUA.

———. "Women at Meadville." Handwritten paper delivered at the semicentennial of the Meadville Theological School, June 1894. MTS.

Niccolls, Samuel J. "Woman's Position and Work in the Church." *Presbyterian Review* 10 (April 1889): 267–79.

Nichols, Mrs. William I. "The Architecture of Liberal Churches." *Unitarian* (September 1907): 301–5.

Olmstead, Margaret T. "Spiritual Education, a Chief Element in the Future Power of the Church." *Old and New* 14 (November 1906): 61–62.

"Our National Conference." *Unitarian* 9 (1894): 459.

Padgham, Estella Elizabeth. Autobiographical essay. Handwritten manuscript. UUA.

———. *Unitarianism: A Religion Good to Live By and Good to Die By*. Rutherford, N.J.: Woman's Alliance of the Church of Our Father, n.d.

Parce, Lida. "Woman and the Socialist Philosophy." *International Socialist Review* 10 (August 1909): 125–28.

Parker, Theodore. *Theodore Parker's Experience as a Minister.* Boston: Rufus Leighton, Jr., 1859.

——. *Theodore Parker's Works,* vol. 7. London: Trubracer, 1864.

"'Parish Calls' from the Lay-Woman's Point of View." *Unitarian* 2 (May 1907): 170–75.

"A Pentacostal Feast." *Christian Register* 59 (24 July 1880): 478.

People's Church Ladies' Society Records, 1890–92. PC.

People's Church Secretary's Book, 1883–94. PC.

Polasky, Mary. "Mary Augusta Safford." Ca. 1928. Typescript. ISHS.

Record Book of the Young People's Religious Union, 1907–13, First Unitarian Church, Des Moines, Iowa. DMUC.

Record of the Orlando Unitarian Church. OUC.

"Religion and Science." *Old and New,* vol. 5 (July 1896).

"Report of a Committee, 1912: The Juvenile Court of Cook County, ILL." Manuscript. CHS.

Report on the Michigan Reconstruction Committee. Lansing, Mich., 1919.

Safford, Mary A. "Experiencing Religion." Handwritten sermon. SHSI.

——. "The Hard Test Being Put upon Our Conference." *Old and New* 8 (June 1900): 1–2.

——. "On Unity Clubs." *Unity* 18 (1887): 264.

——. "Outline of Personal History." Biographical Records of the Iowa Memorial Commission. ISHS.

——. "Ships That Pass in the Night." *Old and New,* vol. 4 (May 1895).

——. "Your Work and Mine." *Old and New,* vol. 4 (May 1895).

——. "Women as Ministers." *Woman's Standard* 8 (1893): 3.

Services at the Ordination and Installation of Rev. Phebe A. Hanaford. Boston: C. C. Roberts, 1870.

Simkhovitch, Mary. "Friendship and Politics." *Political Science Quarterly* 17 (June 1902): 189–205.

——. "The Settlement and Religion." In *Readings in the Development Work,* ed. Lorene M. Pacey. New York: Association Press, 1950.

Staton, Nora McNeill. Interview, 8 March 1985, Orlando, Fla.

——. Telephone interview, 1 June 1986.

——. Telephone interview, 20 March 1988.

Stockman, Cora. "Our Nursery." *Kindergarten* 3 (1891): 337.

"The Story of the Post Office Mission." Ca. 1886. Handwritten manuscript. MTS.

Sunderland, Jabez. "The Liberal Christian Ministry as a Calling for Young Women." *Woman's Standard* 3 (July 1889): 3.

Ten Years of the First Unitarian Church of Sioux City. Sioux City, Iowa: Globe Printing, 1895.

Tunis, John. "Woman in the Ministry: An Appeal to Fact." *Unity* 15 (1885): 92–94.

"Unitarian Church Was Dedicated Last Evening." *Iowa City Republican,* 26 October 1908.

"Unitarians to Build Church in This City." *Orlando Reporter-Star,* 20 January 1912.
Unity Circle History. Des Moines Unitarian Church. DMUC.
Vestal, Pearl Avis Gordon. "Rev. Eleanor E. Gordon, 1852–1942: Biographical Notes." Hamilton, Ill., 1942. ISHD.
———. "Rev. Mary Augusta Safford, 1851–1927: Biographical Notes." Hamilton, Ill., 1949. Typescript. ISHD.
"The Western Women's Unitarian Conference." Ca. 1901. Handwritten manuscript. MTS.
Willard, Frances. *Minutes of the National WCTU at Its 11th Meeting.* Chicago, 1884.
Williams, Fannie Barrier. "The Frederick Douglass Center." *Southern Workman* 35 (June 1906): 334–36.
———. "Social Bonds in the 'Black Belt' of Chicago: Negro Organizations and the New Spirit Pervading Them." *Charities* 15 (7 October 1905): 40–44.
Wing, Amelia Murdock. "Early Days in Clayton County." *Annals of Iowa,* 3d ser., 27 (1946): 257–96.
"Woman Doctor of City Ills." *Literary Digest* 44 (17 February 1912): 350.
Woman's Christian Temperance Union of Iowa: Annual Reports, 1875–1890. Cedar Rapids, Iowa.
"Women Ministers at Mrs. Howe's." *Woman's Journal* (11 June 1904).
Woolley, Celia Parker. "The Frederick Douglass Center, Chicago." *Commons* 9 (July 1904): 328–29.
———. "The Ideal Unitarian Church." Unity Mission Tract no. 32. Chicago: Unity Office, 1889.
———. "The Liberal Church." *New Unity* 5 (7 October 1897): 692.
———. "Our Friendly Critic." *Unity* 68 (26 October 1911): 117.
———. "Practical Service for Negroes." *Unity* 57 (21 June 1906): 308.
———. "The Universality of Democracy." *Unity* 68 (14 December 1911): 232–33.
———. "Whose Ox Is Gored?" *Unity* 76 (9 December 1915): 228.
"Work for All." *Unitarian* 5 (August 1910): 288.

SECONDARY SOURCES

Abbot, Francis. "Modern Principles of Free Religion." *Index* (7 January 1871).
Abell, Aaron I. *The Urban Impact on American Protestantism, 1865–1900.* Cambridge, Mass.: Harvard University Press, 1943.
Abrams, Ray H. *Preachers Present Arms.* New York: Round Table, 1933. Rev. ed. Scottdale, Pa.: Herald, 1969.
Adams, Mildred. *The Right to Be People.* Philadelphia: Lippincott, 1967.
Adams, Samuel Hopkins. "U.S. Inspected and Passed." *Survey* 30 (6 September 1913): 695–98.
Addams, Jane. "The Settlement as a Factor in the Labor Movement." In *Hull House Maps and Papers.* New York, 1985.
Alaya, Flavia. "Victorian Science and the Genius of Woman." *Journal of the History of Ideas* 38 (1977): 261–80.

Alger, William R. "Woman and Religion." *Unitarian* 12 (August 1897): 352–53.

"Amongst Ministers." *Unitarian* 2 (March 1907): 96–101.

"Anniversary of the American Equal Rights Association." *Revolution* (13 May 1869).

"As For Trade Unions." *Commons* 4 (June 1897): 12.

"Attractive Little Church Costs Modest Sum." *Popular Mechanics* (May 1917): 800.

Bacon, Eve. *Orlando: A Centennial History*. Chuluota, Fla.: Mickler, 1975.

Bacon, Margaret Hope. *Mothers of Feminism: The Story of Quaker Women in America*. San Francisco: Harper & Row, 1986.

Bainton, Roland. "The Churches' Shift on War." In *Christian Unity and Religion in New England*. Boston: Beacon, 1964.

Bakus, W. M. "Western Unitarianism." *New Unitarian* 1 (February 1906): 36–37.

"Band of Women Ministers." *Boston Herald*, 5 May 1890.

Bannister, Robert C. *Social Darwinism: Science and Myth in Anglo-American Social Thought*. Philadelphia: Temple University Press, 1979.

Barnes, Harry Elmer. *Revision: A Key to Peace and Other Essays*. San Francisco: Cato Institute, 1980.

Barnett, Ida B. Wells. *Crusade for Justice: The Autobiography of Ida B. Wells*. Edited by Alfreda M. Duster. Chicago: University of Chicago Press, 1970.

Belding, Robert E. "Iowa's Brave Model for Women's Education." *Annals of Iowa* 43 (1976): 342–48.

Bennett, Helen Christie. *American Women in Civic Work*. New York: Dodd Mead, 1915.

Blair, Karen J. *The Clubwoman as Feminist: True Womanhood Defined, 1868–1914*. New York: Holmes & Meier, 1980.

Bordin, Ruth. *Women and Temperance: The Quest for Power and Liberty*. Philadelphia: Temple University Press, 1981.

Bos, William, and Clyde Faries. "The Social Gospel: Preaching Reform, 1875–1915." In *Preaching in American History*, edited by Dewitte Holland. Nashville: Abingdon, 1969.

Bowen, Joseph T. "The Early Days of the Juvenile Court." In *The Child, the Clinic, and the Court*. New York: New Republic, 1925.

Bridgman, Howard Allen. "Have We a Religion for Men?" *Andover Review* 13 (1890): 388–96.

Brown, Alan S. "Caroline Bartlett Crane and Urban Reform." *Michigan History* 61 (1972): 287–301.

Brown, William Thurston. "The Problem of Liberal Religion in the West." *Unitarian* 5 (April 1910): 116–17.

Buell, Lawrence. "Unitarian Homiletics and Emerson's Poet-Priest." *American Quarterly* 20 (1968): 6–10.

Buhle, Mari Jo. *Women and Socialism*. Urbana: University of Illinois Press, 1981.

Calvo, Janis. "Quaker Women Ministers in Nineteenth-Century America." *Quaker History* 63 (1974): 75–93.

Camhi, Jane Jerome. "Women against Women: American Antisuffragism, 1880–1920." Ph.D. diss., Tufts University, 1983.

"Caroline Bartlett Crane: Minister to Municipalities." *Review of Reviews* 42 (October 1910): 485–87.

Carroll, H. K. *Religious Forces in the United States.* New York: Christian Literature Co., 1893.

Cashdollar, Charles D. "European Positivism and the American Unitarians." *Church History* 45 (1976): 490–506.

Catt, Carrie Chapman. "The Iowa Story." In *Woman Suffrage and Politics,* edited by Carrie Chapman Catt and Nettie Rogers Shuler. New York: Scribner's, 1923.

Charlton, Joy. "Women in Seminary: A Review of Current Social Science Research." *Review of Religious Research* 28 (1987): 305–18.

Chodorow, Nancy. *The Reproduction of Mothering: Psychoanalysis and the Psychology of Gender.* Berkeley: University of California Press, 1978.

Christie, Francis A. *The Makings of the Meadville Theological School, 1844–1894.* Boston: Beacon, 1927.

Clark, Clifford. "Domestic Architecture as an Index to Social History: The Romantic Revival and the Cult of Domesticity, 1840–1870." *Journal of Interdisciplinary History* 7 (1976): 33–56.

Clark, Edith J. "Juvenile Delinquency and Dependency: Report of Inquiry at Chicago." *Commons* 6 (1901): 3–4.

"Clergywomen—They Meet for a Conference in Boston." *Boston Daily Globe,* 3 June 1889.

Coe, George Albert. *Education in Religion and Morals.* Chicago and New York: F. H. Revell, 1904.

Coggeshall, Mary Jane. "Woman's Suffrage Society." In *Annals of Polk County, Iowa, and City of Des Moines,* edited by Will Porter. Des Moines, Iowa, 1898.

Cole, Cordelia Throop. "Charge Given at Mary Safford's Ordination." *Unity* 5 (1880): 160–61.

Compendium of the Tenth Consensus (1880), pt. 2. Washington, D.C.: U.S. Government Printing Office, 1883.

Comstock, S. "Public Housekeeper." *Colliers* 45 (30 April 1910): 26–27.

"Contemporary Portraits." *Unitarian* 2 (1907): 91–92.

Cook, Blanche Wiesen. "Female Support Networks and Political Activism." In *A Heritage of Her Own,* edited by Nancy F. Cott and Elizabeth H. Pleck. New York, 1979.

Cooke, George Willis. *Unitarianism in America.* Boston: American Unitarian Association, 1902.

Cott, Nancy. *The Bonds of Womanhood: "Woman's Sphere" in New England, 1780–1835.* New Haven, Conn.: Yale University Press, 1977.

Cooley, Roselle. "Suffrage in Florida." In *Suffrage in the Southern States,* compiled by Ida Clyde Clark. Nashville, 1914.

Crompton, Arnold. *Unitarianism on the Pacific Coast: The First Sixty Years.* Boston: Beacon, 1957.

Crook, Margaret Brackenbury. *Women and Religion.* Boston: Beacon, 1964.

Cunningham, Raymond J. "The Impact of Christian Science on the American Churches, 1880–1910." *American Historical Review* 72 (1967): 887–95.

Dall, Caroline. *College, Market, and Court.* Memorial ed. Boston: Rumford, 1914.

Davis, Allen F. *American Heroine: The Life and Legend of Jane Addams.* New York: Oxford University Press, 1973.

————. *Spearheads for Reform: The Social Settlements and the Progressive Movement, 1890–1914.* New York: Oxford University Press, 1967.

Degler, Carl N. *At Odds: Women and the Family in America from the Revolution to the Present.* New York: Oxford University Press, 1980.

Doan, Mida. "Recollections of First School Days." In *History of Humboldt.* Humboldt, Iowa, 1963.

Douglas, Ann. *The Feminization of American Culture.* New York: Knopf, 1978.

Dubbert, Jack. "Progressivism and the Masculinity Crisis." *Psychoanalytic Review* 61 (1974): 443–55.

Dunlap, Flora. *History of Woman Suffrage,* vol. 6. New York: Fowler & Wells, 1922.

Eastman, Elaine Goodale. "Are D.A.R. Women Exploited?" *Christian Century* (11 September 1929).

Eddy, Sherwood, and Kirby Page. *The Abolition of War.* New York: Doubleday, Doran, 1924.

Eliot, Samuel Atkins. *Heralds of a Liberal Faith.* 4 vols. Boston: Beacon, 1910–52.

Emerson, Ralph Waldo. *Miscellanies.* Cambridge, Mass.: Harvard University Press, 1893.

Epstein, Barbara Leslie. *The Politics of Domesticity.* Middletown, Conn.: 1981.

Faderman, Lillian. *Surpassing the Love of Men: Romantic Friendship and Love between Women from the Renaissance to the Present.* New York: Morrow, 1981.

Fine, Sidney. *Laissez Faire and the General Welfare State: A Study of Conflict in American Thought, 1865–1901.* Ann Arbor: University of Michigan Press, 1964.

Flexner, Eleanor. *Century of Struggle.* Cambridge, Mass.: Harvard University Press, 1958.

Gallaher, Ruth A. *The Legal and Political Status of Women in Iowa: An Historical Account of the Rights of Women . . . 1838–1918.* Iowa City: State Historical Society of Iowa, 1918.

Garfield, C. W. "The Old Church." In *Centennial History of Humboldt,* edited by Oliver De Groote. Humboldt, Iowa, 1963.

Gilley, Keith. "Women and the Unitarian Ministry." London, 1985. Typescript loaned by the author.

Gilman, Charlotte Perkins. *The Living of Charlotte Perkins Gilman.* Edited by Zona Gale. New York: Appleton-Century, 1935.

Gilmore, Albert Field. *Christ at the Peace Table.* New York: Prentice-Hall, 1943.

Ginger, Ray. *Altgeld's America.* Chicago: Quadrangle, 1965.

Glick, Mary Bell. *Furnishings and Friends, 1908–1983.* Iowa City: Iowa State Historical Society, 1983.

Graham, Thomas. "Jenkin Lloyd Jones and the World's Columbian Exposition of 1893." *Colloquium Proceedings* 1 (1979): 61–81.

————. "The Making of a Secretary: Jenkin Lloyd Jones at 31." *Proceedings of the Unitarian Universalist Historical Society* 19 (1982–83): 36–55.

Hamilton, Alice. *Exploring the Dangerous Trades*. Boston: Little, Brown, 1943.

Hapgood, Hutchins. *A Victorian in the Modern World*. New York: Harcourt, 1939.

Hardesty, Nancy. *Women Called to Witness: Evangelical Feminism in the Nineteenth Century*. Nashville: Abingdon, 1984.

Harper, Ida Husted. *History of Woman Suffrage*, vols. 5, 6. New York: Fowler & Wells, 1922.

Hart, Sara L. *The Pleasure Is Mine*. Chicago: Vallentine-Newman, 1947.

Hayden, Dolores. *The Grand Domestic Revolution: A History of Feminist Design for American Homes, Neighborhoods, Cities*. Cambridge, Mass.: MIT Press, 1981.

Hill, Mary. *Charlotte Perkins Gilman: The Making of a Radical Feminist, 1860–1896*. Philadelphia: Temple University Press, 1980.

History of Humboldt County. Chicago and Cedar Rapids, Iowa: Historical Publishing Co., 1901.

History of Kossuth and Humboldt Counties, Iowa. Springfield, Ill.: Union Publishing Co., 1884.

Hitchings, Catherine F. *Unitarian and Universalist Women Ministers*. 2d ed. Boston: Universalist Historical Society, 1985.

Hoeltje, Hubert H. "Ralph Waldo Emerson in Iowa." *Iowa Journal of History and Politics* 25 (April 1927): 62–131.

Holmes, John Haynes. *I Speak for Myself*. New York, 1959.

Hopkins, Charles Howard. *The Rise of the Social Gospel in American Protestantism, 1865–1915*. New Haven, Conn.: Yale University Press, 1940.

Horowitz, Helen Lefkowitz. "Hull House as Women's Space." *Chicago History* 12 (Winter 1983–84): 40–55.

Irwin, Inez H. *Angels and Amazons*. New York: Doubleday, Doran, 1933.

James, Janet Wilson, ed. *Women in American Religion*. Philadelphia: University of Pennsylvania Press, 1980.

Jeffrey, Julie Ray. *Frontier Women: The Trans-Mississippi West, 1840–1880*. New York: Hill & Wang, 1979.

Jones, Chester Lloyd. *Youngest Son*. Madison, Wis.: privately printed, 1938.

Johnson, Kenneth R. "Florida Women Get the Vote." *Florida Historical Quarterly* 48 (1970): 299–312.

———. "The Woman Suffrage Movement in Florida." Ph.D. diss., Florida State University, 1966.

Kipnis, Ira. *The American Socialist Movement, 1897–1912*. New York: Greenwood, 1968.

Kogurt, Alvin. "The Settlements and Ethnicity: 1890–1914." *Social Work* 17 (1972): 22–31.

La Follette, Belle Case, and Fola La Follette. *Robert M. La Follette*. 2 vols. New York: Macmillan, 1953.

Lavan, Spencer, and George Huntston Williams. "The Unitarian and Universalist Traditions." *Caring and Curing*. New York: Macmillan, 1986.

Leach, William. *True Love and Perfect Union: The Feminist Reform of Sex and Society*. New York: Basic, 1980.

Leuchtenburg, William. *The Perils of Prosperity, 1914–1932*. Chicago: University of Chicago Press, 1958.

Lubove, Roy. *The Professional Altruist: The Emergence of Social Work as a Career,*

1880–1930. Cambridge, Mass.: Harvard University Press, 1965.

Luhan, Mabel Dodge. *Intimate Memories,* vol. 3, *Movers and Shakers.* New York: Harcourt, Brace, 1936.

Lyttle, Charles H. *Freedom Moves West: A History of the Western Unitarian Conference, 1852–1952.* Boston: Beacon, 1952.

McDannell, Colleen. *The Christian Home in Victorian America, 1840–1900.* Bloomington: Indiana University Press, 1986.

Macfarland, Charles A. *Pioneers for Peace through Religion.* New York: Fleming H. Revell, 1946.

McGiffert, Arthur Cushman. *Pilot of a Liberal Faith: Samuel Atkins Eliot, 1862– 1950.* Boston: Beacon, 1976.

McGovern, James R. "David Graham Phillips and the Virility Impulse of Progressives." *New England Quarterly* 39 (1966): 334–55.

Madison, James H. "Reformers and the Rural Church, 1900–1950." *Journal of American History* 73 (1986): 645–68.

Mann, Newton. *Import and Outlook of Socialism.* Boston: James H. West, 1910.

Martin, Theodora P. *The Sound of Own Voices: Women's Study Clubs, 1860–1900.* Boston: Beacon, 1989.

May, Henry F. *Protestant Churches and Industrial America.* New York: Harper, 1949.

Mendelsohn, Jack. *Channing: The Reluctant Radical.* Boston: Little, Brown, 1971.

Miller, Russel E. *The Larger Hope,* vol. 1, *The First Century of the Universalist Church in America, 1770–1870,* vol. 2, *The Second Century, 1870–1970.* Boston: Unitarian Universalist Association, 1985.

Noun, Louise R. "Amelia Bloomer, a Biography: Part II: The Suffragist of Council Bluffs." *Annals of Iowa* 47 (Spring 1985): 575–621.

———. *Strong-minded Women: The Emergence of the Woman-Suffrage Movement in Iowa.* Ames: Iowa State University Press, 1969.

"Orlando: History of Its Church Homes." *Orlando Sun,* 14 June 1968.

Parke, David B. "The Historical and Religious Antecedents of the New Beacon Series in Religious Education (1937)." Ph.D. diss., Boston University Graduate School, 1965.

Persons, Stow. *Free Religion: An American Faith.* Boston: Beacon, 1963.

Philpot, Thomas Lee. *The Slum and the Ghetto: Neighborhood Deterioration and Middle-Class Reform, Chicago, 1880–1930.* New York: Oxford University Press, 1978.

Quist, Oval. *Unitarian Church of Des Moines, Iowa: A Brief History of It.* Des Moines, Iowa: First Unitarian Church, 1977.

Raible, Peter. "The Historical Myth Tensions of American Unitarianism." In *Unitarian Universalism, 1984: Selected Essays.* Boston: Unitarian Universalist Ministers Association, 1985.

Reed, Robert L. "The Professionalism of Public School Teachers: The Chicago Experience, 1895–1920." Ph.D. diss., Northwestern University, 1968.

Richey, Clara M. *History of Woman Suffrage,* vol. 4. New York: Fowler & Wells, 1922.

Riley, Glenda. *Frontier Women: The Iowa Experience.* Cedar Rapids: Iowa State University Press, 1981.

Robinson, David. *The Unitarians and the Universalists.* Westport, Conn.: Greenwood, 1985.

Rothman, Shiela. *Woman's Proper Place.* New York: Basic, 1978.

Rousmaniere, John P. "Cultural Hybrid in the Slums: The College and the Settlement House, 1889–1894." *American Quarterly* 22 (1970): 45–66.

Ruether, Rosemary Radford, and Rosemary Skinner Keller, eds. *Women and Religion in America,* vol. 1, *The Nineteenth Century: A Documentary History.* San Francisco: Harper & Row, 1981.

Ruether, Rosemary Radford, and Eleanor McLaughlin, eds. *Women of Spirit.* New York: Simon & Schuster, 1979.

Ryan, Mary P. "The Power of Women's Networks . . . in Antebellum America." *Feminist Studies* 5 (Spring 1979): 66–85.

Rybczynski, Witold. *Home: A Short History of an Idea.* New York: Viking Penguin, 1986.

Schwarz, Judith. "Questionnaire on Issues in Lesbian History." *Frontiers* 4 (Fall 1979): 2–12.

———. *Radical Feminists of Heterodoxy: Greenwich Village, 1912–1940.* Lebanon, N.H.: New Victoria, 1982.

Scudder, Vida. *Socialism and Character.* Boston: Houghton Mifflin, 1912.

Shaw, Anna Howard. *The Story of a Pioneer.* New York: Kraus, 1971.

Sicherman, Barbara. *Alice Hamilton: A Life in Letters.* Cambridge, Mass.: Harvard University Press, 1984.

Simkhovitch, Mary Kingsbury. *Neighborhood: My Story of Greenwich House.* New York: Norton, 1938.

Sklar, Kathryn Kish. *Catherine Beecher: A Study in American Domesticity.* New Haven, Conn.: Yale University Press, 1973.

———. "Hull House in the 1890's: A Community of Women Reformers." *Signs* 10 (Summer 1985): 659–77.

Smith, George Martin, ed. *History of Dakota Territory,* vol. 3. Chicago: S. J. Clarke, 1915.

Smith-Rosenberg, Carroll. "The Female World of Love and Ritual: The Relations between Women in Nineteenth Century America." *Signs* 1 (1975): 1–29.

Snyder, Charles E. "Unitarianism in Iowa." *Palimpsest* 30 (1949): 345–74.

Spear, Allan H. *Black Chicago.* Chicago: University of Chicago Press, 1967.

Spencer, Clarissa Hale. *Saints and Ladies.* New York: Woman's Press, 1925.

Stanton, Elizabeth Cady. *History of Woman Suffrage.* 6 vols. New York: Fowler & Wells, 1969.

Sweet, Leonard I. *The Minister's Wife: Her Role in Nineteenth Century America Evangelism.* Philadelphia: Temple University Press, 1983.

Szelag, Sandra A. "Elizabeth Cady Stanton—Prophetic Theologian of the Woman's Rights Movement: A Model for Being Human Religiously." Ph.D. diss., Meadville/Lombard Theological School, 1984.

Taft, Rev. Stephen H. *The History of Humboldt, Iowa. Address Given . . . on the 11th day of September, 1913.* Humboldt, Iowa: Jaqua Printing Co., 1934.

Taylor, A. Elizabeth. "The Woman Suffrage Movement in Florida." *Florida Historical Quarterly* 36 (July 1957): 42–62.

Taylor, Graham. *Chicago Commons through Forty Years.* Chicago: Chicago Commons Association, 1936.

Tennis, Diane. "We Don't Need Any More Pronouncements." *Presbyterian Survey* (May 1988): 17.

Thomas, Richard. "Jenkin Lloyd Jones: Lincoln's Soldier of Civic Righteousness." Ph.D. diss., Rutgers University, 1967.

Tucker, Cynthia Grant. *A Woman's Ministry: Mary Collson's Search for Reform as a Unitarian Minister, a Hull House Social Worker, and a Christian Science Practitioner.* Philadelphia: Temple University Press, 1984.

Vogt, Von Ogden. *Art and Religion.* New Haven, Conn.: Yale University Press, 1921.

Wade, Louise C. *Graham Taylor: Pioneer for Social Justice.* Chicago: University of Chicago Press, 1964.

Walker-Riggs, Judith. "Cleaning Up the Kitchen and the Theology." In *Transforming Thought: Position Papers on Feminist Theology,* vol. 1. Boston: Unitarian Universalist Women's Federation, 1988.

Weiss, Nancy. "From Black Separatism to Interracial Cooperation: The Origins of Organized Efforts for Racial Advancement, 1890–1920." In *Twentieth Century America: Recent Interpretations,* edited by Barton Bernstein. New York: Harcourt, Brace, Jovanovich, 1969.

Welter, Barbara. "The Cult of True Womanhood, 1820–1860." *American Quarterly* 18 (1966): 151–74.

———. "The Feminization of American Religion: 1800 to 1860." In *Clio's Consciousness Raised,* edited by Mary Hartman and Lois W. Banner. New York: Harper & Row, 1974.

Wilbur, Earl Morse. *A History of Unitarianism.* 2 vols. Boston: Beacon, 1945.

Willis, Gwendolyn B. "Olympia Brown." *Journal of the Universalist Historical Society* 4 (1963): 1–76.

Woodward, Kenneth L. "Feminism and the Churches." *Newsweek,* 13 February 1989, pp. 58–61.

Woolley, Celia Parker. *Love and Theology.* Boston: Ticknor, 1887.

Wright, Conrad. *The Beginning of Unitarianism in America.* Boston: Beacon (for Starr King), 1955.

———. *A Doctrine of the Church for Liberals.* Boston: Unitarian Universalist Ministers Association, 1983.

———. *The Liberal Christians.* Boston: Beacon, 1970.

———. "Social Cohesion and the Uses of the Past." *Journal of the Liberal Ministry* 5 (Fall 1965): 167–76.

———, ed. *The Stream of Light: A Sesquicentennial History of American Unitarianism.* Boston: Unitarian Universalist Association, 1975.

———, ed. *Three Prophets of Religious Liberalism: Channing, Emerson, Parker.* Boston: Beacon, 1961.

Yoder, Jess. "Preaching on Issues of War and Peace." In *Preaching in American History,* edited by Dewitte Holland. Nashville: Abingdon, 1969.

INDEX

CYNTHIA GRANT TUCKER is Professor of English at Memphis State University and author of *A Women's Ministry: Mary Collson's Search for Reform* and *Kate Freeman Clark: A Painter Rediscovered.*